Townspeople and Nation:
English Urban Experiences,
1540-1640

For Anne + Jan,

With admiration
and esteem!

Bob Tittler

Robert Tittler

Townspeople and Nation
English Urban Experiences,
1540-1640

Stanford University Press, Stanford, California   2001

Stanford University Press
Stanford, California
© 2001 by the Board of Trustees of the
Leland Stanford Junior University
Printed in the United States of America

Library of Congress Cataloging-in-Publication Data

Tittler, Robert
  Townspeople and nation : English urban experiences, 1540–1640 /
Robert Tittler.
    p.   cm.
  Includes bibliographical references and index.
  ISBN 0-8047-3868-8 (cloth : alk. paper) —
  ISBN 0-8047-3869-6 (paper : alk. paper).
  1. Cities and towns—England—History.   I. Title.

HT133.T58   2001
307.76'0942'09031—dc21   00-063733
                                                               CIP

This book is printed on acid-free, archival quality paper.

Original printing 2001
Last figure below indicates year of this printing:
10   09   08   07   06   05   04   03   02   01

Designed and typeset in 10/13 Palatino by John Feneron

To Geoff Adams and the late Joel Hurstfield,
both of whom gave me a chance.

Preface

Spend enough time on the early modern records of any well-documented town and a few names are bound to jump out at you and stick in your mind. They do so not necessarily because they are national figures but precisely because most of them are not. They are interesting people doing important but unexceptional things in their communities. Their activities reveal as much about those communities, and about urban life in general, as they do about themselves. It is that very ordinariness which commends them to us. They respond, and they allow us to respond, to the question which students always ask about the past: 'Yes, but what about the regular people?'

This volume aims to see what the experience of particular individuals of this sort can tell us about English towns and townspeople between the advent of the Reformation and the outbreak of the Civil War. It is also intended to demonstrate the importance of towns and cities, and of urban-based activities, to the nation as a whole: a recognition which was just dawning on many English men and women themselves at this very time, and which has too often been lost on us. It is intended for two sorts of readers. I hope that specialists in the field will take on board the original research and the particular interpretive approaches which have guided my selection of subjects, and which I shall discuss at greater length in the Introduction. But it is also written for students, and for anyone else who might be interested in the subject without bringing particularly specialized knowledge to it. I hope it will provide a useful and engaging entrée into the serious consideration of how English townspeople got on in life, looked after their common interests, and thought collectively about their milieu. I hope it will encourage further interest in English towns and cities of this era, and in their inhabitants, and thus bring an often neglected aspect of English history closer to view.

It should be obvious that this is in no way intended to be a comprehensive treatment of virtually anything. It is intentionally selective and suggestive: a sampling of dishes and not a banquet. It omits, perhaps unfairly, many important 'types' of townspeople: clergymen and vagrants and children and adolescents and apprentices amongst them. Somewhat unfashionably, it takes in England alone, without Ireland, or Scotland, or Wales. It makes scant comparison with urban life in other countries at the time. I make no apology for these choices. Introductory volumes have to begin somewhere, and have to create an excitement about the subject before comprehensive coverage can be thrust upon the unwary. Those who are hooked may use the notes as a guide to further reading.

I do still take a few things for granted on the reader's part. A general, if not necessarily sophisticated, sense of English history in the period c. 1540–1640 may come in handy. So may a willingness to engage actively with what has been written, and to take a little initiative in filling in what blanks may turn up. To help the willing novice along, I have provided a concise introduction to English towns at this time and to some of my pet theories about how they functioned. Those eager to get to the essays without this primer on the general subject may skip it if they wish. I've also added a Glossary at the end to define some technical terms which couldn't be avoided. The Introduction should also serve to introduce the contexts and concerns of each essay, and to tie them at least loosely together.

The approach taken here may still strike some readers as novel. It deals with localities and 'minor' people, rather than with the nation as a whole and 'major' people; it takes in some of the newer methodological approaches to the field. Current scholarly concerns such as, for example, the nature and importance of collective memory and commemoration, of political culture, of gender and similar subjects, all find their way to the following pages. Yet whatever the approach, it is useful to remember that all historical thinking and writing must follow a few basic rules, and these rules take on an added twist when we turn to the local rather than the national scene. The first rule is that we must get right the narrative of events. The second is that we must place that narrative in an appropriate interpretive framework, so that it becomes useful and applicable to the subject at hand.

The twist for historians of the local scene is this. With traditional political history, which is national in scope, the narrative history of such nations as England or Britain has been pretty well established for a very long time. One can plunge right in without stopping to explain, for example, that Henry VIII came before Elizabeth I and not after. Those who write about townspeople and particular towns are not always so fortunate in having comparable ground to stand on. Even good town histories, where they exist, often omit many details. Some very important towns and cities, London remarkably amongst them, still lack comprehensive narrative histories of this period. This means that we have to spend much more time establishing what happened before we can get on with the business of interpretation. Much of that groundwork of constructing a basic narrative framework from the sources will be obvious in the twists and turns of the essays which follow. I have not tried to conceal these efforts—they, too, tell us a lot about the historian's task—but I have tried to strike an appropriate balance between narrative and interpretation.

There is a second twist to writing urban history: its sources also tend to be different than those of more conventional approaches. The narrative history of a great many towns has been compiled through the years by local historians who were amateurs in the best sense of the word. They often have had access to materials which have vanished since they wrote, and that makes their work even more valuable to us. We must use their work with great care, but what they frequently lacked in the way of modern standards of documentation or verification they often made up for at least in part by their enthusiasm and diligence.

Many of the surviving sources upon which they relied, and on which we must also rely, are not located in such central archives as the Public Record Office or the British Library. Naturally enough they still tend to remain close to the scene of the action: in the record offices of counties and of the towns themselves. This reminds us that historians no longer necessarily confine themselves as they once did to the central archives, but that they have learned to exploit the full range of archival possibilities in chasing down their subjects. The masterful social historian R. H. Tawney stated a long time ago that a serious historian needs a stout pair of boots. That essential equipment has now come to include a Britrail pass.

Historians of all subjects incur a great many debts as they write up their research. Because comparative urban history of this sort involves research trips to a great many archives and libraries, it may well incur even more than most. In completing this volume, I am delighted to acknowledge the help of several groups of people. First I am pleased to thank the authors, editors, and publishers of works in which small bits and pieces of this book first appeared, and who have agreed to permit me to reproduce that material. They include Edwin DeWindt, editor of *The Salt of Common Life: Individuality and Choice in the Medieval Town, Countryside and Church, Essays Presented to J. Ambrose Raftis* (Medieval Institute Publications, Western Michigan University Press, 1995), in which small bits of Chapter 7 appeared; Helen Ostovich, editor of *Early Theatre*, in which much of Chapter 6 appeared; and the team of Donna Landry, Gerald MacLean, and Joseph Ward, editors of *The Country and the City Revisited* (Cambridge U.P., 1999), in which I first tried out some of the ideas in Chapter 3. Some of these are reprinted here with the additional permission of Cambridge University Press. I am thankful, too, to the City Museum of Gloucester for permission to reproduce the Cookes' portrait. I am especially grateful to Norris Pope, John Feneron, and Martin Hanft at Stanford University Press, and to Paul Seaver, whose helpful reader's comments for that publisher prompted some useful fine-tuning on the eve of publication.

The staffs of county and borough record offices are invaluable guides to their holdings, and are, in my experience, unfailingly courteous and professional in affording access to them. Those of the Lincolnshire, Dorset, Gloucestershire, Cheshire, Middlesex, Herefordshire, and Norfolk county record offices, and of the borough or city record offices of Chester, Gloucester, Coventry, and Greater London, have been especially helpful.

The largesse of the Social Science and Humanities Research Council of Canada and of the American Philosophical Society reminds us that patronage lives on at least some of the time. The policies of Concordia University to grant sabbatical leaves (and not to turn faculty heads with excessive appreciation) reassures us that universities still pay at least some heed to the humanities. This book could not have been completed without financial support of all three institutions. The librarians of Concordia's Vanier Library (especially Judy Appleby, Luigina Vileno, Ursula Hakien, Chris Bober, Susie Breuer, Diane Sauve, Marvin Orbach, and Wendy Knechtel), Yale's Sterling and Beinecke Libraries (Suzanne Roberts and Stephen Parks), London University's Institute of Historical Research (especially Don Munro and Clyve Jones), and McGill's Blackader Library deserve special thanks.

The many scholars who have given advice, support, warning, or encouragement—all those things which remind us that research is never an entirely solitary activity—include Christie Anderson, John Beattie, David Dean, Karen Hearn, Alexandra Johnston, Norman Jones, Sally-Beth MacLean, Lawrence Manley, Shannon Mc Sheffrey, James Moore, Helen Ostovich, Stephen Porter, Ron Rudin, Tim Wales, Joe Ward, Joanna Woodall, Daniel Woolf, and Keith Wrightson. Michael Berlin, Janis Housez, Jason McLinton, and Tim Wales provided valuable research assistance. Finally, Joe Ward, John Craig, Catherine Patterson, and (my one-woman undergraduate market research sample) Laura McAlear bravely read the entire manuscript and made numerous helpful suggestions along the way. None of these fine people should be held in the least responsible for any infelicities, errors of judgment, or sheer foolishness which may remain.

R.T.

February 2000

Contents

Tables and Illlustrations

Tables

Illustrations

Townspeople and Nation:
English Urban Experiences,
1540-1640

Introduction

Nearly thirty years ago, with a volume of essays entitled *Crisis and Order in English Towns, 1500–1700*,[1] Peter Clark and Paul Slack opened up the subject of early modern English urban history as never before. Their title referred to the tension they found in the urban communities of that time between forces of crisis on the one hand and of order on the other. They recognized that such tensions often manifested themselves in political terms, but that they largely arose from social and economic factors. In their view these factors conspicuously included economic decline, unemployment, epidemic disease, inflation, migration (often tending towards vagrancy), and unrest. Although the eight essays which followed the editors' introduction addressed a number of specific issues for investigation,[2] this remained a strong underlying assumption throughout the volume. Four years later, in response to an Open University course on the subject, they wrote a smaller, introductory text on the same subject, *English Towns in Transition, 1500–1700*.[3] This, too, suggested themes of conflict and crisis and, while including a chapter on cultural activities, it sustained the earlier emphasis on economic and social issues pretty much throughout. It would be astonishing if even some of the underlying assumptions of Clark's and Slack's perspectives had not been challenged in the course of this time. Indeed, many have been. Subsequent and more intensive research has sharpened our understanding of a number of their convictions: extended them, qualified them, occasionally rejected them altogether, and sometimes offered alternative models in their place.

Further investigation into the assumption of an urban crisis in the opening decades of the period, for example, has made for a more subtle understanding of the urban economy. One must now look much more carefully at the experience of individual towns and urban types before assuming that they fit broadly conceived notions about growth or decay.[4] Similar cautions have been offered in recent work on social themes.[5]

Another alternative approach has been to place the themes of crisis and order in a context which is much broader than economic and social circumstances alone. Clark and Slack themselves acknowledged political tensions stemming from the general trend towards oligarchic rule, and this has been picked up by others as well.[6] Recent scholarship has further emphasized the cultural dimension of urban life and government. Historians working (especially since the 1970s) towards urban history from the perspective of religion, and especially of Protestantism, have contributed to this approach. Political historians, anxious to examine the context of the Civil Wars, have also played a part. On the whole this has contributed a number of fruitful and essential insights, especially on the politics of religion in the local community, and on the whole questions of urban culture and urban political culture.[7]

Broader developments in our understanding of political culture in urban communities now include research on civic drama and related mimetic activities,[8] on the visual arts (especially on forms of civic architecture and portraiture),[9] and on aspects of urban-centred literature (including city comedy and the writing of local history).[10] We have come to recognize that all of these cultural expressions served in this era as viable forms of political discourse. They did so not only at the top of the political hierarchy, with the projection of royal authority at court and in the nation at large, but also closer to the bottom, with the projection of civic authority in town and city. Together they must now be seen as fostering the communication of political ideas, and the enactment of political behaviour, which make up the culture of political life.

The practical task of writing on this broad subject prompts still another refinement to the Clark and Slack model, one which establishes an appropriate time span for the discussion. Though they had seen the period of their concern as 'transitional', neither

the precise nature of that transition nor its chronological boundaries were ever clearly defined. Perhaps, having taken social and
economic developments as their touchstone for the urban condition, no more precise chronological boundaries than the century
years (1500–1700) were feasible. Certainly some other and also
very impressive recent scholarship has rejected the notion of precise boundaries for particular urban phenomena.[11] Others have
adopted the notion of the *longue durée*, which recognizes few fundamental changes between the late medieval and the early industrial eras.[12]

But if chronological boundaries are to have any value, they
must be custom-calibrated for each topical approach to the past.
'The Tudor and Stuart Era' (i.e., 1485–1714 or, with each dynasty
considered separately, 1485–1603 and 1603–1714) has meaning for
historians of national political history because the dynastic terms
'Tudor' and 'Stuart', and the years associated with each, mark the
formal boundaries of that approach. It has little meaning, on the
other hand, for fields like women's history or the history of tech-
nology, which remain essentially unrelated to dynastic politics.
These approaches, naturally enough, bear their own definitional
milestones: events like the advent of universal suffrage or the in-
vention of the steam engine.

The essays in this volume are set in the century which extended
between about 1540 and about 1640. This time frame should not be
taken to deny continuities in some issues of urban concern which
also run through the period, but it is meant to recognize particular
aspects of the urban experience which are germane to those years.
These include meaningful points of demarcation for the economy
and population, the government, the religious and ecclesiastical
institutions, and the political culture of English towns and cities.
The terminal date roughly coincides with the outbreak of the Civil
Wars, which interrupted many of the normal elements of urban
life in a great many towns. The inaugural date marks the approximate occurrence of two points of change.

First, 1540 marks the approximate point at which the prevalent
economic structures of the late Middle Ages began to shift to-

wards new forms, both in England's towns and cities and in the nation as a whole. A dominant feature of this economic restructuring may be found in the resumed population growth of the early sixteenth century. That population growth, marked by substantial net migration from rural to urban areas, almost certainly pressed most heavily of all on the towns and cities of the realm. By about the middle of the sixteenth century it began to have significantly broad consequences for the economic and the social order, and to elicit an increasingly aggressive and coordinated response from governing authorities.

This also marks the approximate beginning of the Reformation. Though we tend to think of the Reformation chiefly as a matter of doctrine and belief, or as a chapter in the narrative account of high politics, it also had other far-reaching effects. It proved enormously destructive to a traditional and doctrinally based culture which had developed over the course of a millennium.[13] In addition, it profoundly affected the distribution of lands, jurisdiction, and resources throughout the realm. While the effort to define an official formulation of religious doctrine continued for many decades, the break from Rome and, of far greater moment for the urban communities of the realm, the 'Dissolution of the Monasteries', took place just a few years on either side of 1540. In fact, this latter short-hand term connotes much more than the dissolution of monastic houses alone. It refers to the cumulative effect of four separate statutes over the course of thirteen years: for the dissolution and confiscation of the smaller religious houses in 1536 (by 27 Henry VIII, c. 28); the larger religious houses in 1539 (by 31 Henry VIII, c.13); the colleges, chantries and chapels, and related institutions in both 1545 (by 37 Henry VIII, c. 4) and 1547 (by 1 Edward VI, c. 14).

Even the titles of these statutes conceal a great deal. Taken together, those institutions possessed very extensive lands, properties, and material resources (from mills and granaries and water conduits to farm equipment, livestock, and orchards; from church plate, stained glass, and statuary to service books and clerical vestments). The heads of many of them served as feudal landlords, exercising political and legal jurisdiction over communities both urban and rural. They presided over the lion's share of England's schools, alms houses, hospitals, and other such institutions. Even if carried out more gradually than the law allowed, their disappearance from the scene bore vast consequences for the distribution of land and authority throughout the realm.

Emerging at roughly the same time, these complex phenomena, melded with many traditional concerns as well, collectively moved the agenda of urban life, making more emphatic the tasks of governance and impinging on the outlook of individual townspeople. In effect they made this era something of a watershed in English urban life and institutions, and in the life of its towns and cities.

As must by now be obvious, this volume places the theme of 'crisis and order' in a somewhat wider framework than was envisioned a generation ago. Along with traditional but still essential questions about social and economic life, politics, and government, it takes up several issues now associated with the concept of 'political culture'. These include a consideration of, for example, collective memory and identity and reputation, and therefore of civic behaviour and public order as they applied to the urban scene. It dwells on a somewhat more specific time period (c. 1540–1640 rather than 1500–1700) and certainly one which differs from the model of a *longue durée*. Most obviously of all, it presents these perspectives through the life experience of selected but representative townspeople of the day. Their stories remind us that historical themes are often shaped by the collective activity of myriad individuals, and that a nation's history is also a history of the collective experience of its people.

So that the reader may better appreciate the experience of these townspeople in their time and place, some preliminary description of English urban society in these years seems appropriate. This Introduction continues with a closer look at the two primary factors of change which lend shape to the chosen time period, the economic restructuring which took place from about the 1540s on the one hand, and at least some aspects of the Reformation on the other. So as to discourage the illusion that all urban centres were essentially alike, it then considers a suggested hierarchy of urban types, making reference to matters of size, complexity, and governance. It concludes by considering the most dominant English city of all, the unique metropolis of London.

Economic Restructuring

The shortage of reliable information always makes it difficult to be precise about almost any phase of the English economy in the pre-modern era. Yet most scholars accept that the established economic patterns of late medieval England had begun to move in new directions by or shortly after the turn of the sixteenth century. An increase in population, ending a long period of demographic stagnation, appears as one of the signal factors in these changes. From the last quarter of the fifteenth century the long-stagnant birth rate seems finally to have inched upwards, though frequent outbreaks of epidemic disease kept this from translating into sustained population growth until early in the sixteenth century. It would take a very long time before England's population would again reach its early fourteenth century peak, when climate change and then the Black Death had caused a population collapse and long-term stagnation. Still, life expectancy began to rise in the early sixteenth century; the population began to grow.[14] Because the nation's potential supply of food and housing, and its capacity to absorb more wage earners, still comfortably accommodated the rising population levels of the day, this early sixteenth century growth took a few decades to make itself widely apparent, or to surface as a cause for concern. Even when it did so the effect was uneven. Right into the 1530s and 1540s many towns remained underpopulated. They experienced substantial vacancies in their housing stock, relatively low rents, and little economic incentive for landlords to repair older and more dilapidated buildings. This was especially true in some of the older, industrial or commercial centres like Boston, Coventry, York, or Leicester.[15] But in many other towns, and notwithstanding occasional epidemics of plague

and influenza, an increased migration from the countryside and a
closing gap between births and deaths made for more sustained
population growth.[16] Vacant tenements began to fill up around the
mid-century, and derelict urban housing, long neglected and now
often uninhabitable, emerged as a national problem in the face of
rising population.

Also around this time some areas which, in previous years, had
experienced a general shortage of labour now began to experience
a surplus.[17] By or shortly after the mid-century that surplus more
frequently became problematical, driving wage levels down,
placing more people below the poverty level, and encouraging
subsistence-based migration or even vagrancy in many areas of
the realm.[18] Conditions became particularly acute in wool-grow-
ing and cloth-producing areas. The collapse of Continental markets for England's 'old draperies' after 1551 and the collapse of the
Antwerp Mart in the 1560s took their toll. So did the tendency of
cloth producers to move out of traditional but heavily regulated
cloth producing centres like York, Coventry, and Shrewsbury and
into less closely regulated areas elsewhere.[19] Provincial ports like
Hull, Great Yarmouth, Boston, and King's Lynn, many of which
had depended on the wool trade, suffered accordingly.[20] Some
(Great Yarmouth, Rye, Sandwich, Hastings, and others, especially
on the south coast) suffered additionally from severe silting of
their harbours. National legislation began to fortify local efforts to
deal with consequent poverty and, climaxing with the Statute of
Artificers of 1563 (5 Eliz., c. 4)—the longest statute of the century—to defend traditional places and practices of manufacture.

Legislative efforts notwithstanding, remedies to these problems were often straightforward, provided by the natural regula-
tory capacity of the economy. In the case of housing, for example,
landlords often simply fixed up derelict housing to meet the new
demand and raised rents accordingly. But contemporary conditions were not always so simple as to permit such a rational course
of action. In the long era of stagnant rental values, when tenants
had been hard to attract or retain, many landlords let their properties at very long term leases and very low rents: as long as 120

years in the City of York. They now had to wait until those leases expired before they could act. In other cases properties had remained so uneconomical to keep up that landlords simply abandoned them, cutting their losses and turning their interests elsewhere.[21] Both circumstances left vacant or derelict residential buildings in numerous towns throughout the realm. When population began again to push against this potential housing supply, something had eventually to be done.

Individual towns no doubt coped with this in their own ways.[22] Both Norwich, which had suffered housing damage in the great fire of 1507, and King's Lynn, which had suffered similar losses by a series of destructive floods, eventually petitioned Parliament for the authority to assume greater control over, and thus to rebuild, their housing stock. (It is noteworthy that they did not do so for several decades after the destruction itself. We may presume that the loss of housing incurred in the opening years of the century did not become a problem until the mid-1530s.) Both succeeded in gaining statutes for relief of their housing problems in 1536.[23]

MPs from other towns obviously took careful note of this success. Subsequent parliaments produced five more statutes for the rebuilding of local housing stock between 1536 and 1542, pertaining to a combined list of over a hundred towns.[24] The preambles to these statutes described such conditions as 'desolate and voide groundys, withe pittys, sellars and vaultes lying open and uncovered' in what had once been 'pryncipalle and chief stretes' and 'beautyfull dwellyng Howses'.

It is difficult to tell precisely how often these statutes were enforced. Yet some evidence suggests a wide and, indeed, general application over a period of many years.[25] A town's ability to control its housing stock remained critical throughout the century, both as a source of civic revenue and as a precondition to social stability. In an age when the monastic dissolutions created the largest turnover in land-holding since the Norman Conquest, the competition to acquire such properties, by purchase or even forfeiture, became especially acute.

Similar pressures no doubt pertained to the food supply of

various towns, especially in larger centres which had more mouths to feed and required a much larger hinterland to supply their needs. Again the forces of the marketplace came into play and the agrarian economy underwent a restructuring of its own. Following the dictates of profit, some landowners brought marginal lands into production and converted pasture lands to crop production. Pushed especially by the insatiable demands of wholesalers in the London market and a few of the larger provincial centres, some began to specialize in only one or two commodities rather than raising a variety of crops for local consumption in the traditional manner.

But again there were formidable obstacles to what may seem to us rational economic decisions. The tenurial and customary circumstances of land-holding, including strong protection for the legal rights of tenants, and the very force of tradition itself, often made such efforts impossible. Agricultural production did expand, but not always at the rate demanded by population growth. The overall picture here may be focused by the bald fact that, while the population of the nation between 1541 and 1656 nearly doubled, the price of essential commodities over the same span more than tripled.[26] This situation had an obvious long-term effect on the level of 'real' wages, and thus on poverty and opportunity. A relatively low population at the beginning of the century made for scarce labour and sustained high wage levels. Indeed that had been a prevalent pattern throughout much of the fifteenth century. But as population rose, the labour shortage eased. Soon the level of real wages began to fall. It continued to do so, with substantial fluctuations, throughout our entire period.[27] Buying power amongst wage earners was never as high after 1540 as it had routinely been in the opening years of the century. As wage earners fell further behind the pace of rising prices, they found it more difficult to advance in their occupations. Capital remained in short supply, and even when apprentices completed their training, they found it more difficult to set up shop on their own as time went by. Under such conditions, as we will see below, moneylenders like Joyce Jefferies of Hereford (Chapter 8) and philanthropists like

Thomas White of London (Chapter 4) became ever more important, but occupational advancement grew increasingly more difficult despite such efforts.

These trends were not harmful for everyone. For those in a position to raise more food, to transport it or process it, to undertake innovations in marketing, to expand other kinds of production by hiring more labour (and at falling wages), to build new housing, to control more existing property, to lend money, or to raise rents, profits were there to be made. For some people this became an era of enticing opportunity. Traditional patterns of economic and social advancement became more pronounced, and the chance to purchase dissolved ecclesiastical lands and properties came into play for the first time. Prosperity ensued; fortunes were made.

Some of these same opportunities applied to towns as well as to individuals, and some towns did, indeed, benefit considerably in these years. A number, as we will see, were eventually able to make substantial purchases of land and other valuable resources, thus to improve their fiscal capabilities. Many market towns benefited by rising food prices,[28] though some of the smaller ones failed before vigorous regional competition. Specialized centres such as the two university towns of Oxford and Cambridge, or dockyard towns such as Chatham and Portsmouth, did well as their particular specialities grew more important in the latter decades of the century.[29]

Yet Clark's and Slack's characterization of the era as one of tension and unrest, of 'crisis and order', should not be easily dismissed. Shifts in traditional patterns of trade and manufacturing, in agricultural production and patterns of distribution, in employment and housing, and in the prevailing rates of inflation, also left a great many people behind. Subsistence migration and vagrancy became more widespread and alarming; fears of crime, rootlessness, and unrest became ubiquitous, continual, and more systematically addressed. The concern for the regulation of behaviour itself, as Marjorie McIntosh has shown, was certainly not new to this period.[30] Yet many of the pressures which prompted such concerns did grow more widespread and intense, and governmental responses did grow more aggressive and specific, as the period wore on. We see this in the profusion of royal proclamations and parliamentary statutes devoted to regulating social and economic activities in those years, and in the closer cooperation of local officials in enforcing them.

Again, falling material circumstances applied to towns as well as people. Many of the old and traditionally prosperous cloth manufacturing centres, places like Reading, Gloucester, Shrewsbury, Coventry, or Newbury, or ports like Boston, Melcombe Regis, Hastings, and Southampton, found it difficult or even impossible to adapt to changing circumstances and failed to regain their former prosperity. Others, such as York, Hull, Oxford, and Nottingham, recovered only in the last quarter of the sixteenth century, usually by changing their economic function. It cannot be said that social fallout from these circumstances always weighed more heavily on urban than on agrarian life, or that it applied to all towns to the same extent or in the same ways. Yet towns were by their very definition places of concentrated population, and of primarily nonagrarian economic activity.[31] Thus they tended to experience such social and economic changes more emphatically, and to bear the brunt of subsequent pressures more directly than other areas. No reflection on the urban condition of the day can ignore these developments.

Reformation

We must now consider one other profound influence on the urban life of this era. That was the Reformation, or at least its early phases in the reigns of Henry VIII and Edward VI. We may no longer assume that this opening period marked the advent of the Church of England as we know it. In doctrinal terms it merely marked the beginning of the much longer and more complex process which led over the course of many decades to that establishment. Still, these years proved definitive in many respects. In addition to their obvious impact on doctrine and belief, they marked a profoundly important period for the government, economic life, and religious and political culture of England's towns and cities.

One crucial but often overlooked implication of the early Reformation had to do with land-holding, and with the legal and political jurisdiction associated with that land-holding. Most of the property held by ecclesiastical institutions rested with the 'regular' clergy: those who, like the Augustinians or Benedictines, lived by a rule and were governed by the heads of their orders through institutions like monasteries, abbeys, and priories. Especially in urban areas a fair share of properties were also held by the lay religious institutions—religious guilds, fraternities, and chantries—which were more thickly clustered there than in the countryside.

By conventional estimates, both sorts of property taken together amounted to between a quarter and a third of all the land in England. This property itself came in a wide variety of forms, including, for example, agricultural lands, woodlots, fishponds, urban tenements, numerous building types, water conduits, marketplaces, and entire towns. The political implications of those holdings included the right to hold court, collect tolls and fines, determine tenancy, and other elements of feudal lordship. Finally, the Church held moveable goods as well, including such items as jewels and precious metals, paintings, carvings, stained glass, furnishings, vestments, and service books.

Between 1536 and 1547 these institutions, with their wealth, property, and jurisdictions, were dissolved by parliamentary statute and expropriated—much of it to be sold again—by the Crown. This set in motion a more vigorous market for real property, and all which went with that property, than ever before. It is hard to imagine that any urban community in the realm above the level of the very smallest market town could have remained unaffected by the dissolution of a chantry or a guild, or by the wanton and unprecedented destruction of fabric and furnishings in the local parish church. (Indeed, taken as a whole, the sheer physical destruction which marked these years obliterated much of the artistic legacy of a millennium.)[32] In some towns, long dominated by ecclesiastical lords, even the principal political jurisdiction now came up for grabs. To be sure, it often took many decades before a town accommodated to changes in property-holding or jurisdiction. But from 'around 1540' onwards, and in all these many respects, the fat was in the fire.

In many cases, the disruptive effects of the Reformation meant opportunity as well as loss, especially in a pragmatic sense. The period is justly famous for the individual entrepreneurs who snapped up dissolved lands as quickly and advantageously as they could. Though they were on the whole slower to act, many civic governing bodies also saw their chance to acquire the jurisdictions and lands once held by the Church. Such bodies commonly responded, sooner or later, by trying to purchase local properties from the Crown or, later in the century, from those who had initially purchased them from the Crown. Along with the rising population and the pressure it placed on the housing supply, this competition for local resources proved a hot item on many a town council agenda of the day.

In order to ensure that coveted purchases could be made with legal security, local leaders of many towns looked to their legal standing, and often found it insufficient. From about 1540, as we will see in greater detail below, a virtual explosion ensued in legal strategies that allowed local authorities to acquire lands with legal impunity. In the course of this quest, perhaps as a necessary condition to its aims, the governing bodies of many towns also became more oligarchic in form and authoritarian in tone.

A second (and much less familiar) dimension of the old Church's presence in England's towns and cities lay in its cultural role, and specifically its role in shaping the ambient urban political culture of the late medieval town. Over the course of a millennium, the beliefs and practices of medieval Catholicism had come to form a rich and complex culture, one which had been internalized in the civic as well as the religious life of the nation. For residents of individual towns and cities, it had long provided a common social as well as spiritual bond, along with a vocabulary through which that bond could be expressed and sustained. As

Susan Brigden has put it even with reference to so large a place as London, 'Communal religious observance marked the autonomy of the city, and faith might bind the citizenry as nothing else could'.[33]

That 'communal religious observance' included the sacraments, rituals, ceremonies, and regular devotional exercises of traditional religion. All were designed primarily to help parishioners attain personal salvation through the performance of good works, and to sustain a shared fellowship in Christ. By their very nature, all of these were deeply social activities as well. Participation in the Christian life defined one's membership in the civic community just as much as in the spiritual.[34] Just as the eternal salvation of the soul required certain standards of moral behaviour, so did good standing amongst fellow townspeople, and thus the harmony and stability of the community itself required certain standards of civic behaviour. Unless and until one was willing to make retribution and ask for forgiveness, straying from either set of standards invited ostracism: excommunication and possible damnation in the former case, dismissal from the freemanry or corporal punishment in the latter.

An important part of this traditional culture was historical or mnemonic in nature. That is to say, it conveyed a collective memory. This, too, applied in both the universal and the local sense, and to the civic as well as religious identity. The Bible and post-biblical sources for the Christian past imparted a shared sense of heritage to the whole Christian community, and one which, by eliminating papal authority, the Henrician government began sharply to redefine for English communicants. In addition, numerous devices and traditions within that broad framework imparted a sense of identity which was specific to the local community: to the town and especially to the parish. Through their charitable benefactions, one generation of parishioners left its legacy for the next. Through their prayers and commemorations, the latter generation remembered the former for so doing.

There was a material side to this as well. Material objects, serving as what Pierre Nora has called 'sites of memory', could be

counted on to trigger associations with the past.[35] Images of the
patron saint, preserved in the forms of statuary or stained glass
within the church as well as in the very name of the parish, certainly had that effect. The monuments, paintings, furnishings and
plate, the altar screens, reredos, rood screens and clerical vestments, all combined to make the parish church a virtual palimp-
sest for the community. Layer by layer, it recorded and preserved
the lives of parishioners and the historical life of the parish.

The central concern with the terrors of Purgatory, and the fate
of the soul after death, also bore its mnemonic implications. This
'Purgatorial imperative' created elaborate means of remembering
the dead. It invoked such material forms as the funerary monuments and brasses, candles (or 'lights'), and the written list of deceased parishioners known as the bede-roll. It also invoked such
rituals as tolling bells, lighting candles, reading aloud the names
on the bede-roll, singing masses (often by priests employed for
that purpose by the endowments known as chantries), or joining
in ritual processions. Performance of these observances, along
with the sacraments, allowed one to remain 'in charity' with one's
fellows, with one's community, and with the wider Fellowship of
Christ. But through the generations these activities all served to
connect the present with the past. In this manner they engendered
a strong sense of place, heritage, pride, and loyalty: all essential
cultural components of the civic order.

The destruction of the traditional doctrines and practices and
mnemonic associations took much longer to accomplish than the
mere dissolution of properties or destruction of material artifacts
as demanded by statute. Yet, along with other aspects of Protestantism, that destruction does seem to have made very substantial
headway in most areas of the realm by the middle of the Elizabethan era. In Patrick Collinson's words, 'It is only with the 1570s
that the historically minded insomniac goes to sleep counting
Catholics rather than Protestants, since only then did they find
themselves in a majority situation'.[36]

However gradually they came, these changes were just as significant to the ambient culture as were the Dissolutions to land-

holding and governance. Nothing less than an entire, complex, and deeply rooted cultural construct had been ruled out of order; the entire firmament of urban life, and of urban political culture, had been made to shift. And because the perpetuation of civic harmony and perhaps even political stability hung in the balance, an alternative civic culture would have to be created on the ashes of the traditional. New or reconfigured symbolic and material forms would have to be contrived. An alternative and largely secular-based collective memory would have to be constructed. Some of the reconfigured civic culture remained religious in nature, and its concern for the common good remained intact. Yet both the nature of its beliefs and the forms of its expression proved very different from what had come before. Most prominent in this vein lay the emergence of a strongly Calvinistic 'puritan' strain within the emerging Anglican tradition. Aiming to redirect what it saw as the particular moral laxity of the urban milieu, Puritanism presented an alternative doctrinal vehicle for ideas of moral reform. Where traditional doctrine had encouraged benefactions as the road to salvation, the Puritan preachers and lecturers supported civic leaders in striving towards a godly society on earth, one in the image of the New Jerusalem or 'the City on the Hill'. Lectures, sermons, and disputations, often supported by civic patronage, became more common forms of political discourse than ever before.

Naturally enough, these initiatives often provoked deep divisions in particular communities. In town after town, traditionally minded proponents of the Old Faith and of 'merrie England' faced off against the sterner, more disciplinary minded and hotly Protestant folk of the new order. Often, as in Dorchester, this amounted to virtual 'cultural warfare' in which the Puritan-inspired ruling elite recognized an obligation to enforce firm standards of moral behaviour on a partly reluctant community.[37] The story of the Mayor of Chester, Henry Hardware, who replaced the traditional Midsummer Show play-figures of the giant, the dragon, the naked boys, and the 'devil in feathers' with the more pointedly authoritarian image of a mounted knight in armour, told in Chapter 6, allows us to examine this theme at close hand. The essay on Henry Manship's history of Great Yarmouth (Chapter 5) probes some of the intellectual content of the same concern.

But notwithstanding its undoubted significance, we must not overestimate the role of Puritan Godliness in the urban political culture of the day. As we shall learn from the experience of both John and Joan Cooke (in Chapter 3) and of Sir Thomas White (in Chapter 4), many of its ends and even some of its means might be found in the 'civic Catholicism' which preceded it. As Marjorie McIntosh has established, active concern for the regulation of behaviour long preceded the appearance of Protestantism,[38] and even in the period at hand a few towns undertook extensive reform programmes without the inspiration of those concerns.[39] As the experience of Henry Hardware bears out, some acts done under the guise of Puritan reform had as much to do with practical circumstances as with doctrinal commitment.[40]

This reminds us that many other aspects of the new political culture had been rendered pointedly secular in these years. Civic halls (many of them converted from the halls of religious guilds and fraternities) joined or even overshadowed parish churches as key venues for civic culture. New and civic forms of furnishing, iconography, and plate served as post-Reformation analogues to traditional paraphernalia. The civic portraits of mayors and benefactors which first appeared in this era, including those of White and the Cookes, were displayed in the guildhall, replacing in the public consciousness many of the visual images of saints formerly displayed in the churches. Mayoral and aldermanic robes replaced at least some traditional clerical vestments as sartorial images of authority.[41]

As the essays below will attest, some townspeople took the upheavals of the day as an opportunity to feather their own nests. Often, as with the religiously conservative John Browne of Boston (Chapter 1), they placed their financial interests ahead of their religious convictions. Other citizens were more civic minded, and (while rarely denying their own interests in the event) they also worked to strengthen the communities in which they carried out their lives. In some cases, as we will see with Henry Hardware's redefinition of the traditional Midsummer Show in Chester, they worked to adapt traditional institutions and cultural forms to new purposes. In other cases they created new institutions and forms altogether. By the end of our period, they had indeed effectively reconfigured the landscape of urban political culture. This new ethos came to be expressed through a more secular vocabulary, legitimized by an historical rationale, and characterized by the selective retention of many familiar forms and practices.

The ruling elites of English towns did not accomplish this entirely on their own nor, given the political system of the day, could they have done so. They required the active support of both Tudor and early Stuart monarchs, and they got it. Desperate to have the towns and cities governed by 'small knots of reliable men',[42] and thus to remain compliant with its policies, the Crown used a number of devices to sanction effective governing elites in particular communities. Faced with rapid social and economic change, and with an ever-growing concern for the national security, they did so from the mid-Tudor period as never before. The cumulative effect of such efforts changed the nature of urban politics and culture. At the same time, the relations between many towns and the Crown changed as well, bringing them closer together and often eliminating the 'middle-man', in the guise of the traditional feudal landlord who had traditionally held the immediate jurisdiction over most towns, in the process.

Types of Towns: An Urban Typology

Taken together, these changes did indeed make for what Clark and Slack termed a period of transition, but one which was political and cultural as well as social, economic, and doctrinal. In addition, as with all the changes discussed so far, the forces set in motion at this time were of greater consequence to some towns, and some types of towns, than to others. Yet so far the discussion has made no distinction between one type and other. This could give the impression that, save for distinctions in size, urban communities were pretty much all alike. Nothing could be further from the case. In reality, some towns were indeed more 'urban' than others, and some were so marginally urban that they seem hardly different than the countryside surrounding them. Along with our earlier discussions, this begs several questions. What do we mean by 'urban' in the period at hand, and how did urban and rural communities differ, apart from size? Why was it that some towns experienced developments differently than others? And how did towns in general experience them, compared with rural communities? The short answers to some of these questions may be obvious; the answers to others are not. We should not proceed any further before considering them.

In fact, the distinctions between urban and rural communities were not always as sharp as we might think. All urban communities at this time, even the great metropolis of London, exhibited some evidence of such 'rural' activities as crop production and stock rearing. In all but the largest cities major roads led quickly out to the countryside. Many individual building plots backed on to agricultural land. Most towns included some residents directly engaged in agrarian activities, and urban economies were extremely dependent on the state of local crops, livestock, and prices. These factors blurred the distinctions between the smallest towns and the largest villages.

Nevertheless, urban communities shared distinguishing characteristics which set them apart from their rural counterparts. All of them exhibited a significant concentration of population, a primarily non-agrarian economy, a reasonably distinct and sophisticated framework of government, a distinct geographic area (usually with known and precise boundaries), and some economic or cultural or political impact beyond those boundaries.[43] It is generally accepted that something on the order of 650 or 700 or so communities in the period at hand exhibited these basic characteristics, and thus qualified as towns or cities. The ways in which towns exhibited these characteristics, and the extent to which they did so, permits us to arrange urban areas into distinct categories.

Though towns might move over the course of time from one such type to another—a provincial centre at the beginning of the century might decline to mere market town at the end—it is at least a place to begin. It provides a useful typology.

The vast majority of urban centres were small market towns with populations under a thousand.[44] At least at the outset of our period most of these were governed by a manorial lord and his bailiff according to the 'custom' of the manor. John Pitt's Blandford Forum in the County of Dorset, which we will meet in Chapter 2, had long been part of the Manor of Kingston Lacy and, in turn, the Duchy of Lancaster. It would have hovered near the upper limits of such towns, one of eighteen or twenty market towns in just that famously rural county alone. As their name suggests, some of these eighteen would once have had ecclesiastical officials as their manorial lords (e.g., Abbotsbury, Cerne Abbas, Wimbourne Minster); some others may have come directly under the authority of (or have been given autonomy by) the Crown.

Economically and socially speaking, these market towns would not have provided more than the most basic occupations and services, with only a small majority of those in non-agrarian activities. In many cases their economic hinterland scarcely extended beyond six and a half miles: traditionally taken to be the maximum distance from which one could come into a market, carry out one's business, and return home on the same day. The major nonagrarian occupations would have been concerned with processing of food (including, e.g., butchers or fishmongers, grocers, millers, brewers, and bakers), the provision of shelter (including bricklayers, masons, smiths, tilers, carpenters, and thatchers), and the manufacture of cloth or clothing (including, e.g., weavers, fullers, spinners, dyers, tanners, tailors, cordwainers or shoemakers, textile workers, and glovers). Semi-skilled people might have followed several occupations, taking on seasonal or part-time work (including some agricultural work as well) as the opportunity arose. Professionals would pretty much have been limited to clergymen; a bailiff, clerk, or similar official; and perhaps a schoolmaster. Literacy would have been relatively modest in extent, migrants would have come from predominantly short distances, and the social and economic distance between the elite and others would have remained rather narrow.

Every county could boast of at least a few more substantial communities, ones which were more economically specialized and which attracted trade and migration from a wider catchment area. These 'lesser provincial centres' form our second category. The economic activities of these modest regional centres typically included somewhat more specialized trades and industries (e.g., drapers, linen weavers, mercers, silversmiths and pewterers, glaziers and cutlers); more extensive service industries (taverners, inn-keepers, cooks); and professions (physicians, scriveners, apothecaries, notaries and lawyers). Their populations might range from just under a thousand to between two and three thousand. Their governing structure would also usually have been manorial, but they are likely to have secured greater political autonomy during the period at hand. Before the Reformation some may have hosted important religious guilds which drew members from beyond the town's boundaries, or shrines which drew pilgrims or travellers. Like Dorset's county town of Dorchester, they might host those quarterly meetings of the county Commission of the Peace known as Quarter Sessions, presided over by the JPs, or the Assize Courts which also came under the jurisdiction of the Crown.

A step up from these lesser provincial centres would lead us to the thirty or more major provincial centres: towns of even more complex functions, larger populations (perhaps four to seven thousand in c. 1540), and wider external influence.[45] They would have included some of the more substantial shire towns (i.e., the administrative centres of particular counties), the two university towns of Oxford and Cambridge, manufacturing centres like Ipswich, and Worcester. Some cathedral centres (technically—because they held cathedrals—called 'cities' rather than 'towns'), places like Henry Hardware's Chester and John and Joan Cooke's

Gloucester, also belong on this list, as do substantial provincial ports like King's Lynn, Hull, Henry Manship's Great Yarmouth, and (at least in the fifteenth century) Boston.

At the pinnacle of the provincial urban league stood that handful of 'regional capitals' which exceeded all others in all the categories noted so far. Norwich, York, Bristol, Newcastle, Exeter, and perhaps Coventry, Colchester, and Salisbury had populations between about seven thousand and twelve thousand at the start of our period, had substantial traditions of self-government, and were economically dominant over large regions of the realm (Norwich over East Anglia, Bristol over the West, Exeter over the Southwest, Newcastle in the Northeast, and so forth). Interestingly, and not coincidentally, none of them (save for Colchester, which declined as London grew) were situated within a hundred miles or so of London. This reminds us that the more specialized and larger a city became, the fewer of them could be accommodated economically in a particular region. Their economies were simply so highly specialized that there would not be enough custom to sustain those functions unless they took in a very wide catchment area.

Political Typology

One other very important consideration in establishing a hierarchy of provincial town types was their political status. Its importance and complexity demands its own discussion. The constitutional distance between the small market town which functioned politically as part of a manor, entirely subject to the governance of the lord, and such towns of ancient vintage as Gloucester, Bristol, Exeter, Norwich, or York, remained very substantial throughout our period and well beyond. The extent of self-governing authority, the competence and complexity of government structures, and ultimately the political weight of the town in the context of shire and nation, extended over a vast range of possibilities. Even with towns of comparable political standing it was difficult to find two which were exactly alike in their powers, customs, official terminology, by-laws or precise legal entitlements. But fortunately political distinctions, like economic, social, and topographical ones, also lend themselves to sorting by category.

In a handful of the oldest and best established urban centres townsmen had established their own traditions of self-government at such an early time that they had 'from time out of mind', as the saying went, been recognized as self-governing by the Crown. In most cases they were by the sixteenth century among the two most advanced categories of provincial town: either a major provincial centre or one of the handful of elite regional capitals.

Most of the rest of the towns in the realm, easily the vast majority, derived whatever political structures, rights, and privileges they held from the context of manorial jurisdiction. Even in 1540 the majority of English towns, especially towards the bottom of the ladder, were still governed at least to some extent by one or another (and sometimes several) such authorities. An investigation of the political status and development of towns deriving from this context has often been approached as a story of two processes: first, the assertion of the rights and privileges of townsmen against those of their manorial lords; second, the recognition of that assertion through a grant or charter of rights and privileges. Though it fails to recognize the many nuances and exceptions in this complex story, this is still a useful approach to the issue. The assertion of local privileges is easiest to observe through an examination of the charters by which the Crown, and sometimes the landlord, conveyed them.

The ultimate form of such grants was the full charter of incorporation granted by the Crown. This conveyed full corporate status upon the townspeople in question, thereby making their defined collectivity a corporation before the law. In its corporate guise, that town was then able to sue and be sued, acquire and hold property in a secure manner, issue by-laws, hold a corporate seal, and select its own officials perpetually from one generation to the next. Of all the possible types of charter, this is the one which brought a community the closest to full and complete political autonomy under royal authority.

In addition, these charters recognized a more or less standardized form of borough government, spelling out in often fine detail the structures, by-laws, bounds, and other characteristics of community governance. Some charters granted extensive powers and structures which were entirely new. Many other charters chiefly recognized and legitimized conditions of long-standing and customary usage, merely adding one or another item to them as circumstances required.

Charters of incorporation often situated the foundation for local government participation in the institution known as the freemanry. This essentially meant the citizenry: men (and, to a limited extent, women) who had—by apprenticeship, inheritance, or purchase—been admitted to full economic and political rights within the community. The freemanry could include women when, for example (and as in the case of Joan Cooke of Gloucester), they had inherited their status from their deceased freeman-husband. They were then accorded the same full rights and privileges as their male counterparts: to buy and sell at retail, take on apprentices, and, very occasionally, to hold minor office. (We should also note that, as the essay on Joyce Jefferies shows—Chapter 8—some women participated remarkably well in economic activity even without freeman's status.)

All members of the government, save perhaps for the lesser employees who did the lifting and sweeping, had necessarily to be members of the freemanry. It stood as the foundation for the well-understood sequence of office-holding which pertained, at least theoretically, in virtually every corporate and many non-corporate towns. This sequence, the *cursus honorum*, typically included in its middle rungs two councils: a small senior council and a larger junior council, the latter usually twice the size of the former. Criteria for membership in these bodies varied from one town to another, but the small, senior group often co-opted its members from the larger and junior group. This allowed selected individuals to move up the *cursus honorum* to the inner circle of the ruling elite, and it preserved the control of that elite over its own membership. Nomenclature for these bodies was by no means standardized from one town to another (nor did it become so until the Municipal Corporations Act of 1835), but such councils might be known officially as, for example, the small Aldermanic Council and the larger Common Council. Unofficially, they were likely also to be known by their size: the 'Twelve and Twenty-four', or the 'Twenty-four and Forty-eight'.

Atop this official pyramid, and almost always drawn from the ranks of the senior council, sat the mayor. He served a single term of one year, usually beginning at Michelmas (September 29), and then gave over to a successor twelve months later. In addition to these officers and also fixed onto the *cursus honorum*, a town usually had two chamberlains to collect revenues, pay bills, and keep accounts, and a host of lesser employees who looked after the market, public works, the port, and so forth.

Three other officials were essential to the smooth operation of borough government. Because they required specialized skills, and because the incumbents of two of them were not usually resident within the town, their offices were not counted on the *cursus honorum* and they often served for very long periods of time. These were the town clerk, responsible for the town's records; the recorder, usually a professional lawyer who advised the mayor on legal matters; and—in the more substantial boroughs—a high steward, an important national figure who was expected to use his influence in behalf of the town he so served. Neither recorders nor high stewards could be expected to reside in the town. At least the latter should not properly be counted as a formal member of its government. Neither office became common in England's towns and cities until roughly the period covered by this volume. Only then, for the most part, did the growing formalization and responsibility of corporate borough government make them indispensable additions for towns of any importance.[46]

With the help of all three, the mayor and the two councils together shared the law-making functions of the borough. In addition, the mayor (either alone or with the recorder and one or more of the senior aldermen) conventionally presided over the Borough Court (a court with royal authority) and the commercial court known as the Court of Pie Powder. Most important from the Crown's perspective, the mayor and two councils of incorporated boroughs were the legal authorities conventionally responsible for carrying out the virtual deluge of legislative requirements issuing forth from Westminster from about the 1530s on. By the end of the sixteenth century very nearly a hundred statutes—most of them regulating social or economic activity—commanded some form of action specifically on the part of the officials of corporate towns.[47] Non-corporate towns continued to fall under the officials of manor and shire for the same purposes.

The recognition of this form of governing structure by charter of incorporation, and indeed borough incorporation itself, brings us to another distinctive element in the chosen time frame of this book. The concept of borough incorporation, just like the particular governing structure it endorsed, may be traced to well before 1540. Yet as applied to towns the notion of incorporation remained but vaguely understood and little used. Only thirteen boroughs had been incorporated in the first fifty-five years of Tudor rule, from 1485 to 1540.

Yet quite suddenly, around the year 1540, that situation changed sharply. For one, from that time on many more towns clamoured to gain this increasingly coveted status than ever before: 8 in the last years of Henry VIII's reign (1540–1547), 12 in Edward VI's short reign (1547–1553), and an astonishing 24 in Mary's reign (1553–58), before levelling off slightly for the rest of the century. In addition, and perhaps because frequency made for imitation, the content of such charters became much fuller and standardized thereafter. By the end of our period there were a total of 149 borough incorporations and 72 re-incorporations, formalizing, standardizing, and extending the legal privileges of English towns. It is hard to resist the conclusion that the period from c. 1540 onwards not only ushered in a new phase in the use of incorporation as a legal concept, but also in its application to town government. Prior to that time it had been exceptional; well before the end of the period covered in this book it conveyed the normative legal status for towns of any substantial size or importance.

Several factors account for this rapid constitutional development, and for the greater local authority which it established. Some such motivations came from Westminster, and from a Tudor monarchy which was increasingly paternalistic, centralized, and authoritarian. Faced with the challenges of more substantial economic change, and the fear and unrest which came with it, both Crown and Parliament clamoured to bolster local centres of authority which could apply government policy and manage the public welfare at the local level. In this light, borough incorporation may be seen as part of the wider government encouragement for the formalization of all sorts of local corporate institutions, charitable and educational trusts, colleges, trade guilds, and trading companies amongst them.[48]

Some such motivations came from urban communities themselves. Equally concerned about the public order and pressed by the increased weight of statutory responsibility imposed by Parliament, community leaders required greater authority to carry out local government. In towns which had lost the authority of ecclesiastical government, such needs proved especially acute. The sudden availability of dissolved ecclesiastical lands on the market provided another such factor. An incorporated borough had more chance of raising funds, purchasing, and holding newly acquired lands in a secure form of tenure than one which was not incorporated. Lands and resources which had long been physically within the community could now more easily be controlled by its governing body, their revenues enjoyed, their buildings recycled to other uses, and their role in the local identity preserved.

The alternative was to see them sold off to a stranger, and perhaps even to be destroyed for their building materials or other purposes. This had happened in many towns, of which Boston provides a fine example. As we will see in Chapter 1, the Marquess of Northampton managed to snatch valuable properties in that town from under the eyes of its leaders, who had hoped to secure them for the town. At the same time a local entrepreneur, John

Browne, acquired still others so that he could salvage and sell off their building materials. Colourful as it may be, Boston's experience was far from unique. Few issues dominated the attention of town officials at this time more than property, revenues, and resources.

The more modest sized market towns of the day did not often set out successfully down this path to incorporation. They too often lacked the political or financial resources required to stay the course in that involved and costly quest. More of them remained essentially under manorial jurisdiction, with some limited rights of self-government at best, than any of the other types. But the next group up the ladder, the lesser provincial centres with some wider regional importance and some more specialized economic functions, were often better placed to petition for, and receive, incorporation. Many of them had long ago forged limited and de facto institutions of self-government through their guilds and religious fraternities, albeit usually under the superior jurisdiction of a manorial lord. Now they could readily transform those instruments to the more familiar structures of borough government, and have them legitimized by incorporation. Faversham and Maidstone in Kent, Lichfield in Staffordshire, Hertford and St. Albans in Hertfordshire, Banbury in Oxfordshire, Chippenham in Wiltshire, and John Browne's Boston in Lincolnshire typify regionally important towns gaining incorporation shortly after 1540. Abingdon, Lyme Regis, Beverley, Tewkesbury, Thetford, and Congleton are amongst those which did so later in the century.

Of the next class up in our league tables, the major provincial centres, very few if any remained unincorporated by the turn of the seventeenth century. In some of the former cathedral or abbey-dominated towns (including St. Albans, Bury St. Edmunds, and Beverley) where the emergence of self-governing powers had been severely restricted, that move represented a more emphatic break with the past. The familiar 'two-council-plus-a-mayor' format had sometimes to be created almost from scratch. But in most towns of this and other types, incorporation could build on at least some earlier forms and traditions of self-rule.

When we move up to the big five or six regional capitals, we find that incorporation was not always seen as so important in this era. Having been large and important for a long time past, most had received many lesser charters from a very early stage, and had been amongst the earliest to be granted actual incorporation.[49] The sixteenth century found them so well established and jurisdictionally self-confident as to be in no particular hurry to update their charters. Even Exeter, the last of these to receive incorporation (in 1537 and, more fully, in 1550) nevertheless held no fewer than forty-two charters of one sort or another by the turn of the seventeenth century.[50]

Because the initiative of petitioning for incorporation lay open chiefly to those few townsmen who could support the substantial costs involved, and because the petitioners themselves could usually shape a charter to their own advantage, incorporation also had the effect of encouraging oligarchic rule. This, too, served as a motive for leading townsmen to seek incorporation. It was especially typical of the larger communities, where economic and social polarization proved more extreme, and in towns with more extensive rights of self-government than in those still under seigneurial jurisdiction. These petitioners expected to be rewarded for their initiatives by being named in the charter as 'charter' officials. They were rarely disappointed. And whereas earlier charters of incorporation generally permitted reasonably wide participation in the selection of new aldermen, councillors, and even mayors, those powers grew more restrictive as time went on. The freemanry at large saw their rights of nomination and election steadily nibbled away over the course of time. In choosing members of each council, and even the mayoralty itself, the practice of co-option by members of the superior body came steadily to replace more broad-based forms of selection.

Taken in its appropriate context, oligarchic rule may not in all ways have been the Bad Thing which the name suggests. The ruling elites which came increasingly to dominate provincial towns in this era were not necessarily corrupt in the sense of using their powers for personal gain. Many contemporaries considered that they were merely exercising the sort of rule by 'the better sort' which served as the norm for most governing institutions of the day. Then, too, oligarchy usually arose out of a degree of necessity. The more authority a town's government was obliged to exercise, both by statute and circumstance, the stronger and more forceful its leadership had to be. The superior wealth, experience, connections, and reputation of such leaders proved essential assets in the proper ordering of the community. It is thus no wonder that the Crown, ever concerned about the strength of the common weal as a key to national security, wholeheartedly supported and encouraged this development.

The tendency towards oligarchic rule may also be measured over time by careful attention to constitutional forms. Just as the great rush to gain local autonomy by an initial charter of incorporation came principally in the half-century or so after about 1540, a subsequent stage of this development came a half-century or so after that (roughly in the years c.1590–1640). It then became common for the governing cliques of towns already incorporated to petition for new and more extensive charters which would further tighten their hold on power. Only seven re-incorporations were issued between 1540 and 1590. Three of them came in 1589, perhaps reacting to the threat to civil order posed by the Spanish Armada. But between 1590 and 1640 there were no fewer than sixty-five such charters, almost all of them further strengthening the existing authorities and further excluding others from participation.[51] Many were hotly contested. Towns such as Beverley,[52] Ludlow,[53] Abingdon,[54] Chichester,[55] and Totnes[56] left vivid records of litigation over these issues.

In any event, by 1640 the earlier thrust for self-rule had often resulted in narrow oligarchies of townsmen firmly in control. Were it not for the ability of the same middling and better sort of townspeople to re-create a culture of deference and harmony, many more such conflicts might have ensued. That picture should encourage us to consider very carefully the development in this very era of such cultural forms as civic portraiture, civic building, and the writing of civic history. All of those forms, and others like

them, were deliberately cultivated to encourage loyalty and obedience towards local governing elites, and towards the borough
corporation itself. Several of the essays which follow address
these very subjects. Those on John and Joan Cooke (Chapter 3) and
on Sir Thomas White (Chapter 4) demonstrate the political use of
portraiture. John Pitt's efforts to supervise the construction of a
new guildhall in the Dorset town of Blandford Forum (Chapter 2)
tell us something about the purposes of civic building. Henry
Manship's history of his native town of Great Yarmouth (Chapter
5) exemplifies the role of local historical writing in legitimizing the
political authorities of the day.

London

So far the discussion has almost exclusively considered provincial towns and cities. Little has been said about London. The omission has been intentional, prompted by the facts that London operated on a different scale, had different structures of government,
and served a great many more functions than any other urban
centre in the realm. Of all urban places in England, it was (at least
by the middle of our period) its only true metropolis. While of
course it shared many characteristics of other urban centres, London nevertheless merits a discussion of its own.

London stands out in many ways, and certainly in its size and
administrative complexity. Where most towns had but one parish
and even the largest provincial capitals had at most two dozen,
metropolitan London had ninety-seven within its still extant and
functioning walls (four of which parishes extended on both sides
of the walls), and another twenty-five or so in parts of the counties
of Middlesex, Essex, and, south of the River Thames, Surrey as
well.[57] Where most provincial centres had two councils of 'twelve
and twenty-four' or 'twenty-four and forty-eight', London had a
Court of Aldermen with one representative from each of 26 wards,
and a Common Council of 212 members. In addition, it had a large
assembly called the Common Hall which offered direct representation for its several dozen guilds or 'livery companies'. The

twelve most prominent Livery Companies enjoyed a particularly vivid presence amongst this number. London's mayor, called the Lord Mayor, thus sat atop of an extremely large and complex *cursus honorum*. Much more secure in its administrative jurisdiction than other towns and cities, London did not become incorporated until 1608.

At about 50,000 people at the opening of the century, greater London ('The City' within the walls plus Westminster, Southwark, and suburban areas) was at least four times the population of the next largest cities in the realm, Norwich and Bristol. But especially after mid-century, London's population grew at a pace unrivalled anywhere else in England. By c. 1548 the metropolitan area is reckoned to have had between 61,000 and 75,000 residents, with 35,000 to 43,000 in the City alone. Exceptionally rapid growth from the last quarter of the century raised the metropolitan population to at least 200,000 by 1600 and possibly as much as 375,000 by the outbreak of the Civil Wars four decades later.[58]

These huge population levels, based especially on unprecedented suburban expansion, made London one of the fastest growing cities, if not the fastest growing city, in Europe. Whereas by about 1540 London still ranked behind Constantinople, Paris, Naples, and Venice, it had surpassed Venice by 1600 and Naples by about the 1630s to become Europe's third largest city overall.[59] The measure of its growth relative to other English towns and cities is equally dramatic. While London population jumped at what looks like a geometric rate by the decade, the population growth in England's five or six next largest cities remained relatively modest. Indeed, compared to London, some appear hardly to have grown at all.[60]

London's huge size and metropolitan character may be attributed to several factors. Thanks to the Romans, who placed it at the hub of their road system in Britain, it remained the centre of internal communications and transport. This and its link to the sea through the Thames estuary made it the chief port of the realm as well, within easy sailing distance of the commercial centres of northern Europe. Trade and transport, both overseas and domestic, had always lain at the heart of London's economic vitality. Yet though the point is often forgotten, London was also a considerable manufacturing centre, with shipbuilding, brewing, and myriad manufacturing specialities doing especially well by our period. Service industries also played an important part, as a very large proportion of the metropolis made heavy use of eating and drinking establishments, inns and lodging houses, entertainments and professional services, and myriad related occupations catering to its needs. Finally, in a multitude of ways London served England's principal royal residence and the seat of its government in the contiguous Borough of Westminster. Almost nowhere else in Europe did the chief commercial centre of a nation host the royal court and central government apparatus as well.

London's dynamic population growth exemplifies better than anything else the two-edged sword of opportunity and concern created in this period. On the one hand, if there were ever a place of opportunity which projected its siren call throughout the realm, this was it. Betterment migrants looking for improved opportunity through apprenticeship or investment, and subsistence migrants looking for relief in the face of economic hardship elsewhere, flowed in on every tide. Young adults looking for spouses while they worked as domestics or apprentices or journeymen, and older adults fleeing unsuccessful marriages,[61] people of all ages and descriptions seeking the anonymity of the metropolis where they could start life over again, religious and economic refugees from abroad, or Catholic recusants fleeing the threat of discovery in smaller English communities: all flocked there as if their lives depended on it, and sometimes they did.

Under these circumstances it is no wonder at all that men like Sir Thomas White (see Chapter 4), in the image of Dick Whittington before him, could come from the Berkshire clothing town of Reading with promise of a good apprenticeship and end up as Lord Mayor of London and one of England's wealthiest men. Provided with a start of that sort from a well-to-do parent, White found it easy to make his mark in his livery company, his parish, and in the sundry rungs of City government.

But for people of humbler origins, the metropolis proved an enormous challenge, and most failed to connect with the sort of institutions which permitted White's rise to the top. Good connections and ample capital became more than ever the prerequisites for economic success as the century wore on. Yet the sort of kinship networks which were so important for economic advancement elsewhere were often not as strongly established in the metropolis. Economic opportunity for the better trained and more aggressive also meant greater exploitation of the less skilled or confident, or those with few of the right connections. In consequence, social mobility became more difficult, the distance between the top and bottom of the London world grew appreciably, and large areas of the metropolis, particularly on the suburban fringes, seemed disadvantaged and impoverished.

Living conditions spanned a similarly wide range. As with almost all pre-industrial cities, London's death rate was substantially higher than its birth rate. Conditions of housing and sanitation invited overcrowding, ill-health, and gross discomfort. Plague and other epidemic diseases were constant causes of concern, reaching crisis proportions at too-frequent intervals. It is no wonder that, even more than most provincial towns, London depended for its growth on a net inward migration rather than a 'natural' increase of births over deaths.

Efforts to ban further building in the City, and thus check the uncontrolled expansion, were expressed in proclamations and statutes from the 1580s on through the end of our period. Yet they had little effect beyond the fines they generated to the Crown's coffers for non-compliance.[62] Areas which were distinctly rural even in the mid-sixteenth century, especially to the east and in nearby portions of the County of Essex, rapidly gave way to ribbon-like roads, and then in-filling of smaller houses and tenements between those links.[63] This sequence unfolded time and time again, in areas both suitable and not suitable for housing, and often with construction both hasty and substandard. Even in areas of the City and nearby suburbs, houses which had had gardens, or which had been separated from their neighbours' houses by empty lots (the 'void grounds' of contemporary speech) now rapidly filled in, dramatically increasing the density of population. John Stow's oft-cited lament for the dairy farms and milk-maids of his youth, written in 1598, was no idle reminiscence, but an accurate reflection on how the City had grown during his life-time:

> Neare adioyning to this Abbey on the South Side thereof, was sometime a Farme belonging to the said Nunrie, at the which Farme I my selfe in my youth haue fetched many a halfe pennie worth of Milke ... Always hote from the Kine. . . . One Trolop, and afterwardes Goodman, were the Farmers there, and had thirtie or fortie kine. . . .[64]

We also read of Hogg Lane, which 'within these fortie yeares had on both sides fayre hedgerowes of Elme trees, with Bridges and easie stiles to pass ouer into the pleasant fieldes, very commodious for Citizens therein to walke, shoote, and ... refresh their dulled spirites in the sweete and wholesome ayre, which is now ... made a continuall building throughout, of Garden houses, and small cottages'. Similarly, he found the once open fields of the Aldgate highway now 'fully replenished with buildings outwarde & also pestered with diuerse Allyes on eyther side ...'.[65]

Recent research has revealed that London was not by any means as lawless and ungovernable as once assumed, and has emphasized that at least some of its jurisdiction extended well beyond the City walls.[66] Yet no centre of its size and complexity could provide perfect security for its residents. It is no wonder that in the sprawling and untamed colossus which had turned bucolic scenes into teeming streets and narrow lanes, a confidence man and swindler like Robert Swaddon could ply his trade with relative impunity, or that John Pulman and his companions of the demi-monde could make their way for years working on both sides of the law. If the great metropolis allowed the Thomas Whites of the day to find their fame and fortunes, and if its authorities somehow managed to avoid major social upheavals, to wrestle earnestly with problems of poverty, disease, and the occasional riot, it also gave shelter and opportunity to many of less noble intent. This, too, proved a function of the metropolis.

What Next?

The people and towns discussed below were chosen because they represent many of the themes laid out in the preceding pages. With the exceptions of Swaddon the swindler and Pulman the thief-taker (Chapter 7), for whom a degree of anonymity served as a condition of basic survival, all of them were reasonably well known in their own time and communities. Yet except for Sir Thomas White, none of them counted as national figures. The rest stand out in part because of the chance survival of sources which allow us to know them and to reconstruct their activities. Yet in other ways they remain representative types, engaged in activities which were typical, and typically significant, in their time and place.

John Browne's unremitting efforts to use the dissolution and resale of ecclesiastical properties to his own advantage, and thus to make his way in life, demonstrate the sort of wheeling and dealing facilitated by the events of the time. Both he and his town of Boston, which resisted his efforts, engaged in a litigious pas de deux of a sort which was widely paralleled elsewhere. John Pitt's efforts to supervise the construction of the new guildhall in Blandford Forum (Chapter 2) show both the amateur quality of most aspects of borough government and the importance of civic halls in symbolizing the force and integrity of the newly assertive borough governments of the day.

The experiences of John and Joan Cooke of Gloucester (Chapter 3) and Sir Thomas White of London (Chapter 4) speak in their own ways to philanthropic inclinations of wealthy townspeople before as well as after the Reformation. The posthumous enhancement of their reputations, in forms both literary and visual, contributed by century's end to an emerging image of the merchant hero. Such a turnabout reversed the traditional and pejorative connotations of the urban and commercial milieu. Often the effort to boost the reputation of the city had more pointedly political ends, obedience and deference to its rulers foremost amongst them. Henry Manship's 1619 history of his borough of Great Yarmouth (Chapter 5) presents a scholarly and yet gently polemical rationale for such doctrines. A more particularly blunt effort towards the same ends may be seen in Henry Hardware's troubled mayoral term in the City of Chester (Chapter 6), where the threat of social unrest and even violence led to a stunning display of oligarchic imagery in the annual Midsummer Show procession.

Notwithstanding sundry efforts to unify the direction of civic government, urban communities of any substantial size remained complex and pluralistic constructs. Status and occupational groups, neighborhoods, and even age and gender cohorts were indeed 'worlds within worlds'.[67] They continued to flourish within the larger framework of the nation. Perhaps only London could have harboured the parallel criminal milieux both of the 'white collar' swindler Robert Swaddon and the more menacing circle of John Pulman the extortionist and 'thief-taker'. Yet even a sleepy cathedral city like Hereford provided rich and varied opportunities for such allegedly marginal social groups as spinsters, and of women in general. The last essay in the volume (Chapter 8) shows us the complex, highly socialized, and entirely engaged life of Joyce Jefferies, an affluent and independent resident of that community.

Multiplied many times over, the personal experiences presented here are meant to suggest the tenor of urban life at a time of critical transition in the nation's past. Before this time English towns may be thought of as small islands in a sea of agrarian life and culture. The nation itself had far shallower urban traditions than some other parts of Europe, the Low Countries and the Italian Peninsula amongst them. But by the end of our period, thanks in some considerable measure to the sort of people portrayed in these pages, towns and townspeople played a much more significant role in national life, and had come to be regarded as so doing. The links between townspeople and nation had grown much firmer, with the character of each markedly evolving in that process.

CHAPTER 1

Browne, Town, and Crown: John Browne and the Quest for Crown Lands in Boston

Perhaps nowhere in the whole span of English history can we find a larger turnover in land-holding than that which took place after the property dissolutions of the 1530s and 1540s. By the legislation of the 1530s the Crown confiscated or 'dissolved' the lands and possessions of the religious houses (especially monasteries, abbeys, priories and nunneries; their lands, buildings, rental properties, jewels, plate and other endowments). In the following decade it did the same to the chantries, religious guilds, and fraternities, and all of their properties and endowments. These holdings represented something on the order of a quarter to a third of the land in England. Completing what has usefully been labelled a veritable 'tenurial revolution',[1] the Crown resold a great deal of this property in ensuing decades. In addition, the same period saw a particularly tumultuous state of high politics, in which numerous members of the nobility and court circle were done in, in one way or another. Their lands and possessions, often former ecclesiastical holdings, were also usually liable to confiscation and resale by the Crown.

Much of what we know about this vast turnover of property emerged from the scholarly debate, chiefly between the 1950s and the 1970s, over the relative wealth and status of the aristocracy and the landed gentry. Three impressions conveyed by that debate were (a) that the bulk of those lands and resources were rural; (b) that they were confiscated and then mostly sold off by the Crown fairly quickly; and (c) that the recipients were predominantly members of the landed aristocracy and gentry or they were court officials. It is also well established that the new owners often tore down substantial buildings piece by piece, recycling the valuable lead, stone, slates, timber, tiles, and other such materials so as to construct the great country houses which marked the rise of individual fortunes in that era.

Probably because the recognition of these tendencies came forth from the context of a debate about the landed classes, little attention has been paid to the story of dissolved lands which were urban rather than rural, or to purchasers who were townspeople or which were towns themselves. Those few studies which did look at urban property did not see towns or townsmen gaining much. Even such seminal investigators as W. G. Hoskins failed to detect in townspeople 'any sustained interest in urban property' in the years immediately following dissolution, though he left more open the possibility that further gains may have been forthcoming in subsequent years.[2] This verdict led to another common assumption: that both civic corporations and individual townsmen acquired few of the holdings which had been made available in their own communities, and thus lost a golden opportunity to keep control of them in local hands.

But the fact is that many properties dissolved and resold by the Crown do indeed prove to have been urban rather than rural. This is especially so for lands which had been held by the guilds and chantries and were dissolved in the 1540s rather than those held by monasteries and abbeys which went in the 1530s. In addition, though not too many towns or townsmen purchased these properties when they first became available, few efforts have been made to trace the disposition of property further along in time and through subsequent rounds of sales. Later sales and purchases have thus escaped attention. In reality, many substantial urban properties changed hands several times during the course of the century following the initial dissolution, with an ever increasing number coming into the hands of towns themselves or resident townsmen over that duration.

Unfortunately, this point cannot be made with any great quantitative precision. The number, complexity, and means of such transactions makes the evidence for this process incomplete on anything like a national basis. Nevertheless, it isn't difficult to find numerous examples of this activity amongst prominent provincial towns of the day. The farther down the years one looks at the issue, the longer the list becomes. Such towns as Coventry, Leicester, Exeter, Oxford, Bedford, Totnes, Gloucester, and Bristol may not have made many purchases in the early years after dissolution, but they had made some big ones by the end of the century.[3] In addition, because many lands meant rental income, these purchases often allowed those towns to reverse local economic decline, stabilize their finances, and enhance the political position of their governing elites.

It also seems that at least a few towns and townsmen were able to stride quickly off the mark at the beginning and to make very substantial acquisitions. A few even acquired lands in local instances of panic selling by guilds and chantries just before dissolution. Sometimes this was accomplished quite legally, with license from the Crown. Some other holdings were transferred without such a license, and then concealed from the Crown's commissioners who came to take inventory of the lands to be dissolved.

In reality, if we look at the whole century following the first dissolutions (i.e., approximately 1540–1640), the acquisition of dissolved urban property proves just as prominent a theme in the history of some of England's towns (and especially in her corporate towns) and urban families as in some of her landed families. And because there was certainly a strong connection at that time between property and power, that long-range turnover proved as important for the empowerment of some urban interests—both corporate and personal—as for some elements of the landed classes.

These themes, and a few common variations upon them, are particularly well illustrated by the Lincolnshire port town and borough of Boston, and by one of its residents in particular: John Browne. Neither Boston nor Browne himself had much status or many resources on the eve of the dissolutions. Both clamoured mightily—and not always successfully—to seize the opportunity when it arose. Both markedly improved their respective positions in the end. This essay takes up the story of Boston, and of Browne, as they reacted to the dramatically expanded opportunities for acquiring land in the mid-century period. In addition, because this local story sheds light on an unfolding national government policy on the urban condition at a time of rising population and housing shortages, this must be a story of 'Crown' as well as 'town and Browne'.

Boston at the Dissolution

Throughout most of the thirteenth and fourteenth centuries the borough of Boston, some seven miles up the River Witham from that part of the North Sea known as The Wash, had been one of the most important and prosperous of England's provincial ports. It had hosted the only Hansa Steelyard, or mart for Hanseatic merchants, in England outside of London. It had ranked fifth amongst all English towns in the tax quota of 1334, and ninth in tax-paying population (at 2,871 adult males sufficiently well off to be taxed) in 1377.[4] Although its autonomous governing authority remained far less developed than in some other ports of roughly similar importance, we must still consider it one of England's most prosperous and important commercial centres in those years.[5]

By most accounts, however, Boston's fortunes went rapidly downhill from there. By about 1400 the lucrative foreign trade in wine and wool especially, much stimulated by the City of Lincoln, for which Boston served as a seaport, waned sharply as Italian and other continental merchants shifted their attentions to London and Southampton. Even the resurgence of cloth manufacture around Coventry in the early fifteenth century, much of which made its way through the port of Boston, afforded only a few more years of prosperity, so that most of that century found the town in slow but steady commercial decline. The Hanseatic merchants soon abandoned their Boston outpost. Steady silting of the riverbed further accelerated this collapse. By the turn of the sixteenth century, Boston's international trade had dwindled to a trickle, and no particularly strong coastal trade emerged for several decades to balance the loss.[6] Local population levels fell accordingly, from roughly fifty-seven hundred at the time of the 1377 Poll Tax to a little more than two thousand in 1563.[7] Over this long span of time, rental values plunged along with population. Landlords found little incentive to keep up their rental properties, and the quality of the available housing stock—often a reliable barometer to economic conditions—deteriorated accordingly.

Yet despite this long-range decline, the antiquary John Leland could still describe some 'fair dwellings' in his visit of the early 1540s. By then it seems likely that, with many other towns and the nation's population in general, Boston's population may at last have been on the upswing. Measured over the long haul of two centuries Boston may have been a failed port, but it clearly had some life to it yet as a provincial town. It was still one of the largest towns and trading centres in Lincolnshire, at least parts of which enjoyed a rich agricultural economy of mixed farming and fertile soils.[8] At a time of resumed national population growth and rising food prices, Boston could reasonably hope to reinvent itself economically as a centre for regional marketing and local industry. At this bullish time, its leaders were anxious to establish greater political autonomy so that the town could control as much as it could of the resources within its boundaries.

Amongst the weighty burdens imposed by this broad economic transition were issues of legal jurisdiction and civic finance. Boston's governing structures on the eve of Reformation were still largely manorial, leaving the townsmen to control only their religious guilds and fraternities. Over the course of several centuries these institutions had come to possess extensive monetary endowments and real properties—buildings, agricultural lands, rental properties, and so forth—which had accrued from the pious bequests of members and townspeople. In the absence of other secular and locally controlled institutions of local government, it often fell substantially to the guilds and fraternities to look after the community's resources: streets and market, seawalls and harbour, poor relief, education, housing, and so forth. It was especially important to carry out repairs to the town's seawall, which had been badly damaged in the serious storms and floods of the year 1543. This had caused flooding over several square miles of surrounding farmland as well as damage to local shipping.[9]

The townsmen's ability to cope with these demands, and to take advantage of what seemed to be more prosperous times on the horizon, remained hobbled by their subordinate and complex legal status. As an unincorporated borough, Boston was largely subject to seigneurial authority exercised from elsewhere. But unlike many smaller seigneurial boroughs, which were subject to the control of a single manorial lord, Boston remained additionally subject to the authority of several distinct and external jurisdictions: to the Fees of Tattershall and Croun, to the feudal Honour of Richmond and to the Manor of the Borough of Boston itself which formed a part of the Honour. In particular, Bostonians had traditionally depended on the earls of Richmond, lords of the Honour and thus also lords of the Manor of Boston, for the exercise of most legal authority over the community. Even the town's bailiffs and stewards were in reality the earl's officials, appointed by him rather than by the townsmen themselves. There were other rival authorities to consider as well. The bishop of Lincoln claimed sundry jurisdictions of an ecclesiastical and fiscal sort, the towns of Cambridge and King's Lynn as well as the merchants of London claimed various commercial privileges, and so forth.[10] Even aside from such important obligations as finances, public works, and legal jurisdiction, the townsmen's weak corporate position had sometimes proven an obstacle in restraining unruly elements in their own community.[11]

The financial implications of this situation remained particularly irksome. Unlike many other, more independent, towns of the same size, the lack of its own governing authority had hampered Boston's ability to hold property and bring in income from rents. In its heyday as a leading port, taxes and tolls derived from commerce satisfied most local requirements. Rents had been less important. In fact, during the long period of declining population, vacancy rates were so high and rents so low, it hardly mattered who controlled them. But by the early sixteenth century, when rental values began to rise with the renewal of population, the town's ability to meet its fiscal obligations, to maintain public works, and to do a great many other things, still remained very insufficient. External authorities like the earls of Richmond collected much of the rents as was their due, but they repaired only what and when they wished. Only the guilds and fraternities could be seen as indigenous holders of rental properties, even though they were of course not strictly speaking secular institutions of local government.

Dissolution of numerous local and income-bearing properties, (along with the Crown's repossession of the Honour of Richmond for quite other reasons) and the resale of all those holdings by the Crown, provided a unique opportunity to reverse this very subordinate legal status. On the one hand Bostonians could perhaps gain control of these very substantial properties whose revenues had been controlled externally. On the other, the dissolution of the guilds and fraternities could mean alienation of even more lands from local control if those properties were bought up by outsiders. Clearly, this was not an opportunity to be missed.

In a sense the dissolutions of the monasteries, abbeys, and nunneries in the 1530s proved something of a trial run for Boston: relatively little Boston land had been held by such institutions, and, though the borough initially bought very little of it, it hadn't lost much either. The death of Henry Fitzroy, the King's illegitimate son and earl of Richmond, in 1536, had meant that the lordship of the Manor of Boston reverted to the King, but neither the properties nor the lordship were sold off immediately thereafter. The same could be said of the extensive Boston holdings of John, Lord Hussey, who was attainted for treason in the following year: his lands also reverted to the King.

But the calamitous flood of 1543, and the great and expensive destruction left in its wake, emphasized to Bostonians more starkly than ever the importance of controlling their own resources. When rumours began to circulate in the early 1540s of a second phase of dissolutions, one which would take in the chantries, guilds, and fraternities, Bostonians could wait no longer.

Given the willingness of a number of leading townspeople to contribute towards the potential purchase from the Crown, only one obstacle stood in the way. Before the Borough could receive such lands in this or any other manner, it had first to obtain the legal status which enabled it to hold lands as a corporate body. This meant securing a charter of incorporation. The development of this legal device may be traced well back before the Tudor era, but only at this very time was it becoming a common practice for individual towns. Only thirteen towns had sought and received incorporation in the first fifty-five years of Tudor rule, but many (a total of forty-four between 1540 and 1558 alone) would do so from this time forth, often for motives which were similar to Boston's.

Amongst its other implications, incorporation would allow Boston to gain for itself, as a corporate borough, the several legal authorities which had traditionally been exercised by outsiders, and which were now held, or (in the case of the guilds and fraternities) about to be held, by the Crown. This authority would then allow the borough to purchase property and to hold it with security of tenure. In a larger sense, incorporation would make the freemen of Boston masters in their own household, able to determine and shape their own future as a community for the first time.

Thus a group of the leading townsmen embarked on two big steps at virtually the same time. They petitioned the Crown for a charter of incorporation, and then they petitioned for the purchase of a large number of properties, both formerly ecclesiastical and others, which had come into the Crown's hands. Though neither document has survived, we may infer that in the first petition they described the structure of government and the rights they wished to have. Amongst them were the rights to hold several courts, to collect several forms of toll, to be exempt from a variety of external jurisdictions, and to hold lands in mortmain, the most secure form of tenure for their needs.[12] In the second petition, they asked to purchase the lordship and Manor of Boston and numerous other properties. These included scattered Boston properties which had belonged to several distant abbeys and monasteries and also some of the more extensive properties of the local religious guilds and fraternities, including those of Corpus Christi and St. Mary. The request included jurisdiction over the inhabitants of the suburb known as Skirbeck Quarter, traditionally considered part of the Fee of Richmond, though that claim was heatedly disputed by Skirbeck residents.[13]

To their great delight and relief, both petitions were granted, almost at the same time: the charter of incorporation on 14 May, 1545;[14] the grant of lands on May 28.[15] Ironically, the Act of Dissolution for Chantries, Religious Guilds and Fraternities (37 Henry VIII, c. 4) was passed by Parliament and signed into law just six months later. Boston had managed to purchase at least some of these guild and fraternity properties before they could be dissolved. In addition, as eventually became known, it appeared informally to have annexed some local guild and fraternity properties which had not previously been included in the grant, effectively concealing those acquisitions from the Crown and then collecting their revenues without full legal entitlement. All things considered, the newly corporate townsmen, led by a mayor, twelve aldermen, and eighteen common councillors, had reason to anticipate a rosier future for the borough. In all, they agreed to pay the Crown the hefty sum of £1646 15^s 4^d over a period of twelve years for lands rated at an annual rental value of £526, to which could be added the value of the guild lands informally annexed. Once the annual payments had been made, this appeared to assure the borough of over £300 in annual income during the repayment period and even more thereafter. It seemed sufficient to establish fiscal stability even in a borough whose best days as a trading centre were well behind it.[16]

Yet things were not to run as smoothly as they had hoped. The concealed guild and fraternity lands which the borough had illicitly annexed, those of the Guild of St. Mary and the Guild of St. Peter and St. Paul, were granted in January 1552 by King Edward VI to the marquess of Northampton.[17] In order to take possession of these properties, Northampton challenged the borough's control. After much controversy with the marquess and divisions amongst themselves, the Mayor and burgesses were compelled to acknowledge his rights. They ceded the lands to him in July of that year, winning in exchange a commitment for the foundation of a grammar school.[18] Northampton was not the borough's only competitor for available lands. It also faced competition for local resources from within its own community.

This brings us at last to the interesting and, in many ways, typical figure of John Browne. If the 'Mayor, Alderman and Common Councillors of the Borough of Boston' (for that was now the official name of the town's government) had hoped to seize this particular moment, so did he. The nature of the competition between those two interests, and the manner of its resolution, proves an equally revealing window on the politics of local resources after the Reformation. It shows how individual townsmen, no less than towns themselves, sometimes seized the opportunity to profit by purchases of dissolved lands, and to gain wealth, status, and influence by so doing.

John Browne

One might well say that John Browne is important to us in our time because he was so relatively unimportant—and so typical—in his own. He began in almost complete obscurity and ended life as a gentleman, and moved along that road in ways which were characteristic of other men on the make. We know little of his early life. We may speculate that he was born sometime between about 1505 and 1515; we know that he died in 1582.[19] He probably migrated to Boston from elsewhere in the shire: possibly from Brothertofte, a few miles outside of Boston,[20] or from West Deeping, some twenty-five miles to the southwest.[21] There are indications that he passed through each of those opposite poles of propriety represented by study of the law at Gray's Inn on the one hand,[22] and incarceration in Marshalsea Prison on the other.[23] He was certainly not in that group of town leaders who secured the charter, or successfully petitioned for the lands gained in 1545, nor did he serve in local government for some time to come.

We do know of his connection to a middling gentry family from that part of Lincolnshire known as Holland. From the mid-1540s to the early 1550s, his relative Thomas Browne served as a customs official for the Port of Boston, a Justice of the Peace, a Commissioner for Sewers, and in a number of other capacities in royal administration at the shire level.[24] Another Thomas Browne, a middling gentleman of Fishtofte outside of Boston, made John an executor to his will in 1557, referring to him as 'gent.'[25] By then Browne had become well known to his fellow Bostonians, made his residence there, and had begun to be accepted in at least the outer circle of the ruling elite. But this had not always been the case. Members of Boston's governing elite knew Browne as an adversary long before they took him for a colleague. Browne was not alone in his efforts to acquire local properties for himself, but to a far greater degree than anyone else, he challenged or flouted the borough's authority in pursuit of his own ends. He worked aggressively and litigiously, engaged quickly in controversy, and was clearly a man on the make.

These assertions seem to have begun in 1547, if not beforehand, when he brought a lengthy petition against the borough to the Court of Star Chamber. It amounted to nothing less than the first cannon shot in a sweeping legal challenge to the borough's acquisitions of 1545 and to its very incorporation. Browne claimed that the Mayor and alderman had received their lands under false pretences. They had appeared to want the lands so as to protect the town from the 'ruin from the sea', and so that revenues deriving from those lands might be employed in relief of the local poor. Browne charged that some of the borough's aldermen involved in the purchase had been officials of the very guilds which were being purchased, thus constituting a conflict of interest in the transaction. He alleged that the Mayor and aldermen had sold off the jewels, plate, and moveable goods of the former guilds for roughly £1,000, and proceeded to use those considerable funds for their own purposes. He noted, too, that the borough government had begun to charge townsmen a fee for becoming freemen, which had not been done before. Finally, Browne charged that the Mayor and aldermen had set out to do him personal harm and to have set a certain sum of money aside for that purpose.

In conclusion, Browne saw these actions as a deceitful violation of the newly acquired charter of incorporation. He at least affected a concern that it would lead to the undoing of the town and to its inability to pay the King's customs on trade. He asked the Star Chamber to create a commission of enquiry, with the clear implication that, should it sustain his allegations, the borough's control of these lands, and perhaps its very charter, should be nullified. Following the normal procedure upon receipt of such a petition, the Court struck the desired commission in August 1547. Amongst its members was John Browne's kinsman Thomas.[26]

Browne's allegations were neither implausible nor, as it transpired, completely unfounded. The jewels and plate of the local church and guilds had been the object of several schemes before the time of his suit, forming the crux of a Star Chamber case in Boston itself a few years before incorporation.[27] Sale of such riches had become very common in the Edwardian years. As for Browne's other charges, even the defendants admitted imposing freeman's fines, though they noted that their new charter allowed them to do so. And as for conflict of interest, the same John Margery who as Alderman of the Guild of St. Mary deeded the guild and its properties to the borough according to the terms of their purchase, was also one of the charter alderman of the borough, taking his oath on the first meeting of the new corporation.[28] Indeed, in a small community where guild activity was one of the few forms of public life open to leading citizens, this sort of 'conflict of interest' must have been very common.

Browne's motivations for bringing this suit against the borough are not as clear as one would like, but the circumstances suggest several possibilities. Clearly the suit indicates a degree of antagonism between himself and at least some elements of the borough leadership. In addition, he may have been acting in what he hoped would appear to be the King's interest in uncovering a deceitfully obtained charter: the wording of the petition certainly conveys the sense that the burgesses had deceived King Henry in their petitions for both the lands and the charter. For this revelation he no doubt hoped to be rewarded. It was the sort of action which held out hope of a career in the King's service, perhaps with some royal office in the Boston area.

There is also a third possibility, and one not incompatible with the first two. Browne may have been a committed Roman Catholic, loyal to the traditional religious guilds and to that faith which they had been organized to serve, and anxious to sabotage any strategy for curtailing their activities or confiscating wealth emanating from pious bequests. A continued devotion to the traditional faith is certainly suggested by the formula in his will, even though he wrote it as late as 1578. Amongst his requests of the court were that it investigate whether the pious bequests which had created the guilds' wealth had been honoured since the borough's acquisition.[29] In a town which became known as an early Protestant stronghold, this alone could well have alienated him from the mainstream.[30]

But when all is said and done, it is hard not to imagine that Browne must also have hoped to obtain at least some of the properties in question for his own benefit. Because the borough actually made most of its purchases just a few months before the official dissolution and resale of the guild lands in question, Browne had not had the same fair chance to bid for them as would normally have done if the Crown had actually dissolved them and put them up for sale. He may well have intended the suit to nullify the borough's purchases so as to reopen the prospect of purchasing something for himself. His later activities in acquiring other properties in the town certainly support such a suggestion.

The borough's response to Browne's accusations, as articulated by its Mayor, Nicholas Robertson, and the leading alderman, John Wendon, proves very revealing.[31] It tells us a great deal about the goals and strategies of a provincial town faced with the imminent dissolution of its traditional religious guilds, and with the loss to civic coffers of the income brought in by the endowments of those institutions.

Robertson and Wendon affirmed that there was a genuine and critical need to keep up the sea dikes and coastline, which the King, as the resumed Lord of the Honour of Richmond, could not effectively do.[32] The particularly bad storm of 1543 had indeed wrought great destruction to surrounding farmland and destroyed part of the sea-dike belonging to the Honour. As the King could not or had not expeditiously repaired this, so they claimed, a good deal of trade had been lost to the port and extensive farmland lay open to further destruction. Burdened by these concerns, they had gone for advice to the duke of Suffolk, a friend to the town. He had advised them to petition for an incorporation which would facilitate the purchase and control of local guild lands. These, in turn, would provide the financial resources to permit the purchase and repair of all the dikes and also many buildings which were decayed in the town itself. With Suffolk's support, the measure had gained approval of the King's Council and a charter came forth along the lines which the townsmen had envisioned. This coveted document enabled the Mayor and twelve aldermen to annex the guild lands in question to the borough, to charge entry fines for new freemen, and to take various tolls in the marketplace.

But Robertson and Wendon also reported that two local men, William Spynk and Thomas Browne (the latter described as a 'malicious JP'), had opposed the very petition for incorporation, which they saw as threatening to their own interests. In their view Spynk and Thomas Browne had conspired to get John Browne, whom they described as recently released from the Marshalsea Prison, to challenge the petition for incorporation before the Privy Council. Why they could assume that a recent guest of His Majesty at the Marshalsea should have had sufficient influence with the Privy Council to carry out this task remains unclear.

In the end, the defendants alleged that Browne had failed to sway the privy councillors, who then approved the incorporation in the early months of 1545. Robertson and Wendon then tell us that instead of accepting that decision with grace, Browne and his two supporters had joined with other local opponents to the incorporation and continued to conspire against it, carrying out a campaign of harassment against the borough. They allegedly challenged the town's control of certain lands, embezzled some of the borough's records, tampered with witnesses, and both harassed and tried to divert ships coming into the port, causing a marked loss of trade and custom. Robertson and Wendon also maintained that the borough had met its payments for the guild lands on time, that it had spent money to aid the poor and repair the dikes, and that no one had conspired against John Browne.

Though the judgments in this case have not survived—a common but very frustrating outcome of research in court cases from this era—there is an indication in a document of 1592 that some of Browne's allegations may have hit home. In explaining why it needed an exemption from paying some of the parliamentary subsidy to Queen Elizabeth in that year, the town's officers of the day alluded to the borough's loss of its lands by a Star Chamber suit in the reign of Edward VI. Although, as we will see, the marquess of Northampton, and not John Browne, may have been the eventual and real winner in Browne's challenge to the borough's possessions, this probably refers to Browne's suit of 1547 rather than any action brought by the marquess five years later. And, though no record of purchases has been found, Browne's litigation may have gained him something after all. In one way or another, he had obviously come to hold a number of former guild properties by the end of Edward's reign.

In any event, Browne's suit against the borough did not end his efforts to gain Boston properties, or in other ways to use the opportunity of the great land transfers of the day to launch his own fortunes in life. By 1552 we find him engaged in further conflict with the Mayor and burgesses, but this time on the defensive. It seems that Browne had managed to obtain a number of houses in and around Boston, perhaps from his suit and perhaps not. But instead of using them for rental income, he had begun to pull them down so as to sell off the building materials for his own profit. There is even evidence that he pre-contracted with others to acquire and pull down certain buildings for this purpose, and sold their materials virtually on consignment. This was also all too common in that pragmatic, entrepreneurial, and iconoclastic age. Though we usually think of those who did such things as working for the great landed families of the day, anxious to recycle building materials in the construction of their great country houses, this was obviously an urban occupation as well.

In this instance, the Mayor and aldermen secured an intervention by the Privy Council, where the Lincolnshire-based William Cecil, already Secretary of State and a close friend of the borough of Boston, spoke in their behalf. But the Council's subsequent letter, forbidding Browne to continue, came too late. As the Mayor explained to Cecil, Browne had already torn down 'a fair mansion' where several people had lived, selling the materials and converting the land to a yard for raising hogs. Then, in partnership with a William Turpyn, Browne sold St. Peter's Hall—probably the guildhall of the defunct Guild of St. Peter— 'the slate of which is carried away with part of the timber'. And he was alleged to have bought another 'fair house' called St. George's Hall (probably the guildhall of that guild) for the same purpose despite its being inhabited by a local craftsman. There was reason to fear, the letter continued, that 'there will be few houses standing in the marketplace or elsewhere that may be sold' unless Browne and others desisted. Yet they claimed that Browne had 'showed a very light countenance' when he received the Council's letter, and threatened to do even worse if the Mayor persisted in opposing his actions. Responding as best they could, the privy councillors bound Browne in an obligation not to proceed further with those activities, or to begin the same with other buildings.[33]

The injunction did not work for long. Two years later, in 1554, we find the Mayor and aldermen of the day sending two representatives to London to pursue further business against Browne, and to secure a reissue of 'ye councils letter for non pullyng downe of houses'.[34] They seem to have wanted broader support for preventing not only Browne himself but others as well from the business of pulling down houses and reselling the building materials,[35] and this intervention seems to have resolved itself more successfully. After about 1554, Browne's activities seem decidedly more conventional, and he seems to have begun shortly thereafter to gain the good graces of his fellow townsmen as a respectable gentleman: we will pick up this last phase of his life below.

The Policy of the Crown

In appealing to the central government for its support in stopping Browne's actions in pulling down local housing, the Mayor and aldermen of Boston invoked a third player in this story. They did so in the reasonable certainty that they would find the desired support at Westminster. In several statutes passed between 1534 and 1544, collectively called the 'Re-building Statutes of Henry VIII', Parliament had hammered out a policy to preserve the physical integrity of urban houses and other buildings.[36] The initiative for this legislation had come from large numbers of towns which faced the same problem: a declining and decaying supply of houses and other buildings at the very time when urban populations had begun to grow. In short, housing had begun to be a problem for many English towns in the 1530s and 1540s. Even where population pressure seemed more moderate, civic authorities became alert to the possibility of a similar problem just over the horizon in their own communities. The Re-building Statutes attended to these concerns by giving local authorities the power to enforce the repair of decayed housing or, failing compliance by the intransigent or absentee landlord, by allowing them to seize the properties altogether.

Technically speaking, this legislation applied only to those towns listed in the specific statutes, and Boston was not amongst that large number. Possibly the lack of a well-defined local governing structure prior to 1545 had prevented Boston's interests from being represented in parliament when these statutes were being drawn up. Several other Lincolnshire towns (including Stamford, Grimsby, Grantham, and Lincoln) were listed, and Boston burgesses must surely have known of both the statutes and the policy which they conveyed.

Yet the larger point is that the Crown seems to have stood by the principle of the legislation: houses in towns should not readily be pulled down for building materials or other reasons, but they should be repaired and made habitable instead. This is certainly the policy which lay behind the Privy Council's willingness to grant letters against Browne and others who were trying to exploit this opportunity for personal gain at the expense of the local housing stock. Even though the town had been unprepared or unable, in its pre-corporate state, to get itself listed in the statutes, its leaders were not too backward to apply for government support to stop Browne and others from their destructive efforts when faced with that reality thereafter.

Browne Again

By the early 1550s, Browne had become a wealthy man, but not a happy one. He had failed to nullify the borough's incorporation by his suit in the Star Chamber; he had failed to buy and strip more houses for their materials; and he could not have enjoyed much esteem from his fellow Bostonians. After about 1554, he seems to have determined that, as he couldn't beat his neighbours, he may as well join them. Perhaps he had also acquired sufficient wealth by then to support his newfound respectability. In any event, Boston was not a large borough, and it had few men with Browne's legal training or enterprise. Though they were never willing to elect him their mayor or their MP, the borough leaders needed Browne as much as he needed them. Oligarchies were often more accessible than they seemed.

This new phase of Browne's career seems to have been signalled in March 1555, when he legitimately purchased land of the borough corporation.[37] By January 1556, Browne gained appointment as an attorney on the town's business in London, and received his first assignments within the opening week of his service in that capacity.[38] By September 1557, the year in which his kinsman's will referred to him as 'gent.', he was first listed as a member of its Common Council. Three months later he was selected to fill the place of a deceased alderman, one of twelve on this senior and more prestigious governing council.[39]

Browne did not change his stripes entirely. He engaged in a few more spats with fellow townsmen over the years, and was fined for misbehaving towards a mayor in 1562.[40] Yet he went on to hold various other offices and responsibilities in the borough's behalf in these years. He made an inventory of the borough's possessions in 1558, became Town Auditor in 1559 (reaffirmed in 1560), helped to select a new town clerk and served with four others to sort the borough's records in 1562, settled numerous local wills, and so forth. While apparently maintaining his own residence in suburban Skirbeck, he continued to purchase income-bearing properties throughout the area, keeping them in good repair for his tenants. These included the advowson of the nearby parish of Tofte in 1574 (which he sold, presumably at a profit, a year later),[41] and a 'long house' which housed several families in the borough itself for the considerable sum of £40 in 1578.[42]

John Browne seems to have matured late in his personal life as well as in the public esteem. When he drew up his will in 1578, over thirty years after he first appeared in local records as a litigant at court, at least one of two daughters was still under twenty years of age and his son was under twenty-four. His legacies were substantial if not enormous. To his wife, Jane (elsewhere he referred to her as Joan, though this is probably a simple problem of orthography), he left £200 in goods and chattels; to his son Joseph, £200 plus his £20 to £30 worth of books when he attained the age of twenty-four; to his unmarried daughter Margaret he gave 200 marks, and a smaller sum to his married daughter Agnes. And of course there were properties as well, most of which he left to his wife.

His will also tells us that Browne valued education: perhaps this, too, marked his maturity. In addition to his books, he asked his executors to see that his son received appropriate schooling. Finally, in the event that both Joseph and Margaret should die before coming into their inheritances, he willed that their legacies be applied instead to pay for a schoolmaster in what would be called

'John Browne's School' in the borough of Boston. There is no indication that this came to pass, though it is an interesting echo of the
gesture made by the marquess of Northampton to soothe the
feelings of the borough leaders back in 1552. Perhaps that promise
served Browne as a model of genteel behaviour.

Browne lived on for four more years after writing his will.
Shortly after his death in 1582 his widow delivered to the Mayor
and aldermen of Boston 'two baggs of books and papers tuchinge
ye accompte of this Corporation' which her husband had kept for
the borough until his demise, a faithful civic official to his death.
John Browne had managed in the end both to feather his own nest
and to serve his town. In both regards his success exemplified the
opportunities opened up both for towns themselves and individual townsmen by the vast land exchanges of the 1530s and 1540s.

Conclusion

In some small details, the story of Boston's acquisitions of local
resources at the time of the dissolutions remained untypical. Not
many towns had major lawsuits brought against their incorporation and purchase of lands, or lost some of their acquisitions to
rising court figures of the day, or regained most of them when
those same men, in this case Northampton and Throckmorton, fell
out of power. But in other ways its experience was much more
common than we have usually recognized. Boston's ruling elite
took a keen and aggressive interest in the borough's control of its
own resources. They understood that, at a time of generally rising
population, the income derived from rental property could be the
most effective bulwark against fiscal chaos, especially when receipts from trade and tolls had long stagnated. They understood
the value of enhancing Boston's legal and constitutional status in
order to have sufficient authority to acquire and manage local resources, though at the same time (and also like a number of other
towns) they were not above concealing and annexing some properties when it suited their interests. And they understood, too, the

value both of friends at court—Suffolk and Cecil especially—and of the support by the central government for their interests.

Browne, too, seems rather typical in a number of ways. A man of no particular inherited wealth or standing, he exhibited the sort of aggressive and entrepreneurial self-reliance, even ruthlessness, shared by many others in that age of opportunity. Educated in the law and convinced of the importance of education in general, he moved expeditiously from Marshalsea to mansion house in the course of an active lifetime. He seized the opportunities of the age for social mobility and, unencumbered by traditional occupational patterns or expectations, he made his way by his own wits. The tenurial revolution of the day served him as it served many others, as a springboard for personal respectability and modest success in the society of a middling provincial town.

This story also shows that third player, the central government as represented by king, council, courts, and parliament, surprisingly interested in local affairs and more receptive to the interests of individual towns and townsmen than many have realized. It responded even-handedly to Browne's suit against the borough, to the borough's entreaties to stop Browne from selling off building materials from standing houses (a response echoed in extensive legislation of the 1530s and 1540s), and finally to the borough again in its need for tax relief at the end of the century. The close-knit concerns of all three parties—town, Browne, and Crown—prove a fitting introduction to some of the salient realities of civic governance in the Reformation era.

CHAPTER 2

John Pitt and the Building of the Blandford Forum Town Hall

The period after the mid-sixteenth century saw a number of dramatic changes in the built environment of England's provincial towns, and few of those changes have yet been satisfactorily explored. Pressed by expansion of both population and boundaries, early modern English towns took important steps towards controlling and building up urban water supplies.[1] Supported by legislation of Henry VIII's reign, and pushed by the expanding need for housing, they worked hard to renovate derelict residential properties.[2] Ports such as Boston and Great Yarmouth on the east coast and Hastings, Rye, Weymouth, and Melcombe Regis to the south had to cope with the substantial silting up of their harbours. The Elizabethan Poor Laws encouraged the construction of new almshouses and workhouses in the last years of the century. Most obviously of all, the dissolutions of religious houses and their associated institutions in the 1530s and then of guilds, fraternities, chantries, and similar institutions in the 1540s, meant a great deal of destruction and conversion of ecclesiastical buildings and properties throughout the realm. There can have been very few towns of any size at all which were not affected.

And finally, this period saw considerable activity by provincial towns in the construction and/or conversion and renovation of civic halls: a point closely related to the dissolution of the guilds, whose halls then became redundant. Between 1500 and 1640, something close to half the provincial towns in England probably built or rebuilt a civic hall, or converted a former guildhall to that civic use. Though towns were building civic halls as seats for their governing institutions as early as the twelfth century, if not before, this represents a dramatic acceleration in this sort of civic construction, and one which contrasts sharply with the relative lack of civic hall construction in the six or eight decades prior to about 1540.[3]

Several factors account for this dramatic expansion. As many standing halls were already old at the opening of our period, some simply had to be replaced as worn out or dilapidated. A number were severely damaged or even destroyed by some calamity: fire, or flood, or simply the collapse of structural parts. Others seem to have been built or rebuilt as a statement of local pride, especially in the effort to keep up with the building record of neighbouring towns in the same region. In addition, a very substantial number which were constructed in the period after 1540 resulted from the anticipation or acquisition of greater governing powers on the part of the town itself. This strengthening of local authority often came at the expense of traditional borough lordship, and often in the form of a charter of incorporation or a deed of enfeoffment. There were, after all, 149 new borough incorporations in the period between 1540 and 1640, plus 72 reincorporations. Almost all of these represented substantial increases in the powers of local government.[4]

In these many cases, such halls served both practical and symbolic purposes. In the first instance, the acquisition of new powers and the expansion of local government jurisdiction simply required a larger and more elaborate space in which local institutions could carry out their responsibilities. In the latter sense, the newly authoritative government of post-Reformation provincial towns required a building which would, in its layout, design, iconography, and even its site, symbolize the authority of those who governed. Taken together, new civic halls served as both seats and symbols of local authority. Both functions were required ever more urgently in these years of rapid jurisdictional expansion, and also at a time when traditional elements of the local political culture, bound up with the traditional religious faith and practice, had been uprooted.[5]

Some measure of the importance which provincial town governments came to place on such buildings may be gauged by the financial challenges involved in their construction. For many communities building a town hall could well be the largest single expenditure of the century, and it was not unusual for a town to lay out for such projects sums amounting to several times the average annual civic income. These efforts thus often demanded great financial resourcefulness, careful supervision, and both efficient and diplomatic management.

Some of the towns which undertook this process were the large provincial centres or county towns which one would most expect: places like Chester, Exeter, Bristol, Norwich, Gloucester, Leicester, or King's Lynn. But a greater number would have been found at the very opposite end of the urban league tables, as towns of even very modest size and complexity also gained new jurisdictions and expanded powers of self-government in these years.[6]

These scores of hall-building towns included the small but thriving market town of Blandford Forum, nestled in a bend of the River Stour in central Dorset. Blandford built a new town hall as the seat of its local authority in 1593, though its efforts to gain a full charter of incorporation would not bear fruit until the next decade. A large part of Blandford's importance to us lies in its very ordinariness amongst those roughly two hundred towns which built or otherwise acquired a town hall between 1540 and 1640.

Blandford's population has been estimated at somewhere between five and seven hundred people for the year 1562.[7] In accord with population trends in the nation as a whole, and despite extensive destruction from a great fire which swept through the town in 1579,[8] Blandford probably grew at a modest rate in the Elizabethan period.[9] By 1593 its population may have grown to roughly six hundred to eight hundred people. Though the rental income on town property seems also to have grown slightly in these years, the annual receipts brought into the town's coffers from its property holdings amounted to only a very modest £22 a year.[10]

Beyond the business of regional marketing, Blandford cannot be said to have had a particularly specialized economy. Still, strategically located on the border between the sheep/corn raising downland to the east and the dairying and swine-keeping pasture lands just to the west, it served as a natural point of exchange between two distinct agricultural areas.[11] Its site on the main road from the county town of Dorchester and the port of Weymouth to the southwest and the cathedral City of Salisbury to the northeast (or, as the Dorset historian John Hutchins put it, 'from Land's End to London'),[12] no doubt facilitated this trade, as did its five-arch bridge over the Stour. This location and these roads had been Blandford's raison d'être from the very beginning. They helped support the town's reputation for the sale of sheep and cattle, both being raised in some numbers nearby.[13] Extensive shambles adjacent to the site of the town hall suggest a large-scale butchery trade had long been well established.[14]

In addition to its lively overland trade, Blandford's merchants also appear regularly in these years as coastal and overseas traders through the Dorset ports of Poole, Weymouth-Melcombe Regis, and Wareham. They served as middlemen for goods from elsewhere as well as primary merchants for those of local provenance, produce, and manufactured items alike. The appearance of Blandford merchants in Dorset port records fell off somewhat in the early to mid Elizabethan years, but then revived markedly in the last decade or two of the century.[15] Competition for the letting or purchase of Blandford shops also appears to have become very keen in these latter years of the Elizabethan era.[16] All of this suggests that the town was undergoing an economic revival at about the time the new town hall was constructed in 1593.

Blandford's political structure seems similarly modest in its extent and complexity in this era. It had long been classed as a borough, had on two occasions (1304–5 and 1348–49) sent members to parliament, and possessed from the Crown the right to hold markets and fairs. Throughout most of the period from Domesday forth to the reign of James I it had been divided between two or more external jurisdictions, including the Duchy of Lancaster and the Canons of Windsor. But as its manorial lords had always been absentee, townsmen had long since learned to fend for themselves. They had informally developed their own institutions to provide effective local government. Revenue officials called 'stewards' and administrative officers known as 'bailiffs', both no doubt technically subordinate to the manorial authorities, seem to have been selected by the townsmen themselves and to have carried out fairly extensive governing authority by the sixteenth century.

These practices were finally sanctioned by the incorporation of 1605, Blandford's first, with some additional rights and privileges tacked on.[17] The same charter either recognized an existing council or created one anew, but in any event it called for a 'common council' of eleven capital burgesses, with the bailiff, as chief administrative officer, to be one of them. In addition, a 'seneschal' was to be elected for a life's term. Though the title had become rare in England by that time, the requirement that he have legal training probably made Blandford's seneschal somewhat like the recorder of other towns. Finally, the charter sanctioned the modest amount of income-bearing property which the town seems already to have held.[18]

Though no map of Blandford exists from the period at hand, we know that it included a roughly triangular street plan with its substantial (and much prized!) bridge over the River Stour, the hundred-foot-long parish church of St. Peter and St. Paul, a school (said to be famous in the mid-century), a town hall probably located in the east end of the north marketplace, and the shambles adjacent, an almshouse, and the remains of St. Leonard's Chapel (see p. 65).[19]

Most of these characteristics made Blandford much like a good many towns of the same category, but it does stand out in two important respects from the rest. Thanks to the efforts of one particular townsman put in charge of the project to build its new hall in 1593, Blandford has preserved the most extensive set of building accounts of any town, large or small, known to have constructed a civic hall in this entire period.[20] That man was the local merchant John Pitt. It is to him that we owe as close a knowledge as we are likely to gain about the finance and construction of a town hall in this period. Though neither Blandford Forum itself nor its construction of a town hall may be anything out of the or-

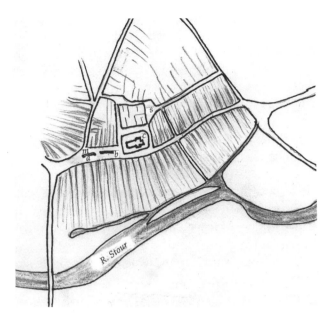

The Market Area of Blandford Forum to 1731.
(*a*, shambles; *b* town hall; *c* church; *m*, market place;
s, sheep market)

dinary for this era, both Pitt and his accounts commend Blandford
to our attention. They help us understand 'the ordinary' to an extraordinary extent, and to use the Blandford experience as a model
for comprehending similar experiences elsewhere.

John Pitt had been very much in the thick of Blandford's economic and political life since the mid-1560s, some thirty years before he was asked to take charge of building the hall. (Though
Pitt's appointment as 'Keeper of the Funds for the New Guild
Hall' is not recorded until 1593, he had clearly been serving in that
capacity for at least a year and probably longer.)[21] Unfortunately
the destruction of almost all of Blandford's records in a fire of
1731—the fourth great fire to visit Blandford in the pre-modern
era!—and the fact that John Pitt was a common name in the Dorset
of his day, makes him more of a shadowy figure than one would

like. Still, a thorough combing of local records allows us to know at least a few things about him.

He is probably that John Pitt whose father, William, came from the rural Dorset hamlet of Iwerne Steepleton, and who was the younger of William's two sons. We do know that John married Joan (sometimes written 'Joann') Swayne, the daughter of another minor gentleman from rural Dorset, John (sometimes called Richard) Swayne. And we know that John and Joan Pitt had four sons and at least three daughters, and that Joan was still alive when John died in late 1601 or early 1602.[22]

One of the characteristics of economic life in this age was that it was by no means as occupationally specialized as it would become. Like many other townspeople of the time, John Pitt made his living in a number of ways. A late Elizabethan lawsuit, naming Pitt as a defendant in a case of miscarriage of justice for his role as a juror, refers to him as a yeoman, which may indicate some lingering involvement in agricultural enterprise, carried over from his rural upbringing.[23] We also know him as a landlord. His will records some lands which he had inherited from his father-in-law both in Blandford and elsewhere in Dorset. It identifies two other houses (one of which he lived in) plus several Blandford shops and tenements which he acquired on his own. It seems safe to assume that he let out most of these holdings for a steady rental income.[24]

Though he may have been a landlord of modest proportions, he made the lion's share of his money in commerce. Customs accounts (known as 'port books' after 1565) show him shipping a variety of products through the port of Poole, which was about seventeen miles southeast of Blandford, from the early 1570s to shortly before his death. We may assume that he dealt in a much greater volume of trade by land, which is not recorded in any customs accounts, throughout central Dorset as well. Pitt's recorded shipments through Poole consisted of wheat and several kinds of wine plus raisins and pitch. Most shipments went to other south-coast merchants in Falmouth, Lyme Regis, and Southampton, as well as to London.[25] These incomes must have added up, for the assessment for the 1593 parliamentary subsidy rated Pitt as one of the wealthiest men in Blandford. In addition to his properties and some store of moveable goods, he was able to leave his wife and each of his surviving children considerable cash and a silver cup.[26]

Pitt's father-in-law, John (or Richard) Swayne, also made the move from village yeoman to Blandford merchant. He frequently shipped iron out of Poole for other south-coast ports, and had (with other Swaynes) bought up monastic lands outside of town.[27] Swayne, too, appears in the surviving records as an active member of the Dorset merchant community in these years, and his descendants also figure prominently in local affairs for some time to come. Pitt's will indicates that he remained close to his Swayne in-laws, suggesting again the importance of marriage ties in the business of getting on in life.

The final means by which John Pitt seems to have made his way probably brought in very little income, but it directly related to his expertise in supervising the building and finance of the hall. From his very first appearance in the town's accounts, we find him laying out monies for civic expenses and being repaid either in interest or in leases on local properties. It is not easy to interpret these references. Some of them suggest that his expenditures on the town's behalf are in the form of personal loans. Others are clearly charitable contributions to defray particular civic expenses. Still others came in Pitt's official role as one of the town's five bailiffs (noted for 1567 and 1589) or one of its two stewards (noted for 1583–85 and 1598–99).[28] Because of the ambiguous recording of these sums, it proves impossible to total them up and draw any conclusions about the return which they yielded Pitt in the long run. But we can say that these expenditures occurred almost every year and that they were for small and irregular amounts. They probably did more for Pitt's reputation than for his pocketbook. In addition, we do know that a good many of the expenses of all three types had to do with civic building and maintenance of the town's physical infrastructure. Even his entry fine for the office of bailiff in 1598 went for building expenses.[29]

Blandford may not have engaged in civic building more than many other towns, but it did so at a steady rate and over the entire period covered by its single surviving book of accounts. Indeed, the amount of building activity in even such a small town as this—one which seems not to have been uniformly prosperous throughout the period—indicates how common and important such activities must have been in towns of any and all sizes. Some of Blandford's building no doubt resulted from the damage done by the fire of 1579, or by the need to keep up the local schoolhouse, the parish church, the bridge, the marketstead and shambles, and the old town hall.

Above all of this, the construction of the new town hall was clearly the town's single greatest undertaking during Pitt's lifetime. For a number of reasons, including his long experience as a merchant with connections throughout the region, his long involvement in Blandford's finances and government, his experience as a landlord and manager of property, his leadership in restoration efforts on the old hall, and the trust which his fellows seemed to place in his judgment, he was the logical choice to direct it. When asked, he agreed to do so.

In understanding the scope of Pitt's task, it helps to realize that the building industry at that time did not include the sort of hierarchy of personnel which would come in a later day with the advent of the general contractor. The Tudor analogue to that useful role was still the master craftsman, usually a master mason, carpenter, or bricklayer. And of course the work needed to be supervised by a representative of the town as 'employer'. This role was also not yet professionalized. Some trusty lay person, not necessarily a craftsman himself, had therefore to shoulder a very great responsibility to represent the town's interests. So it was with Blandford, and with John Pitt.

Pitt's role as the local expert on the town's building projects began well before the town hall project loomed into view. He had supervised repairs to the old hall from as early as 1585.[30] It was probably not until 1591 that he and his fellow townsmen recognized that these efforts were futile, and that the ancient building was beyond repair. Pitt laid out on the town's behalf in that year a sum for the construction of a saw pit, and for hewing and sawing timber.[31] This implies the new fashioning of timber from hewn tree trunks rather than mere repairs to parts of the standing structure. Thus 1591 seems the most likely point at which construction on the new hall may be said to have begun. But this was a preparatory stage, and the rest of the accounts tell us that the main part of the building itself went up in 1592 and 1593, with bits and pieces being finished off as new funds permitted for several years thereafter. (Perhaps the delay may be explained by the need to season the timber once it had been sawn into the required lengths: sawn timber often lay to season for many years before it was considered fit to use.)

The accounts show that Pitt's duties seem to have taken in several areas of expertise. We may presume that he chose most of the master builders for the project, that he oversaw the purchase and transport of building materials—many of them from outside of the immediate area of Blandford—and that he closely supervised the work itself. We know for certain that he took charge of raising financial support for the project, kept track of expenditures, kept the accounts (probably in rough form in his own hand before they were copied by the town clerk into the account book itself), and submitted them at the required regular intervals for the scrutiny of his fellow freemen. We cannot assume that he bore sole responsibility for the design of the structure, including its layout, features, and decoration, but he must surely have had a prominent voice in those decisions. And certainly those decisions would have been made to serve the interests of the leading men of the town, amongst whose number Pitt must surely be counted. But the accounts are best at showing Pitt as financial manager, this role being (naturally enough) recorded more directly than any of his other functions.

Blandford's strategies for financing such a project seem typical of the way most small towns went about that critical task, save that Pitt's work in Blandford as an overseer of the works would probably have been done in some towns by the regular chamberlains as part of their normal responsibilities for local finance. As the 'Keeper of the Funds for the New Guild Hall', an ad hoc title created specifically for Pitt's performance of this task, Pitt received from the town coffers a certain sum each year for building expenses. He would lay this out to defray expenses as they occurred. At the end of the year he would submit his account, either returning unspent sums to the civic coffers or claiming reimbursement himself for laying out any expenses beyond his budget. These are the records, entered into the regular 'Town Account Book', which survive for our scrutiny. When expenses exceeded Pitt's building allowance for the year, as happened several times, he made up the difference out of pocket. The town would then reimburse him as best it could, though not necessarily in cash. In fact Blandford seems to have been indebted to Pitt each year from 1595 to at least 1599, giving him some of its income directly or, in 1598, allowing him use of the churchyard (for what purpose it is not clear) to make up the difference.[32]

One would assume today that fund-raising comes before construction, but that was not necessarily the case in small market towns in the Elizabethan era. Both activities went on more or less simultaneously for several years: building from about 1592 to 1597 (though with £197 13s of the total being spent in 1592–93) and fund-raising beginning as early as 1590 and continuing until about 1597. The funding sources shown in Table 1 indicate a range of devices, with support of leading townsmen, essential to the project, appearing in the form of voluntary contributions of cash or supplies (including nine oak trees from a nearly landowner).

Though such devices as holding fund-raising festivities for financing a huge civic building project and reimbursing the Keeper of the Funds with use of the churchyard may seem quaint to us today, they were common enough at the time. The fact is that the cost of building a town hall for almost any town of this period far exceeded almost any other form of civic expense, and it elicited a wide range of fiscal strategies to meet the challenge. Blandford's average annual civic revenue in these years, as can also be deduced from the accounts, hovered around the very modest figures

TABLE 1

Sources of Funding for the Blandford Guildhall

Source	£	s	d	% of total
Individual Gifts (22 in all)	26	7	8	10.3
Group Contributions	25	0	4	9.8
Regular Civic Revenue	61	15	4	24.1
Sale of Old Hall and Shambles	21	12	0	8.4
Fund-raising Festivities (especially Ales)	43	14	6	17.0
Sale of Building Materials	1	2	0	.4
Loans (4 in all)	62	0	0	24.2
Other/Unknown	14	5	4	5.6
TOTAL	£255	17	2	100.0

of £30 to £40. Yet in addition to contributions in kind, including some timber, transport of materials, and a few other items which were provided by benefactors in the town or region,[33] the cash outlay for the project came to about £255. This was not out of line with what little we know of building costs for other halls. Though far below the extensive additions for the large and lavish Exeter Guildhall of 1593–96, it equates roughly to similar expenditures elsewhere: to the Dorset port of Poole's expenditure of approximately £300 in 1568–70 and—given the prevailing rates of inflation—to the Warwickshire town of Alcester's approximate £300 from 1618 and to the Wiltshire town of Marlborough's approximate £400 in 1630–31.[34]

Still, this was an enormous sum for a town of fewer than nine hundred residents, and it required considerable ingenuity and several years to raise. Here too, there was a wide range of experiences upon which Pitt and his fellows could draw. The neighbouring borough of Bridport, also building a hall, canvassed private individuals throughout the shire of Dorset, passing the hat amongst strangers on the road, those attending Quarter Sessions, and in local inns. We know that Pitt was aware of this technique, because he shows up himself as one of those who contributed to the Bridport hall![35] In some towns large bequests were received for hall building from private citizens. In others church plate and jewels were sold (including, in Poole, the communion cup from the local church!); ales and other fund-raising activities were held; building materials from old halls were sold off.[36] Deddington in Oxfordshire and Leeds in Yorkshire were amongst those towns dipping into their poor relief funds for such construction.[37] In this company Blandford's fund-raising seems conservative and even unimaginative, but by and large it did the job.

What, then, can we tell about the hall that Pitt supervised to completion, and what may we infer of the town's goals in designing it? The decision to construct a new town hall seems to have unfolded gradually after the fire of 1579, which presumably damaged or even partly destroyed the former hall. We know almost nothing about this earlier edifice save that there were periodic expenditures recorded through the 1580s for its repair, and that parts of it were sold for building materials in the effort to finance the new hall in the early 1590s. The word 'guildhall', as it was known, had several possible meanings. It is likely that, although the hall of 1593 was clearly intended to serve as an administrative headquarters for Blandford's government, its predecessor may have been either the hall of a local guild (and thus literally a 'guild hall'), or else a 'yeldhall' or 'geldhall', first employed as a place where revenues could be collected for the town and/or manor of Blandford.[38]

Like its successor which Pitt helped bring into being, it seems safe to assume that the old hall stood in the middle of the widened out street which served (and was known) as the marketplace. Along with the butchers' shambles just to the west, from which it also stood apart, the hall stood on an isolated site in the middle of this area, just west of the Parish Church of St. Peter and St. Paul.[39]

As the 1593 hall burned down in another fire in 1731, along with something like 80 percent of Blandford's other buildings, it is of course impossible to know exactly how the building may have looked. Only one Blandford building of the period, St. Leonard's Chapel on the outer rim of the borough and dating from the late fifteenth century, still exists in anything like its original form from before the mid-seventeenth century.[40] Yet Pitt's accounts are re-

Conjectural Appearance of the Blandford Forum Town Hall, from the Southeast. (Based on the 1731 Survey plus features found in other contemporary buildings from central Dorset; *HM, Central Dorset*, pt. 1 (1970), Plates 104, 105, and pts. 1, 2, passim.)

markably precise. They describe the building materials in considerable detail, down to the species of certain trees squared for timber or flooring. They give the place of origin for some of the stone and slate. They indicate precise quantities of virtually all materials. They name most of the workmen and, in some cases, their occupations. They note at least in passing the names of specific rooms and other quite distinctive features. Added to what we know of St. Leonard's Chapel and contemporary central Dorset buildings elsewhere, they allow us to offer at least a conjectural image of the building's size, shape, and features. From that record, as we will see, other points may be inferred as well.

The resulting picture is of a two-story, rectangular building (dominated by an 'upper hall' and 'lower hall') with an attic or 'loft', framed with oak. Its length ran parallel to the long end of the rectangular marketplace, its front probably looking south across the narrow width of the same area. Its walls were timber-framed and covered with both tile and stone. In this they seem to have followed the distinctive pattern of contemporary Dorset vernacular buildings whereby walls were clad in alternating courses of two materials, giving the effect of horizontal stripes.[41] In most cases those materials would have been some form of stone and then brick, but Pitt's accounts make no mention of brick.

In another distinctive form well documented in contemporary central Dorset buildings, the roof consisted both of blue slates (imported along the coast through Poole and probably quarried in Cornwall or Devon) and some flat, rectangular stones known as 'hillingstones', both of which were held up by oak supports or 'battens'. Slates would have covered the majority of the roof area, with the larger and perhaps less fragile hillingstones on the bottom two or three courses above the lead rain gutters.[42] Stairs, probably internal to the building rather than external, were constructed of elmwood; floors of deal boards. Gables protruded from the upper story, and must have held some of the fifteen leaded casement windows recorded for the whole building. Oddly, the buildings may not have had chimneys: neither they, nor the bricks from which they were usually constructed, nor fireplaces, are mentioned.

As there is no indication of an open ground floor for marketing, we must assume that this hall was not the familiar 'box-on-stilts' type of hall, such as we may still see at Ledbury, in Herefordshire, and elsewhere.[43] Several other factors point to the same conclusion. The earlier Blandford Hall, and thus Blandford's accustomed use for a hall, seems to have begun as a guildhall (chiefly for administrative and devotional purposes) rather than a market hall (primarily for commercial purposes). The very large Market Place itself included the shambles, which conventionally housed the fishmongers and butchers, and the area covered (as we will see) by the pentice (see below) extending out from the hall itself. It undoubtedly offered as much space for marketing as was required without having to raise the hall up on pillars to shelter marketing below.

The accounts identify several specialized spatial features with certainty. These include a kitchen, a 'pentice', a 'blind house', and a decorative lantern or turret over the lower hall which enclosed a clock. Each of these elements tells us something about the intended uses of the whole structure, and thus the objectives of those who commissioned and designed it. They allow us to employ the accounts not only as a source for building history, but for social and political history as well.

Kitchens were commonly featured in halls of this era, and were no doubt carryovers from the days when 'guildhalls' were indeed the halls of guilds. They facilitated preparation of food for feasts and celebrations, and sometimes for serving the poor.

'Pentices' were also common features. Sometimes the word meant a self-contained building, as in Chester, but often a pentice consisted of nothing more than a sloping roof projecting out over part of the street and supported by pillars. A free-standing pentice, not attached to a building, would require at least four pillars, one at each corner. But the Blandford Accounts note only three pillars, leading us to assume that Blandford's pentice conformed to the latter type: a sloping roof extending over a walkway, attached to the building on one side and held up by the three pillars on the other. It would have afforded a sheltered and shaded space against the hall. There it would have made a useful and specialized part of the marketing area, affording maximum shade for the most perishable goods. The Accounts record payments for paving and, as the interior flooring seems to be wood, it is the pentice area outside the buildings which was most likely to be paved.

One is tempted to read the reference to a 'blind house' as meaning a small apartment or individual room in which blind people could be housed. The word 'house' did sometimes mean a mere room in contemporary usage. But it is more likely to refer to an enclosed room used as a holding cell or lockup: 'blind' in this case meaning windowless or enclosed, as in the architectural terms 'blind arcade' or 'blind tracery'. The fact that the new hall served the town's courts of law (and would by the eighteenth century sometimes even host Quarter Sessions) makes the idea of a windowless lockup even more likely.[44] The term appears in reference to a similar structure in the town hall of Painswick, Gloucestershire, built in 1628, and was in wide usage in the West Country during the eighteenth century.[45]

In the context of Blandford's hall, the incorporation of a lockup in the town hall itself served purposes which were both functional and symbolic. The functional aspect derived from the convenience of having a lockup in a building facing the marketplace. Here the constables could keep petty thieves until they could be brought to the market court in the hall itself or—for more serious crimes— sent on to Quarter Sessions if they were being held elsewhere. This not only had its obvious and practical uses, but it also instilled confidence in market-goers that they could trade secure in the knowledge of a well-policed market area. The close proximity between the cell, the rest of the hall, and the market symbolized the authority of the town government to enforce regulations and to keep the peace. It provides a common but vivid illustration of the connection between building and authority in the provincial town.[46] To men like Pitt, whose livelihood depended primarily on trade, and thus on the ability to attract consumers to the town, this was of obvious importance.

Clocks began to appear on churches before they were affixed to town halls. The latter usage was just becoming common in this period. Some thirty town hall clocks have been documented throughout the realm from the period up to 1640.[47] Yet they were still not 'standard equipment' on civic halls in Dorset or elsewhere in England at this time. While clocks in public view have been identified elsewhere in Dorset from as early as 1409 in Wimborne Minster, 1525 in Bridport, and 1570 in Corfe Castle, all were on ecclesiastical buildings. They were useful in telling the hours and thus the times for prayers in the daily devotional cycle of pre-Reformation times.[48]

The fundamental purpose of the newer, civic clocks, and of their display on civic buildings, was of course simply to tell the time. Thus they needed to be placed in a central and visible spot in the physical layout of the town. This was often the open area of the marketplace in which market and town halls were often sited. So it would almost certainly have been in Blandford.[49] But it is no accident that they were constructed and placed by civic authorities in this era and not much beforehand. The more complex significance of the time-telling function, especially after the demise of the need to tell the hours for devotional exercises in the local abbey, seems to have been to impress upon the members of the community at large the importance of a time-related, well-disciplined mode of behaviour.

This is, after all, the period in which the demands of a revitalized economy throughout most of Western Europe, and an early capitalist economy at that, had need to measure time in precise units. It is in this same period that contracts came to call for obligations to be fulfilled by the specific calendar day rather than the saints' day or the season. Apprenticeship indentures and similar labour regulations came then to demand precisely measured units of work-time. Naturally enough, this rather modern and rational outlook came first to urban areas, and with the economic elite— usually equated with the freemanry—in those areas, before it came to rural areas or to the workforce in general.[50] As the ruling elite of Godalming, in Surrey, put it less than three decades after Blandford built its hall, '. . . the use of a clock in the said town is very necessary for the inhabitants thereof for the keeping of fit hours for their apprentices, servants and workmen'.[51]

As in the construction of a 'blind-house' or lockup, the addition of a clock on Blandford's hall was carried out with the display of civic authority very much in mind. And here again John Pitt must have endorsed these associations. He was precisely the sort of individual—a leading merchant, freeman, and town official, entrusted with supervision of the town's chief construction project— who would most have supported such facilities and the messages which they conveyed.

The fact that the clock, or 'horlodge' as it was called in the Accounts, was encased in a 'lantern', or small clock tower, also bears some interest. Clocks could easily be mounted on the facade of the building, as was the clock on the market hall of Shrewsbury built in 1596, with the 'works' set into the facade for protection from the elements. But the construction of a 'lantern', with its additional expense, suggests two implications. The first is to identify this device as most probably a 'turret clock', which required a long drop area for the heavy weights which were essential to the mechanism.[52] Assuming that the clock had but one face, it would be interesting to know which way it faced: east, towards the church, or, more likely, westwards, where it could best be seen along the length of the marketplace.

The second and perhaps most important implication is an aesthetic concern. Lanterns often signalled the introduction of the newer Renaissance style of building which, even before the well-publicized and mature designs of Inigo Jones, was beginning to seep into England from abroad.[53] Such 'lanterns' became much more common in decades to come, but were obviously already making their appearance even in such small towns as Blandford. Pitt and his fellows would almost certainly have been familiar with the rather precocious example of Renaissance architecture in the facade of Waterston House in nearby Puddletown, built in 1586, if not in their wider travels on business. They may very likely have emulated its style in constructing the lantern to house the hall's 'horlodge'.[54] Civic booster that he was, Pitt may quite plausibly have wanted to indicate by this architectural flourish that Blandford could keep up with the times. (How *could* they allow themselves to be outdone by Puddletown?)

A last word must be said concerning the reasons behind this major and very costly construction project. We cannot doubt that Blandford built its new hall first and foremost because the old one had outlived its usefulness. But why did such a small town put itself to such a great expense in constructing a hall of this apparent structural integrity and complexity? And secondly, what had the choice of Pitt to do with the town's deeper purposes in taking on the project to begin with? Some of the explanation may lie with the recognition that the old and probably fire-damaged hall was no longer worth keeping up. Then, too, several other Dorset towns had recently constructed halls, and there was the matter of civic pride to be considered. Poole, Shaftesbury, and Melcombe Regis had built new halls in the late 1560s, Poole added a market hall as well in 1570, and Bridport decided to build a new market hall at about the same time as the men of Blandford came to the same decision: it, too, came to completion in 1593.[55]

But it is difficult to escape another probable factor, one which in the end was both common to other towns at the time throughout the realm, and likely to have been especially decisive in Blandford. As we have seen, the years immediately preceding the hall project seem to have been years of growth for the local economy, and thus to have provided Blandford merchants with an enriched stake in its continued prosperity and stability. In England generally, and no doubt in Blandford as well, these years also saw increased anxiety created by problems of crime, vagrancy, and rootlessness, and by the demands of war and of government finance. All over the country the Crown was having to depend more than ever on what Clark and Slack have called 'small knots of reliable men', to keep the peace and represent its interests. Following from this necessity, the Crown and parliament invested local governing elites with greater authority than ever so that they might get the job done. It has recently been argued that many towns not only received such greater authority, in the form of incorporations and re-incorporations, but that they also engaged with increasing frequency in the construction of civic halls to symbolize it in the eyes of fellow townsmen.[56]

Though in this case the hall came on the anticipation, and not the actual achievement, of incorporation, Blandford seems to fit this explanatory model very well. The long-standing jurisdiction of absentee landlords had, by default, left the townspeople pretty much to their own devices in matters of local concern. Through the years they had risen to the challenge, though never to the point of becoming a formally corporate town. But whereas that may have been good enough in former times, the demands of the late Elizabethan era must have made it increasingly difficult for ruling elites to protect their interests and to continue to govern on the basis of little more than custom.

John Pitt would have felt this very keenly. Over a period of several decades he had been one of the local officials himself, and he was obviously one of the merchant elite who ran the town. He would not live to see Blandford receive its charter in 1605. Yet it is not hard to imagine him, had he lived longer, amongst the ruling circle which must have pressed for its acquisition, and who then became, literally, the 'charter officials' of the new corporation. The first capital burgesses of the corporate borough of Blandford Forum included his sons Thomas and John Pitt and his nephew by marriage, Robert Swayne. Blandford's seneschal was another in-law, the lawyer Richard Swayne.[57] When the ruling elders of Blandford chose John Pitt to oversee the construction of the new town hall, they were not merely choosing a municipal employee, useful for his experience, or a knowledgeable consultant, unfamiliar with the community. They were choosing one of their own, whose interests coincided with theirs, and who could best be trusted to see the work to its desired end.

As his meticulous accounts bear witness, John Pitt did not let them down. He oversaw the project over the course of its several years' duration and to its completion. So far as the records reveal, he did so with remarkably little controversy, and retained the esteem of his neighbours to the end of his days. More than that, he must have encouraged those symbolic elements of the new building which conveyed a sense of its builders' authority. Not only in its chambers and its layout, but in its clock, and 'blind house' cell, and probable Renaissance elements of style, it conveyed the symbols of command which would have been clearly understood by anyone who saw them.

In the end it may also be said that, not only did Pitt help shape the building, but he was perhaps shaped by it as well. When he came to write his last will, in September of 1599, he agreed to leave his rental properties to his two sons, but only on the condition that they promise to keep the buildings in good repair![58] As for the hall itself, it met the fate of its predecessor, being destroyed by the fire of 1731.[59] The borough replaced it very shortly thereafter.

CHAPTER 3

John and Joan Cooke: Civic Portraiture and Urban Identity in Gloucester

Wandering through the rooms of the Gloucester City Art Gallery makes for a pleasurable experience on a leisurely afternoon, offering a fine introduction to the regional landscape painters of the eighteenth and nineteenth centuries. One painting in particular stands out for its distinctiveness and incongruity in those surroundings. It is a smallish double portrait of a man and woman, dressed in the styles of the late sixteenth century, painted on wood panel. It strikes us immediately both for its primitive style and the gravity of its mood and content. As an inscription on the upper left-hand corner of the picture itself tells us, this is the double portrait of John and Joan Cooke, Mayor and Mayoress of Gloucester (see p. 82).[1]

As the single most common form of painting in England by far, portraits are on display in every art museum, and certainly every functioning country house has its share. But even a cursory inspection shows the Cookes' portrait to be dramatically different in several ways from the very great majority of contemporary portraits.

Against the merest suggestion of a dark brown drapery, we see John Cooke, in his scarlet mayoral robe trimmed with fur, standing rigidly on our left. He seems to be staring blankly, indeed almost catatonically, off into the distance over our right shoulder. His wife, Joan, clasps his right hand in hers, and she draws it leftwards across his body as if to lead him forward.

Joan is also well but simply dressed, in what appears as a dark-coloured (perhaps originally deep maroon), short-sleeved gown or kirtle, opening in the front to reveal an embroidered underdress. This extends beyond the sleeves of her gown, ending in

Portrait of John and Joan Cooke, Mayor and Mayoress of Gloucester (courtesy of the Gloucester City Museum).

delicate lace cuffs. Her right hand clutches a pair of brown leather gloves. Unlike her husband, she stares right at the viewer and strikes a pose as the dominant figure: she looks younger, bright-eyed, and more alert than John; she stands slightly in front of him, and she alone makes eye contact with us. Her side of the painting, on our right, seems better lit, as if the artist wished to place the emphasis on her rather than on him. In giving her 'crow's feet' around the eyes, he seems to be attempting to show her smiling at a time when it was still considered gauche to depict such smiles with visible teeth. Both figures wear the ruffed collars fashionable in the Elizabethan and Jacobean periods, and Joan wears a small beretlike cap of the same era. Her only additional adornment is a curious necklace from which hang four pendants, and a simple chain clasp tying together both sides of her collar. Neither figure wears a ring. Both the depiction of each figure individually and the positional relationship of each to the other engage our curiosity.

Several other elements command our attention. One is the 'label' in the upper left-hand corner, next to John's head, telling us that he is 'MA[ster] Iohn Cooke, Maior of the Citie of Glocester 4 Times'. A much longer inscription, in the form of a poem, runs in four vertical columns along the bottom few inches of the portrait. It reads as follows:

> Though death hath rested these life mates
> Their memory survives
> Esteemed myrrors may they be
> For Majestrats and wives
> The School of Crist ye Bartholomews
> The Cawseway in ye West
> May wittnes wch ye pious minde
> This Worthy man possest.
> This vertuous dame perform'd ye taske
> Her husband did intend
> And after him in single life
> Lived famous to her end
> Their bountye & benificence
> On earth remaines allways
> Let present past a future time
> Still Celebrate yr praise.

This is more writing than most pictures offer in explanation of the subject. Those who designed it obviously wanted us to know the full story without having to contrive a visual, iconographical representation of such a detailed message.

Unfortunately, the portrait bears no artist's signature or date. Ordinarily, assuming that the City commissioned the picture, this sort of information, along with the cost of the work, would be recorded in the City's chamberlains' accounts. Yet Gloucester's accounts no longer survive for any but three years between 1597 and 1635: the very period in which, judging from stylistic and sartorial evidence, the work appears to have been done.

In its lack of formal convention the portrait conveys to us a charming crudeness which seems closer to the characteristics of folk or naive painting than to the conventional portraiture of the period. The figures appear lifeless and stiff, though John's more so than Joan's, and it isn't even entirely clear whether they are meant to be sitting or standing. The brush strokes are broad and unsubtle, even crude. The bodies exhibit very little sense of natural form, with the hands being rendered in an especially schematic manner. Virtually no attempt has been made to offer even conventional suggestions of either figure's physical attributes: strength through musculature, sensuality through close-fitting clothes or alluring poses, physical vigour or prowess through such props as horses or weaponry. John is cloaked in his official rather than his personal attire, attesting to the mayoral office he is said to have held four times, but this tells us nothing about his personal life, his affluence, occupation, or sophistication, in the conventional manner. We perceive virtually no background scene and only the merest hint of an architectural framework which usually offers such clues in other portraits. Efforts at conveying the subject's character seem concentrated on the impression of age, wisdom, and the cares borne of responsibility. Even the colour range remains fairly limited. This, too, adds both to the crudeness of the portrayal and the gravity of the scene.

Certainly in most of these respects, this painting departs sharply from almost any of the contemporaneous portraits we would find reproduced in the standard literature on the subject for that time: far from anything we might have seen at the great *Dynasties* exhibit of Tudor and Jacobean painting at the Tate Gallery in 1995–96 or, indeed, the National Portrait Gallery, or other public repositories of what might be called English courtly painting of this era.

It is equally unlike what one would find in the picture galleries which were becoming essential features in the country houses of the gentry and aristocracy. Those galleries would have held portraits of the family and its ancestors, commissioned by the family head, plus copies of pictures of royalty and chief figures of state. The former and larger category commemorated the status, accomplishment, and associations of the sitter. Such paintings displayed personal wealth by opulent costumes, jewellery, and background scenes; sophistication by means of a neoclassical archi-tectural setting, or books or even other paintings shown as background; fecundity by tight, stylish clothes or frequently by offspring on view in the foreground. Such displays in country house picture galleries served to reinforce the impression of the sitter's social standing and ancestry. They would, in short, have been meant to fulfil what Lawrence Stone has called 'the frenzied ancestor worship of the age' by attesting visually to 'the sitter's position and wealth by opulence of dress, ornament and background'.[2] But we have none of that here.

The contrast between these conventional characteristics and objectives of the courtly and aristocratic tradition on the one hand and the Cookes' anxious and roughly painted visages on the other leaves us wondering what to make of this visual dog-in-the-manger. Is this a unique painting, a curious oddity standing on its own, or is it merely one example of a distinct, if less familiar type of portrait? Why does it differ so sharply and in so many respects from what we take to be the conventional portraits of the era? What was it intended to communicate at the time and in the place and context of its creation, and—perhaps most important of all—what can we wring from it about the nature of urban society during the course of the sixteenth century?

Let us begin with the sitters themselves, John and Joan Cooke, the Mayor and Mayoress of Gloucester. Even the idea of a portrait of a mayor and his wife departs sharply from the conventional notion of who served as the subjects for portraiture in this era. A closer look, first at them and then at the painting (for which, as it turns out, they did *not* sit in any literal sense!), turns up a few surprises and reveals a good deal more than meets the eye.

Like many who rose to civic prominence in the provincial towns of our period (and like so many in this volume), John Cooke was not, strictly speaking, a native son of Gloucester, but rather a successful migrant from a nearby village. He turns out to have been born in Minsterworth, Gloucestershire, around the 1450s, and he died in 1528.[3]

Contemporary documents refer to him as both a brewer and a mercer,[4] both lucrative and influential occupations in that day and age. Brewers had come within the century of Cooke's birth to produce beer (as well as the more traditional ale), facilitated by the preservative qualities of hops, in much larger quantities than before, expanding their potential scale of production, capital equipment, and wealth. By extending credit to growers of the grain (in effect, buying these crops well in advance of the harvest), they were often involved in money-lending activities as well. Mercers, who were dealers in fine textiles, were at the top of the heap of the English merchant hierarchy. They could become extremely wealthy, they often had very extensive commercial networks, and their influence often spread as widely as their trade goods. More often than not they composed a significant share of the leading citizens in the larger towns and dominated positions of local government. Involvement in both occupations suggests that Cooke was very likely an extremely enterprising and well-to-do man. In addition, he was undoubtedly a self-made man. The village of Minsterworth (three miles west of Gloucester as the crow flies, but five miles as the road goes round and across the upper part of the River Severn) was unlikely to have given him a start in these activities, which by their nature required an urban setting and a substantial population base.

It also seems likely that Cooke's success came relatively early in life, because he was able to employ his wealth and influence in the City of Gloucester over some five decades. Coming up through the familiar ladder, or *cursus honorum*, of City and guild organizations in the 1480s, he served twice as sheriff in the 1490s, and as Mayor four times between 1501 and 1518. He can easily be seen as one of the most dominant figures in Gloucester City affairs in the several decades following that City's incorporation as a county in and of itself in 1483.[5]

And, as the inscription on his portrait suggests, he was a generous benefactor to his City at his death as in his life. His will tells us that in addition to pious bequests to local churches and for the care of his soul, and bequests of his lands and tenements to his wife, Joan, he gave widely to civic causes. He supported the poor of St. Bartholomew's Hospital and the repair of the great West Bridge of the City and of two of its main roads. On John Speed's map of 1610 this was the only bridge over the River Severn at Gloucester,[6] though modern research shows a smaller one below it.[7] The bridge served to link Cooke to his home village and the City both to Wales and the West Midlands north and east of the river. Its serious decay in the fifteenth century had been a major and persistent problem.[8] Finally, he endowed the foundation of a free grammar school in the parish of St. Mary de Crypt for the 'erudition' of its children.[9]

To see that these bequests were carried out John named his wife, Joan, née Messenger, as his sole executor. He entrusted her brother, Alderman Thomas Messenger, and several other prominent townsmen with the foundation of the school. This came to be known as the Crypt School because of its location adjacent to St. Mary de Crypt Church in Southgate Street. The building still exists and indeed has housed the portrait itself even in recent times.

Joan herself outlived her husband by about fourteen years. She never remarried, and she did indeed perform 'ye taske Her husband did intend'. It is this carrying forth of his wishes which we see conveyed in the juxtaposition of the two figures in the painting. By grasping his right hand in hers, she is not only engaged in a conventional gesture of affection but appears to be leading him forth. She purchased much of the lands of the former Llanthony Priory after it was dissolved, and used the site, adjacent to St. Mary de Crypt Church, to build the intended school. It was completed by 1539. By her will of May 1544, she, too, left sums to the Church and for pious bequests, and she, too, left money to keep up one of the main roads out of Gloucester. She also endowed the Cathedral

Church of St. Peter and its High Altar, and also a perpetual chantry to be governed by a board of feoffees. It was probably one of the last chantries to be founded anywhere before the dissolution of such institutions which began shortly thereafter. Joan rounded out her bequests by remembering the inmates of three local hospitals and the poor prisoners in the City's gaols.[10] Neither will mentions children, suggesting either that the couple remained childless or that their children predeceased them.

These wills, traditionally Roman Catholic in their testamentary formulae, suggest that both John and Joan Cooke were first and foremost benefactors of their community. John left to its various causes the bulk of his considerable fortune, while Joan carried out his bequests and thus completed his work. Along with everyone else at the time, the Cookes were obviously concerned with the salvation of their souls through the performance of good works. But unlike many of their contemporaries, they saw such activities consisting of civic as well as religious benefactions. The classic study of charitable patterns before and after the Reformation emphasizes the small proportion of pre-Reformation bequests which went to civic betterment.[11] The example of the Cookes (like that of Sir Thomas White elsewhere in this volume) nevertheless strengthens the notion of a highly developed 'civic Catholicism' at work prior to the Reformation, if not amongst the majority of benefactors, then at least amongst some of the more enlightened and well placed.

The same concern for civic benefactions extends to the commissioning of the portrait itself. Not only is there no evidence that the sitters commissioned it themselves, but the chronology of their lives and the creation of the portrait makes such a suggestion impossible. The inscription makes clear that the portrait was obviously painted after the deaths of its subjects. There is nothing in their will suggesting a desire for a portrait and—though again we do not have a date for it—it is obviously a posthumous painting. Precisely how posthumous is another question.

The mode of the Cookes' attire, simply as it has been rendered,

is characteristic of a much later period than the lives of either subject. Ruff collars and delicate ruffed cuffs can hardly be earlier
than mid-Elizabethan. Given that the painting was almost certainly done locally and thus far from the centres of fashion at court or
in London, it was probably done even later. It is likely that the artist patterned these styles after Southern Netherlandish paintings
of the last decades of the sixteenth century, with which he seems to
have been familiar. However, he obviously lacked the technical
skills which would have been apparent in paintings of that time
and place.[12] Finally, the fact that no record of payment for the
painting appears in the City chamberlains' accounts before they
are interrupted in 1597 suggests that it was painted after that date,
though probably, if the evidence of dress is any indication, by only
a few years.

A further bit of circumstantial evidence regarding the probable
dating of the Cookes' portrait may be found in the eleven other
civic portraits of this type which have survived in Gloucester—the
second largest surviving collection in any single town after Norwich—which have been dated to the same approximate period.
They, too, exhibit many of the same stylistic characteristics as the
Cookes' portrait. (Perhaps even more appropriately, in view of
their modest artistic merit, we find them today not in the Art gallery on Brunswick Road at all, but in the City Folk Museum several
blocks away on Westgate Street!)[13] All things considered, the
Cookes' portrait seems most likely to have been completed around
1600.

But why should a portrait of a mayor and his wife, even if they
were such important benefactors, have been commissioned so
long after their deaths, and probably not even representing an accurate likeness?[14] The question seems more pressing still when we
consider that Gloucester had already become dominated by a
strong Puritan element of the sort not presumably given to enthusiasm for personal celebration or to support for the visual arts.
And in the absence of the sort of self-celebration or self-fashioning
which seems to have been a dominant motive for most (which is to

say the courtly and aristocratic) portraits of the time, what did the artist, or those commissioning his work, intend this painting to signify?

In the absence of almost any element of the painting which would refer to the subjects in their personal, as opposed to official, capacities, the suggestion emerges that the purpose here was indeed to commemorate their lives not as individual people but as citizens: in John's case as a civic official and benefactor; in Joan's as his helpmate in civic affairs. This is not only conveyed by the inscription, which tells as much, but also by John's mayoral robe and Joan's gloves. In a sense it is also conveyed by the absence of almost any other element of furnishing, dress, background, or architectural setting which could allude to their private lives, and thus distract from the intended message. Given this privileged position in the picture, the robe and gloves seem worth an explanation.

Mayoral robes or gowns were conventionally tailored of red velvet and often trimmed with fur (in many towns, of course, they still look the same today) and were conventionally meant to reflect the dignity of the wearer. Local records commonly emphasize that they were to be 'made after the gravest and most seemely fashion' (Gloucester, 1601), or refer to 'gownes of the gravest sort' (Bristol, 1594).[15] All these features conform closely to the invariable demand of town by-laws that the mayors and aldermen wear their proper gowns when going 'abroad' from their homes. These were elements of the borough 'livery', reflecting the desired public image of civic rectitude and sobriety rather than any display of personal wealth and fame. As the contemporary writer John Earle put it in 1628 referring to the figure of the London alderman: 'He is venerable in his gowne . . . wherein he setts not forth his owne so much as the face of a City. . . . [H]is scarlet gowne is a monument, and lasts from generation to generation'.[16]

Gloves had broader and more complex meanings, rendered slightly confusing because they bore a multitude of connotations and because they figured—with a different symbolic intent—in courtly portraits as well. In this painting they seem to serve two functions. First, they symbolize membership in the freemanry, and the virtue of fair trading: both were conventional and well understood meanings in urban communities throughout the realm. In the Somerset town of Wells, for example, gloves were given as gifts by the new member of the freemanry to his fellows, not only as a sign of thanks for admitting him but also as a pledge of fair trading and fair dealing in upholding the reputation of the community.[17] In many other towns a glove, or a model of a gloved hand, would be displayed at a market or fair, signifying the hand of authority which guaranteed justice and fair trading. In towns like Chester, Portsmouth, Southampton, and Barnstaple, the erection of a glove or gloved hand on a pole signalled the opening of the day's marketing, as it continued to do well into the nineteenth century.[18] In the context of the Cookes' portrait, then, the gloves must be considered a sign of John's freeman's status, and of his reputation for fair dealing.

In the portrait, it is of course Joan who carries the gloves. This tells us that she had inherited John's freeman's status at his death (inheritance being the most common way for a woman to achieve such status herself) and that she faithfully carried forth his reputation just as she carried forth the gloves which symbolized it. The fact that she is holding them (bringing them more emphatically to our attention) rather than wearing them (meant for him, they would presumably not fit her) adds to this impression.

Secondly, gloves also played a role in the symbolism of marriage, and here we have the one exception to the artist's refraint from commentary on the Cookes as people. Throughout European society at this time an exchange of gloves served as a means or symbol of plighting troth, or promising fidelity, at an engagement or marriage itself. This message is further conveyed in the familiar and highly meaningful gesture of hand-clasping—right hand in right hand—which is also so evident in the portrait before us.[19] And there is tenderness here, too, in Joan's gestures towards John. The crow's lines at her eyes are meant to suggest a smile in the artistic conventions of a time when rotting teeth made for closed mouths on the portrait. In sum, these images surely make something of a statement about John and Joan as people. They remained faithful to each other in life; she to him after his death.

Yet even this emotional element of the painting, so charmingly rendered in its stylistic naiveté, has its distinct civic purpose. Surely in a host of political theories beginning with Aristotle and very much alive in the sixteenth century, the marital union and the family which it formed lay at the heart of the civic weal: an example of harmony and tranquility of manner, and also the most elementary form of political organization. Then, too, of course, the context in which the painting places Joan's loyalty to her husband is patently civic: she carries forth his freeman's responsibilities and his civic benefactions.

But if this is intended as a commemoration of civic virtues, we still need to think about why it was painted as much as a half-century or more after the death of its subjects, and even at a time when Gloucester had already become known as something of a Puritan stronghold.[20] Surely the virtues displayed by the artist were as valued in the lifetimes of the Cookes as after, and yet no one seems to have considered commissioning their portrait any earlier. The answer to this conundrum appears to lie in two themes, one having to do with the disruption of civic memory occasioned by the Reformation, and the second having to do with the urgent need of the post-Reformation city governments to reconstruct an alternative civic memory which served their needs. Let us take up these possibilities in turn.

We may think of a 'civic memory' as nothing more than the collective sense of the past which was held in common by members of a particular civic community. Some such communities could be very large indeed. Christendom and the sense of the Christian past which were shared by all communicants, and the sense of England's past which was shared by an ever-growing number of English men and women, weigh in at one end of the scale. Residents of Gloucester, like those of Henry Manship's Great Yarmouth and John Pitt's Blandford Forum discussed elsewhere, would also have shared a sense of the past. That image would have embraced the town's identity, its history, its place in the history of the realm, and its own particular heroes and worthies.

Before the Reformation, communities like Gloucester would have fostered collective memories which were local versions of the larger picture. That is to say that part of that memory had in general terms to do with being Christian, with being English, and so forth. Closely tied up with these elements of heritage, part also would have had to do with the particular events and historic figures in the history of Gloucester itself. The patron saint for which a parish church or cathedral or religious guild would have been named, icons and images of various sorts in ecclesiastical buildings, stained glass windows, plate, and other such items would all have commemorated the religious heritage. Noteworthy individuals would have been remembered by the preservation of funerary brasses, in prayers for their souls offered in obits and anniversaries, and in the periodic reading aloud in the Sunday service of the names on the parish bede-roll. In addition, very important people were commemorated in funerary monuments, by lavish gifts of plate or in statuary on biblical or related themes. These elements of collective memory obviously played an important part in spiritual terms as a means of encouraging prayers for the souls of the departed. But they also served as important cultural icons of the local identity, and as political markers engendering respect for the community, its traditions, and its leaders.

Many of these doctrinal foundations of the collective or civic memory were disrupted and almost completely destroyed in the course of the Reformation. Much more lay at stake in this loss than a change in doctrine or a superficial redecoration of the parish church or similar building. With the wholesale iconoclastic destruction of the material elements of the old faith—especially of the icons and images, the bede-rolls and brasses—those changes effectively erased many central elements in the community's heritage. Much of the sense of its own particular past simply disappeared. In a national culture with relatively weak traditions of urban identity to begin with, certainly as compared with a number of other Northern European cultures and traditions,[21] this was a very serious loss. It threatened to impinge on the continuity of behaviourial conventions, on the maintenance of law and order, on the operation of a local identity, and on the common respect for civic traditions and leadership.

Especially in the era of rapid economic and social change which characterized the second half of the sixteenth century, when the very population of towns turned over so quickly, civic leaders in many towns strove to reconstruct whatever elements of heritage they could. They hoped thereby to restore the traditional pride, respect, and deference to the civic weal. In consequence, these years exhibited (as we will have seen in Blandford Forum) the polemical use of civic architecture and furnishing,[22] and also (as in Great Yarmouth) the enhanced and intense interest in the writing of civic history.[23] Civic ruling elites frequently adopted a version of Protestantism which encouraged civic discipline and the perfection of the city as a moral ideal.[24] The creation of a secular form of civic portraiture, specifically dedicated to the commemoration of civic worthies of both the past and the present, worked toward the same end.

The portrait of the Cookes in Gloucester exemplifies these tendencies in several respects. As prominent citizens and pious Christians in their time, the Cookes had in fact been commemorated in the traditional ways of the old faith. Traditional funeral rites, for example, were very much intended as occasions for remembrance, and occasions memorable in themselves. The bodies of the deceased would have been surrounded by candles and crosses before and during the procession to the grave site. The procession itself would have moved to the accompaniment of public prayers by attendant priests, and perhaps by monks and friars as well. Knells would have been rung, and mourning cloths would have been distributed to the poor in exchange for their prayers. John left the very substantial sum of £20 to the poor at his burial, and another £40 at the first anniversary of his death for pre-

cisely such observances. Both John and Joan asked in their wills
for prayers to be said—aloud and in the hearing of many parishioners—for their souls. They had provided funds for that, too, to
be done, and in perpetuity.

John had bequeathed to one of Gloucester's churches an alabaster table with a carving of St. John the Baptist, and had provided for his own burial at the high end of the altar, next to the image of the same saint, in that church.[25] Joan arranged to be buried
next to her husband, and listed many bequests for the singing of
prayers for her soul and for the upkeep of several churches of the
City. She left an altar cloth for the Mother Church of the Diocese
(St. Peter's, created as a Cathedral in 1541), money for the poor
inmates of St. Bartholomew's Hospital to pray for her soul, and the
same to the poor of several other hospitals. The perpetual chantry
she founded was intended to provide prayers sung in perpetuity
for her soul as well as for John's. Tapers were to be lit for the same
purpose, and the indigent residents of three different poorhouses
were to sing prayers. Finally, both John and Joan had been the
subject of a funerary brass, probably (though this is not mentioned
in their wills) at their own expense. These actions and bequests
may largely have been undertaken for purposes of pious interces-
sion, and out of a concern for the salvation of their souls after
death. But they also had the effect of enshrining the Cookes in the
memory of their community, if not perpetually, then at least for as
long as it remained possible to observe them in the traditional
manner.

As fortune would have it, of course, that was not to be for very
long. With the Reformation, and with the Cathedral Church given
to the episcopal care of the zealous John Hooper in 1551, much of
the traditional paraphernalia of remembrance came to an abrupt
end. The obits, anniversaries, tapers (or 'lights'), the chantry and
the Hospital of St. Bartholomew in their traditional forms, and
probably both the altar cloth for the Cathedral and the alabaster St.
John Baptist, were all removed. And so the principal means by
which the Cookes' model of civic service and benefaction would

traditionally have been conveyed to later generations—forming a chapter in the unwritten history of the community—were almost entirely destroyed during and after Joan's lifetime.

Not until the post-Reformation government of the City had a chance to sort itself out, and to work out that alternative form of civic memory required by the demands of civic order and obedience, did a means come forth to revive their image—or at least the secular part of it. It may strike us as ironic that this came forth at a time of increasingly Puritan influence in Gloucester's affairs, but in many respects the Puritan ethos shared many of the same goals—of a religious doctrine which could be applied to the goal of moral perfection—as its Roman Catholic predecessor, and the expectation that Puritans would have opposed the use even of secular images ought not to be taken too far.

In any event, whether Puritans or not, civic leaders in the post-Reformation era faced in two respects a difficult task in their effort to govern their communities. First, as men without hereditary status, title, landed property, or even long tenure in office as commonly shared by those who ruled in county government, Gloucester's officials, along with those of other provincial towns, required some other means of inculcating deference and obedience to their authority. And secondly, they had to accomplish this in the wake of the destruction of the ambient political culture which had served that purpose prior to the Reformation. Central to that ethos was the civic memory, conveyed in sundry traditional forms, and embracing such exemplary figures as John and Joan Cooke. It is against this profound need, to resurrect a civic memory which would inform a post-Reformation civic culture and thus facilitate the business of maintaining order in difficult times, that we must see the creation of the Cooke portrait, and of its eleven surviving fellows.

As it happens, the Cooke portrait is not unique in kind, but one of several dozen civic portraits, as we must now label this type, which have only recently been identified for the period at hand.[26] Fascinating in its own right to be sure, it bears a wider significance as well. It suggests something about the political culture of turn-of-the-century Gloucester, and of the role of civic portraiture in the political culture of many provincial towns at this same time. Although this particular work remains extremely unusual in showing both Mayor and Mayoress,[27] it shares virtually all of the essential characteristics of those civic portraits which have been identified in this age: characteristics of chronology, aesthetic merit, civic as opposed to personal virtues, public provenance, and display.

Of all the civic portraits which have been dated, only one derives from as early as 1549: that of Alan Percy of Norwich.[28] Two derive from the 1560s,[29] one from the 1570s,[30] and two from the 1580s,[31] before we find a greater abundance around the turn of the century. Most of those which can be dated, and where the death dates of the subject are known, were painted during the lifetime or shortly after death. But even in Gloucester the Cookes were by no means unique in being painted so long after their demise. Thomas Bell (d. 1566), John Falkner (d. 1545), Joan and William Goldston (d. 1579 and 1569), and Richard Pates (d. 1588) provide other examples. The portraits of all of them are considered to have been done around the turn of the seventeenth century, well after the deaths of their subjects.[32]

Even longer durations between death and portrait come from elsewhere. Three of the impressive series of portraits from Norwich, the largest single concentration of civic portraits and the one most likely to have been conceived as a series from this era, came forth in that manner. Robert Jannys, one of the wealthiest men in all England in his time, last served as Mayor in 1517 and died in 1530. John Marsham, who succeeded Jannys as Mayor in 1518, died in 1532. Augustine Steward (d. 1572) served three times as Mayor and was perhaps the most prominent Norwich citizen of the mid-century years. But all were painted (perhaps from earlier drawings) in the early seventeenth century.[33] In similar fashion there may have been a contemporary or near contemporary drawing of the fifteenth-century Bury St. Edmunds benefactor Jankyn Smith, but the town did not acquire an oil portrait of him until 1616.[34] Nicholas Thorne, Mayor of Bristol in 1545, was first painted in 1624.[35] Clearly the ruling elite of Gloucester seems not to have been alone in hitting upon the device of painting portraits of its deceased as well as its living worthies around or after the turn of the seventeenth century.

The Cookes' portrait also seems typical of its type in terms of style and merit. True, it and its eleven companion pieces from Gloucester are overshadowed by the greater artistic merit of some other civic portraits, especially some from the Norwich collection. But many other portraits in provincial towns were artistically just as crude. In addition, the human form generally took a beating in these renderings. Heads, arms, and trunks are often disproportionate with each other, poses are stiff and unnatural, and both hands and fingers are often extremely wooden and schematic even when they are given gloves or similar devices to hold onto.

The Cookes' painting is also par for the course in terms of its ornamentation or iconographical references. That is to say that these are few in number, simple, and limited almost entirely to civic themes. The mayoral or aldermanic robe is the most common such device, though a few subjects wear seal rings to provide identification, and there are sometimes simple props relating to the sitter's contribution. Giles Tooker of Salisbury, for example, holds the charter of the City which he did so much himself to obtain.[36] Several others hold a book, which may indicate their level of learning or legal training. But we pointedly do not find in any of them an occupational reference which might form an analogue to the country house, or fertile fields, or scene of war, which figure in the background of many an aristocratic portrait of the same time. Save for the Cooke portrait and that of Laurence Seldon and his wife of Exeter,[37] which is documented archivally but has not survived, we do not find any reference to marriage or family, or heritage, or dynasty, or, for that matter, to physical vigour or youth, as we frequently do in the more conventional portrait type. These associations may have been vital to the contemporary imaging of the aristocracy and landed gentry, but they were of far less moment to the office of the mayor, serving his single year's term before returning to his counting house or his shop.

All this is meant to suggest several related themes in contemporary portraiture. We have long known that the familiar type of aristocratic/gentle/royal portraiture played the prominent role which was described by Lawrence Stone. Such 'courtly' paintings certainly provide rich sources for what we know of the landed society which still dominated in almost every aspect of English life, and which would do so right on up into the modern era.

The Cookes' portrait, on the other hand, opens a window onto quite a different world, and one which was very far from being dominant in the society and culture of its time. This is not even the world of the merchant so much as that of the citizen, in which the virtues of civic benefaction and citizenship itself were the most essential element for public display. Coming at the time and in the form in which the Cookes' portrait and others of the same era may be seen, this distinct type answered a profound social and political need of the governing element. Even when it meant stripping away references to traditional religious preferences, the civic leaders of late sixteenth and early seventeenth century provincial towns were most anxious to retrieve worthy models of civic behaviour which they could hold up to the citizens and (perhaps especially) the newcomers in their midst. In so doing they displayed models for behaviour, engendered respect for civic government, and strengthened the traditions of urban identity upon which the civic order, and the ability to govern, substantially depended.

Sir Thomas White of London: Civic Philanthropy and the Making of the Merchant-Hero

Perceptions of the Merchant

Save for scattered literary references in Chaucer and elsewhere, few perceptions of urban society and of city dwellers them-selves—merchants, craftsmen, journeymen, and so forth—can be seen as flattering before the Elizabethan period. In contrast to the ordered three-part conception of traditional society (peasants, clergy, and the landed classes), towns and cities, and their in-habitants, represented a distinctive and intrusive element in the social hierarchy. Urban communities were founded for different economic purposes and run by different rules. The road from mercantile to landed society in the course of a generation or two was not infrequently travelled. Yet social advancement by means of material wealth alone threatened a society which still valued status and lineage more than such wealth. This was particularly true in a society where conventional ideas of status derived from one's relationship to the land.[1]

The city's reputation for sinfulness and corruption, for disorder and instability, and for the avarice and rapacity of its citizens, stood in sharp contrast to the image of the honest ploughman and the familiar, ordered mores of the landed classes. The moral con-trast, and the metaphorical battle, between merchant and gentle-man became a stock theme of Elizabethan drama.[2] The contest between Sodom and Jerusalem formed almost as prominent a theme in the sermon literature of the same time.[3]

Yet towards the end of the sixteenth century these perceptions came to be balanced by one which was more favourable, so that

the contest between merchant and gentleman, Sodom and Jerusalem, evened out. Some Elizabethan observers of English society,
men like Thomas Churchyard, William Harrison, Sir Thomas
Smith, and William Camden, began at least to find a legitimate
place for city dwellers, including merchants, in their descriptions
of social structure.[4] By c. 1585 playwrights began to write often
enough about the urban milieu to justify the term 'citizen comedy'
for some of their efforts. Though their view of the merchant was
often negative, it was not always so.[5] And of course the 'respectable' classes came more than ever in this era to rely on the wealth
and benefactions of such figures. The taking of interest became effectively legalized by the Usury Act of 1571 (13 Eliz., c. 8), and the
lure of commercial investments became too enticing for them to
resist.[6]

At least some types of merchants came to have their proponents
amongst the writers and theorists of the day. It is true that an appreciation of the merchant's skill as merchant was only occasionally voiced,[7] and the business of business itself only sometimes
figured as a subject. But there did appear considerable approval
for what merchants did with their money after they made it. Those
who engaged more directly and positively in public life, or who
spent their gains altruistically and honourably, found their place
in contemporary plays and essays,[8] and gained approbation
amongst the ranks of the land-owning classes. Some, like Sir
Thomas Gresham or (posthumously) Simon Eyre and Dick Whittington, came even to be lionized.

And, with the recognition of at least some of the positive attributes of the merchant figure came a more balanced view of urban
life in general. What had been seen as avaricious, alien, vulgar,
and dangerous, and marked by social climbing of the crassest sort,
now came to be seen at least in some quarters as providing opportunity, as both civilized and civilizing, and as the potential
source of the good things which wealth could obtain. The potential of the city as a civilizing force became a common theme in
contemporary Puritan sermons,[9] and of course formed an underlying assumption of their sermons and lectureships.[10]

These are vital issues for the study of urban society in this era. They bring into focus that exceptionally important time, and that process, which established the respectability of trade and manufacturing and thus facilitated the eventual commercial and industrial pre-eminence of Great Britain. They focus, too, on the turnabout in the common perception of urban society, and of the merchants who dominated it, whence much of that pre-eminence came to fruition.

In this reversal of perceptions John Stow's works on London, and his high regard for the deeds of London's ruling elite through the years, form a prominent landmark. That theme continued to build through subsequent decades with the work of such popular writers as John Webster, Richard Johnson, and Thomas Deloney, and such dramatists as Thomas Dekker, Thomas Heywood, and William Haughton. These writers reflect the growing perception in contemporary popular literature that at least the elite amongst merchants displayed some attributes of gentility associated with the landed classes. With this attitudinal shift, and with contemporary advances in the vocabulary of public celebration, the last decades of the sixteenth century saw the birth of the merchant-hero as a literary type.

By any such measure, that status must be accorded to Sir Thomas White (1495–1567), whose career affords us useful insights into all of these phenomena. His entrepreneurial achievements as a member of the Merchant Taylors' Company of London and almost certainly as a draper and clothier,[11] his remarkable and far-reaching benefactions, and his commemoration within a very few years of his death as a heroic figure in the popular literature and portraiture of the period, afford him a prominent place in the history of English mercantile—and urban—society. In addition, his experience as a merchant led him to what was for his time a remarkably imaginative and sophisticated approach to economic problems and policy, and one which anticipated government strategies in several respects. Let us consider White's career as a prime example of these themes.

The Rise of Sir Thomas White

Alone amongst the cast of characters assembled in this volume, White was a man of national prominence in his own time and enduring reputation even into ours.[12] Born in 1495 to a Reading clothier,[13] White was apprenticed at the age of twelve to Hugh Acton, a prominent master of the Merchant Taylors' Company of London. Acton was a generous man both to apprentices in general, for whom he established a loan fund, and to his own apprentices in particular. When Thomas White completed his apprenticeship with Acton, sometime before 1520,[14] Acton gave him £100 with which to set out on his own: an act of generosity which White would replicate manyfold.[15]

The money soon proved well spent, as White did very well for himself in business. Despite some years of instability from the mid–1540s to the early 1550s caused by war and stoppages of trade abroad, and the lingering effects of an early-century slump in some quarters, White's career coincided with years of general prosperity for the Tudor cloth industry. It would last until the heightened political friction between England, Spain, and the Spanish Netherlands from about 1558, the Dutch stop of English trade in 1563, and the outbreak of the Dutch Revolt itself shortly thereafter. All those events destabilized that sector of the English economy for some time to come.[16] Yet at their peak, and in the person of such figures as Thomas Spring of Lavenham and William Stumpe of Malmesbury, the clothing trades gave rise to some of the wealthiest merchants in the kingdom.[17] White himself became a member of this rarefied circle by the mid-1540s. By 1544 his wealth allowed him to join with other London liverymen in a large loan to Henry VIII. By 1559 he is reckoned to have become the richest man in London.[18]

While he was accumulating his fortune, White rose rapidly through the ranks of the Merchant Taylors, becoming Master of the Company by 1535.[19] The senior ranks of this powerful company provided him with a springboard to office in the city itself. He served as alderman of Cornhill Ward by 1544, and sheriff by

1547. The first (and very eventful) year of Mary's reign, 1553–54, proved the apex of White's public career. In the tumultuous days of her disputed accession, he had been one of Mary's most conspicuous and powerful supporters in London. Appropriately enough, he was also one of the five City officials to ride out and greet her as she arrived for the first time on the outskirts of London on 29 July, 1553, only ten days after her victory had been assured.[20] White received his knighthood shortly thereafter and served as Lord Mayor of London from 1553 to 1554.[21]

There may have been many reasons for his Marian sympathies, but one of them surely was his continued loyalty to the Roman Catholic faith. White drew much of his inspiration from the revelations of Elizabeth Barton, the seer known as the Maid of Kent.[22] His foundation of St. John's College, accomplished over a several year period following the receipt of a royal patent of May 1555,[23] seems the most overt expression of his religious persuasions. He dedicated the College to the patron saint of the Merchant Taylors' Fraternity, thus ensuring a continuity of that tradition. Its statutes (including the requirement for mandatory confession) stood as White's statement in the battle against heresy. The College stuck to that rubric even after the accession of Elizabeth and thereby attracted many adherents of traditional doctrine to its fellowship. When White's funeral came to be held there the future Jesuit Edmund Campion preached the sermon in the College chapel.[24]

During his year in office as Lord Mayor, Mary clearly relied on White to maintain the support of the City for her rule and her policies. In response, he helped rally Londoners against Wyatt's rebels in February 1554, supervised the expulsion of Protestant intellectuals who had flocked to London and Westminster under Edward VI,[25] and took charge of the London reception for Mary and her consort Philip after their marriage in Winchester Cathedral.[26]

These accomplishments in affairs of the City and nation would have earned White an honoured place amongst his contemporaries regardless of his other achievements. But his role as a philanthropist, begun as far back as 1542, loomed far above them in forging his personal reputation, and it endured far longer. It was in that year that White established his long charitable association with the City of Coventry. It would be only the first of his magnanimous schemes; in fact, it proved to be but the first of two centred in Coventry, with whose declining cloth trades White had no doubt long familiarity and deep sympathy.

By a patent of 19 July, 1542, the mayor and burgesses of Coventry purchased lands in Coventry and Warwick which were worth at the time £70 a year in rental value.[27] They did so with a gift of £1,400 from White, who conferred it '. . . thereby to Relieve and prefer the Comon Wealth of the said City of Coventry being now in Greate Ruine and decay . . .'.[28] This observation about the state of Coventry City was no exaggeration. It had suffered a severe and precipitous decline between about 1518 and 1525, in large part because of a failure in its traditional broadcloth industry with which White would have been intimately familiar, and it had not at all recovered by 1542. Indeed, it has come to stand as the classic example of urban decline in the sixteenth century.[29]

In return for White's gift, Coventry's leaders agreed, in a covenant signed in 1551, that after White's death they would dispense a fixed proportion of the annual revenue in two distinct ways.[30] The first provision was simply to support an alms fund to support twelve poor but virtuous men each year with a sum of £2 each. But the second provided for a rotating loan fund whereby four young freemen of Coventry ('. . . being of good name and fame and towards in thrift, and such as be Ffree and have bin Apprentices in the saide Citty of Coventry') would receive each year for nine years the sum of £10 each from the profits of the lands. These were interest-free loans, to be repaid in nine years' time. Thereupon the sums would immediately be lent out again on the same terms to four new recipients, and the scheme would continue in that manner, nine years by nine years, in perpetuity. Eventually, as capital continued to accrue from the lands which served as the principal, the scheme would extend, one at a time, to four additional clothing towns as well: Northampton, Leicester, Nottingham, and Warwick.[31] White entrusted the supervision of the scheme to the Merchant Taylors' Company. And, save for the absence of any

stipulation regarding the occupation of the recipients,[32] the structure of this scheme served White as a model for two additional
loan funds of the same sort.[33] Recipients were to have served a full
apprenticeship, to have been admitted freemen, and to remain
resident in their cities for the duration of their loans. The scheme
was to extend to additional cities in the course of time, with the
Merchant Taylors presiding over the whole.

The second scheme again focused on Coventry, and again there
were other cities involved: Worcester, York, and Lincoln.[34] In this
undated scheme the annual revenues produced by the landed endowment extended to £220 p.a., the loans were to amount to £25
each for the same nine-year term, and the scheme was to apply
only to those young men who 'woll promys to make clothe'.[35] In its
final form, as with the first scheme, monies repayed at the end of
the first loan period, added to additional revenues which continued to be generated from the landed endowment, would continually expand the fund's available capital at a constant rate, and
more loans could be made each year. It was reckoned that at the
end of six years, twenty-four men would have been helped; thirty-
two men at the end of eight years, and so on until there were forty
recipients of the loan in Coventry alone in the first twelve years. At
that point the loan was to be extended in the same manner to the
other cities in turn, again at intervals sufficient to allow the principal to grow.

Not content with these benefactions to Coventry and other
towns and cities, White also turned to educational endowments.
In addition to his foundation of St. John's College Oxford in 1555,[36]
he played a substantial role in the 1561 founding of the Merchant
Taylors' School.[37]

But above all these achievements, and even considering these
impressive forays into the world of charitable endowments, the
one bequest which did the most to establish White's reputation
even to our time, and for which his other charitable schemes seem
to have served as dress rehearsals, is the rotating charity, administered by the City of Bristol, for the clothiers of twenty-four different locales. This plan, too, was complex, both in its terms and in

the provisions made for its endowment and administration.[38] It hinged on White's bequests to the City of Bristol which eventually amounted to £2,000. Some of this sum had been given to pay for Bristol's purchase of former ecclesiastical lands in 1544,[39] an endowment which produced income of £76 a year from that time.[40] The rest seems to have been given later on, probably in the early 1560s, and it sufficed to bring the total annual revenue to £120 a year. By an agreement worked out over several years,[41] and affirmed in a deed of July 1566, to which White, the Mayor, Commonalty, and Burgesses of Bristol, St. John's College, and the Merchant Taylors' Company, were parties, that sum was earmarked as the income to sustain the scheme.[42]

For the first eight years of the arrangement, from Martinmas 1567, monies derived from White's gift were to be expended in Bristol itself. They were for the purchase and resale of corn to the town's poor, beginning in 1575, and to extend two annual loans of £50 each to merchant tailors, interest free. The principal of these loans was to be repaid, and lent out again on the same terms, after ten years, and thus again every ten years forever. But by 1576, with £1,000 having accrued through the annual rental of lands plus the repayment of some of the £100 loans, the main part of the scheme would come into effect.

At that time, Bristol was to begin to operate a rotating and perpetual charity to provide interest-free loans to young clothiers in twenty-three cities plus the Merchant Taylors' Company itself: a twenty-four-year rotation, in which each specified town (plus the Merchant Taylors) would be the recipient once each twenty-four years in turn. Every year, from 1577 and perpetually thereafter, on the feast of St. Bartholomew (August 24) and at the Merchant Taylors' Hall in London, representatives of the City of Bristol were to convey the sum of £104 to representatives of the recipient corporation for each year. Four pounds of this sum were to go to the recipient corporation for administrative costs. The other hundred were to be divided four ways to provide interest-free loans of £25 each to four young clothiers for a period of ten years. In addition, each recipient had to provide guarantors for their repayment, and to return the principal, without interest, in ten years' time. Upon that repayment the Mayor and burgesses of the particular town would immediately re-lend the same £100 to another four young men. In addition each town would gain an additional £104 every twenty-four years, this to be lent in the same manner. The scheme emphatically insisted that the recipients be 'of honest name and fame, occupyers and inhabitants within the sayed Citie and ffreemen of the same [conditions to which we will return below] . . . And Clothyers to be preferred aboue all others to be named'.[43]

Additional provisions were contrived to organize supervision of the scheme's operation by representatives of both the corporation of Bristol and St. John's College. After twenty years' operation, these two would visit every one of the twenty-four recipient corporations to see if the bequest had been duly administered as required. Any one of the twenty-four found to have failed in its obligations was to forfeit its part of the bequest to St. John's College, and to be replaced in the rotation by another town. Recipients were:

1.	1567 Bristol*	13.	1588 Lincoln
2.	1577 York	14.	1589 Winchester
3.	1578 Canterbury	15.	1590 Oxford
4.	1579 Reading	16.	1591 Hereford
5.	1580 Merchant Taylors' Co.	17.	1592 Cambridge
6.	1581 Gloucester	18.	1593 Shrewsbury
7.	1582 Worcester	19.	1594 King's Lynn
8.	1583 Exeter	20.	1595 Bath
9.	1584 Salisbury	21.	1596 Derby
10.	1585 Chester	22.	1597 Ipswich
11.	1586 Norwich	23.	1598 Colchester
12.	1587 Southampton	24.	1599 Newcastle

In practice, then, this meant that, for example, Chester received its first sum of £104 on 24 August, 1585, and (retaining £4 for ad-

*Bristol to receive £100 a year during the years 1567–76 inclusive, and then £104 every twenty-fourth year thereafter as the recipient town for that year.

ministrative costs) lent it out to four recipients.[44] These four repaid their loans in 1595 so that they could be lent out again, setting up a ten-year cycle of repayment of the initial subsidy to the City of Chester, in 1595, 1605, 1615, 1625, and so forth. But in addition, Chester would receive another £104 every twenty-four years, keeping £4 to defray administrative costs, and dispersing the remainder in four more loans of £25 each. Each of these loans would also be repaid in ten years, to be recycled at the same ten-year interval. The second payment of £104 would accrue twenty-four years after the first—that is, in 1609, and be repaid and re-lent in the '09' year of each decade thereafter. Over the long haul, after Chester's first receipt of £104, this means that Chester could extend loans of £25 to four recipients in each of the following years, with the frequency increasing steadily.

TABLE 2

Loans and Repayments in the City of Chester in the Sample Years 1585–1791

1585	1609	1633	1657	1681	1705	1729	1753
1595							
1605							
1615	1619						
1625	1629						
1635	1639						
1645	1649	1643					
1655	1659	1653					
1665	1669	1663	1667				
1675	1679	1673	1677				
1685	1689	1683	1687	1691			
1695	1699	1693	1697	1701			
1705	1709	1703	1707	1711			
1715	1719	1713	1717	1721	1715		
1725	1729	1723	1727	1731	1725		
1735	1739	1733	1737	1741	1735	1739	
1745	1749	1743	1747	1751	1745	1749	
1755	1759	1753	1757	1761	1755	1759	
1765	1769	1763	1767	1771	1765	1769	1763
1775	1779	1773	1777	1781	1775	1779	1773
1785	1789	1783	1787	1791	1785	1789	1783

NOTE: Dates of the £104 payment to the City of Chester, accruing every 24th year from 1585, are written left to right across the top of table. Dates for repayment of the various loans roughly within each decade are written from top to bottom. These years could be extended to the present.

From what we can tell, chiefly through the reports of the Charity Commissioners who were charged by the House of Commons in the early nineteenth century with investigating the state of the endowed charities in the realm, the scheme worked remarkably well right from its inception. A few challenges had been launched regarding the disbursement of funds between 1810 and 1820, but the scheme continued in operation as, indeed, it does in a number of the recipient towns to the present time.

The Meaning of White's Benefaction

By the time the Bristol scheme had been worked out in its final form and ensured with the indenture of July 1566, White's health began to decline. He began to withdraw from his aldermanic responsibilities and to turn his thoughts to the disposition of his estate. In subsequent months White wrote out his fourth will and concluded arrangements for the succession of the College's direction after his death.[45] The trepidation with which he greeted this final period of his life is further attested by the writing of yet another will, his fifth and last, in early November 1566.[46] He continued to fuss about the disposition of the College's finances and statutes, and about his wife's welfare as well, until he succumbed, in his London home, to what may have been a stroke on 12 February, 1567.[47]

But if White ended his days with these problems weighing heavily upon him, he also had every good reason to find solace in his accomplishments. These were manifest in his own lifetime, even more so within a few years thereafter, and just as impressive, albeit perhaps for different reasons, for us in the present day. For most of the time since White's death (and notwithstanding his other signal achievements) his fame has rested chiefly on his benefactions. And yet there is even more to them than meets the eye. At closer examination, they suggest (along with other aspects of White's career) some important developments in the role of the merchant, and thus in the nature of both mercantile and urban society. They also have much to tell us about the perception of both merchant and urban society in White's own age. Let us consider some of the elements of White's importance a little more closely.

For one, White's benefactions symbolize an important period in the development of philanthropic activities. They are part of a more vivid awareness of social and economic problems, and they were carried out on a broader scale than before. It cannot be said that the idea of an interest-free loan fund to a particular class of urban dwellers was novel in itself. His own master, Hugh Acton, had done the same thing, albeit on a far more modest scale, and W. K. Jordan has estimated that some 2 percent of all charitable bequests in the period 1480–1640 (almost all of them after 1540) fell into this category.[48] But the very nature of money-lending in past times, and even in White's own time to some extent, had been based on a number of pre-capitalist notions. Loans were seen principally as morally worthy ways of helping relatives, neighbours, and friends rather than as opportunities for profit. They were rarely extended to recipients who dwelt beyond the lender's own town of residence or who were unknown personally to the lender. The taking of interest had long been frowned upon, and its boundaries carefully prescribed in both law and custom. Loans were extended without particular regard for the borrower's occupation.[49]

White's benefactions, to journeymen clothiers in present and future generations and in twenty-four locales, embraced some of these ideas but moved them much further along. They were still without expectation of profit, either to White himself or the institutions and towns which administered the loans. In this they embraced a cardinal point of traditional morality on the subject. But they extended well beyond his own community, and to perfect strangers. They were greater in scope and magnitude than any previous effort of the same sort. Finally, they reveal White's remarkably sophisticated understanding of the English clothing industry of his time, and his recognition of how it could best be strengthened.

The scale and decisiveness of White's actions invite a closer analysis. Though most of White's years saw general prosperity in the English clothing industry, the picture was not unrelievedly bright. Booms and slumps occurred frequently and with dramatic effect. For the most part they were determined by the activity of the greater European market upon which England, a trading nation, had to depend. Continental competition, foreign wars, stoppages of trade often associated with those wars, the wildly fluctuating nature and value of English coinage and of its purchasing power, and (even at that early time) the vagaries of fashion were all facts of life in the Tudor economy. They made for a precarious and constantly volatile situation. Some towns (Coventry conspicuous amongst them) experienced difficulty vending their traditional cloths throughout the period.

Under these conditions, some sectors were more vulnerable than others. The better established merchants and manufacturers found themselves able to spread their capital around and diversify their interests. Many of them invested in the capital-intensive industries of shipping and brewing; butchers became graziers, and mercers and clothiers invested in agricultural lands and even—especially in the Midlands—in the metal trades.[50] But merchants generally found it easier than manufacturers to diversify. They were not tied down to capital resources required in the manufacturing process, nor were they tied to a labour force trained for a particular set of tasks. (Indeed, labour was the least mobile factor in the Tudor economy, and the hardest hit at times of slump.)[51] Finally, merchants were also far less vulnerable to the illicit manufactures carried out outside the jurisdiction of guilds and civic authorities.

All things considered, as Barry Supple has put it, 'In a slump it was normally the clothier, not the merchant, who first besieged the Privy Council with complaints'.[52] Indeed the recorded Acts of the Privy Council as well as the Statute Book itself bear out the truth of that corollary throughout the period. Of course White knew this, too. This is what led him to direct his charitable resources to the clothing trades generally (including clothiers, drapers, and others, as well as mere tailors) and not to the merchants.

Yet even amongst manufacturers there were diverse levels of

vulnerability. The better established and more affluent amongst them could afford to diversify, and thus to hedge their bets against a slump in any one area more readily than the smaller operator or the novice. In addition, in London, where the greater competition had already begun to push out the smaller manufacturer, most of the survivors had both sufficient resources to diversify into other enterprises and a sufficient variety and depth of stock to cover fluctuations in demand. The provincial trader, often a much smaller operator, generally had a narrower range of stock to cushion against the instability of the market, and very few resources which would allow him to diversify. Though he therefore required a faster rate of turnover to meet his obligations, his sales were more vulnerable to the fluctuations of the market. Manufacturers in general thus required a constant and reliable supply of liquid capital. They needed it to tide them over the rough times, to keep their labour force secure, and to allow them to keep pace with demand. Since the cloth and clothing trades were the nation's most important export trades, and the critical mainstay of many of her provincial towns, these realities applied to them more keenly than perhaps any other occupational grouping.

These conditions pertained throughout the sixteenth and seventeenth centuries, and in fact arguably grew even more pronounced as time progressed. The slump of 1621 would come to be seen as the most critical in memory, and by the latter years of the same century the government had progressed in its understanding of these economic realities to experiment with a Board of Trade and, in its foetal stages, a Bank of England. But save for the precocious observations of a few like Sir Thomas Gresham and Sir Thomas Smith, and despite the fact that the decades of White's own activity were marked by sharp fluctuations in trade and manufacture, the accurate understanding of economic forces barely appeared on the horizon in White's day. Nevertheless, these fluctuations proved very troublesome indeed both to the nation as a whole and to numerous individual provincial towns which had long-standing involvement in such manufactures. Too small and limited in their resources to diversify their economies to anywhere near the extent possible in the great metropolis of London, these found themselves perhaps most vulnerable of all communities to the commercial uncertainties of the age.

White himself came to a precocious understanding of these threats to the traditional system, and he designed his schemes accordingly. Though his Coventry scheme of 1542 bore no reference to specific occupations, he directed his later schemes specifically to the clothing trades. In order to protect traditional manufacturing from non-guild producers setting up in the countryside (and thus outside guild jurisdictions), White insisted that recipients apprentice in the traditional manner, that they be accepted as members of their guilds, and that they retain residence in their home cities (and neither in the countryside nor in other cities) for the duration of their loan. After ten years of established residence therein, White could well assume that they would have too much at stake to pick up and move outside town and guild jurisdiction.

And though £25 may not seem like much of a boost to a clothier setting up in business (and though its real value obviously declined over the course of time), it went rather further in the mid-sixteenth century than we might think. Even in the early seventeenth century £25 bought a lot for the provincial recipient. It would pay an admission fine to the Merchant Adventurers (£25 for members from the outports even in 1634), to the Levant Company (£25 to £50 even in the 1620s) or the Eastland Company (£20 in the same decade). It would cover entry by redemption to the freemanry of the City of London or virtually any provincial town.[53] More pertinent to most of White's recipients, it would allow a clothier to stock a modest shop in a provincial town and still have change left over.[54]

A second dimension of his fund's value may also be found in the large and ever-expanding number of individuals helped by it. In Coventry, which benefitted from two of White's schemes, no less than two-thirds of the sixty clothiers admitted to the freemanry between 1579 and 1614 received help from one or the other of his benefactions.[55]

White's keen awareness of the difficulties of contemporary

clothiers is matched by his awareness of the problems of cities themselves in his age. Here again he was ahead of his time when he first took it up in the early 1540s. To most articulate observers, cities were still perceived as corrupt and problematical in all sorts of ways. Though they may have been foreshadowed by such prescient publicists as Thomas More and Thomas Starkey in the 1520s and 1530s, it was only midway through White's career that some of the important writers on political and economic matters begin to suggest that urban societies had redeeming features, or that the economic problems which so many of them exhibited could be understood and perhaps remedied. And only from the late 1540s did the national governments of the day begin to look seriously at urban problems, and to take tentative steps towards their solution.[56]

White's concern for the state of England's cities extended well beyond the loan schemes for young entrepreneurs. We see it of course in his long and distinguished career as a citizen, alderman, and Lord Mayor of London. We also see it in his provisions for St. John's College, where a certain number of entry scholarships were to be reserved for boys from the four clothing towns of Tonbridge, Reading, Coventry, and Bristol.[57] And we certainly see it in other parts of his bequests to Coventry, Bristol, and the other towns associated with them.

Most of White's favoured towns were old manufacturing centres which had flourished in earlier times but which, especially with the tremendous mid-century volatility of England's trade in the 'old draperies', had typically stagnated by the time White singled them out. A few (especially Bristol, Chester, Southampton, Ipswich, Colchester, and Newcastle) were also port towns which depended upon the cloth trade as well as on its manufacture. With the curious exception of his birth-town of Reading itself, they had all been listed on one or another of the Henrician statutes for the rebuilding of decayed towns, most of them passed in the 1530s and 1540s.[58] Although not all the towns so listed may necessarily have been as impoverished as one might assume, or as badly hit as Coventry seems to have been, it seems safe to say that most of them were feeling the adverse effects of volatility in the clothing trades which so emphatically marked the mid-Tudor period.

In taking all this into account in his benefactions, White's thinking as early as the 1540s, on both trade and manufacture and on the condition of towns and cities, recognized how critical these factors were becoming to the nation's urban structure and economy. That is not to say that, in retrospect, his outlook would prove especially enlightened, though it may have looked that way at the time. Our own hindsight allows us to understand that White was defending an old, pre-capitalist system, represented both by traditional guild organization and the civic jurisdiction which upheld it. In addition, he was at least implicitly trying to shore up the traditional production of what were called 'old draperies' just as contemporary European fashions began to swing towards the lighter and finer 'new draperies' produced abroad. Nevertheless his ability to conceptualize economic and urban issues on a national scale, coupled with the equally broad scope of his charitable initiatives, mark him as a perceptive and imaginative participant in the domestic issues of his age. And notwithstanding what seems to us their retrograde character, his analysis and solutions were considered forward-thinking at the time. His goal of strengthening corporate towns by allowing them the resources to stimulate their own economies—and by requiring his borrowers to maintain residence in them—and especially his defense of the guild system against pressing competition from the countryside, find clear echoes in the landmark Statute of Artificers (5 Eliz., c. 4) of 1563, passed into law some two decades after White's first exposition of those ideas.

Finally, White's bequests bear implications for our prevailing views about charitable giving in the age of the Reformation. They certainly run counter to what we have been led to expect by the classic authorities on the subject. To W. K. Jordan, for example, the pre-eminent modern authority on charity in Early Modern England, charitable giving in the Roman Catholic tradition had been indiscriminant in focus and driven by hopes of personal salvation. The advent of Protestantism, by contrast, had meant a sharp secularization of the charitable impulse. In Jordan's view, the rapid development of a social conscience or other, more purely altruistic, motives thus led almost immediately to an outpouring of bequests for schools, public works, poor relief, and the like.[59]

White, on the other hand, presents the example of a Roman Catholic motivated by the sort of social conscience which Jordan thought chiefly characteristic of Protestants. His loans came not only interest free, but prayer free as well. When Christ's Hospital in London, built on the ruins of the Greyfriars, gained its charter as a City-run institution, White did not let his adherence to the old faith keep him from serving as one of its Governors from 1556 until his death.[60] And yet his benefactions may be seen as a very traditional striving to obtain a state of charity with the sundry communities to which he belonged, including the Fellowship of Christ.[61] They suggest that the charitable impulse in White's time may have consisted of more than a stark choice between God or Mammon, and that both the secularization of charity and the Reformation itself may have been a much more gradual and complex process than Jordan and others of his generation had assumed.

The Image of the Merchant-hero

There is still one aspect of White's life to consider, and it concerns the reception he met amongst his contemporaries and near contemporaries. As has been noted at the outset, the image of the merchant which prevailed at the time of White's birth and for most of his life remained almost uniformly negative. Articulate opinion saw the merchant as liable to flout the traditional economic morality of the guild system and to be led by greed, cunning, and self-interest. And yet, by the last years of the century—perhaps as the links between writers and the world of commerce grew ever closer—this image began to give way. In its place, or at least along side of it, merchants, craftsmen, and apprentices became the stock heroes of numerous popular literary works, both plays and essays.

And in this turnabouts, Sir Thomas White came readily to the fore: not, to be sure, immediately after his benefactions went into

effect, though acts of such magnanimity and geographic application must have been widely known, but in the years and decades
thereafter. Only then did it became fashionable to hold such mercantile benefactions up for celebration.

John Stow has been identified as amongst the first to write of
merchants (again defined broadly) in a positive light, and to write
of White amongst their number. Though a wider reading of contemporary literature would add names to that short-list,[62] Stow
does indeed seem to have played an important role in turning the
tide. A lifelong citizen of London and student of its history, Stow
could hardly have viewed merchants otherwise, and we must
consider his voice as in most respects representative of the merchant's own. In addition, though White would have been nearly
three decades older than Stow (born around 1523), the two had
much in common and undoubtedly knew each other. Fellow Merchant Taylors after Stow became a member of that Company in
1547, they shared as well a sympathy with the Old Faith, and numerous associations with many of the same parts of London.[63] It is
also noteworthy that Stow devoted a few lines to White in his 1565
Summary of the Chronicles and much greater space to him in several
of his subsequent writings. White does indeed get a brief mention
in the former,[64] but that slim notice expanded to a full two pages
(sixty-three lines) in the miniature edition of 1573, and similarly
substantial attention in subsequent writings.[65]

But if Stow was (so far as we know and outside the historical
traditions of St. John's College[66] or similar beneficiaries) the first to
recognize White after his death, he would not be the last. In Richard Johnson's *Nine Worthies of London* of 1592 we find, in lines
given to the figure of White himself, this praise of his own success
and its altruistic effects:

> The English Cities and incorporate townes
> Doe beare me witnesse of my Countrys care
> Where yearely I doe feede the poore with crownes
> For I was neuer niggard yet to spare,
> And all chiefe Burrowes of this blessed land,
> Have somewhat tasted of my liberal hand

He that did lende to me the grace of wealth,
Did not bestow it for to choake with store
But to maintaine the needie poore in health,
By which expence my wealth encreased more
The oyle of gladness ever cheared my hart
Why should I not then pitie others smart.[67]

Another such recognition came in John Webster's *Monuments of Honour* of 1624, in which the author places the figure of White in a pagaent entitled the 'Monument of Charity and Learning'. White is seated under an elm tree, an allusion to the legend that White received instructions in a dream to found a college where he saw two elm trunks arising from a single root. He wears his mayoral robe. He is flanked by the figure of Charity on one side and Learning on the other, with a model of St. John's College ('exactly molded') behind him. Ringing this centrepiece around the perimeter of the pagaent, Webster placed twelve of the twenty-four cities which were endowed in White's bequest: More, as he tells us, 'would have overburdened the pagaent'![68] Coming as vignettes in writings intended for a broad and popular readership, White's career must have been seen by these writers as broadly familiar in that time. They thus reflect his contemporary notoriety as well as they magnify it for us.

And finally, there were commemorations of another kind as well, in the form of nearly a score of portraits painted and hung in the places of his benefaction. In the decades following his death they appeared in Bristol, Canterbury, Coventry, Exeter, Gloucester, King's Lynn, Leicester, Lincoln, Norwich, Oxford (two for the City and two for St. John's College), Reading, Salisbury, and Southampton.[69] Most of these which survive to be examined show White in the same pose and with the same expression, and are obviously copies of some as yet unidentified common ancestral painting. Those two done for St. John's in 1580 are actually described as 'counterfaytes of our founder'.[70]

But if we do not yet know which was the first portrait of White, and thus the presumed model for the others, it seems safe to assume it was a fair likeness. It would have been commissioned, viewed, and possibly painted by those who knew him personally. The manner in which White is portrayed, as a thin, serious, hollow-cheeked man, little humorous and all business and earnestness, certainly supports what we know of him. And if the inscription affixed to the White portrait in the guildhall of Leicester is any indication, these were intended for two purposes: to commemorate his benefactions (as opposed to his mercantile skill) and to hold them up as examples for others to emulate.[71] It reads as follows:

> Lo here a ship a merchant roial fraught
> With store of wealth: from whoes rich sid's vsovght
> Plentie of mettall hath been larglie given
> White name: white gifts, white sovle, white saint in heaven
> Whoes arms wee: (lest wee shew ovr selfs ingrate),
> properly blazond here doe celebrate
> The which eternall monvmente shal be:
> Of White's renowne to all posteritie,
> Dye then and rot and stinke yov hvlks of shame,
> Who charg'd with wealth have nothing bvt the name
> Of dying rich: whoe's tombs shall never speak
> Yovr praise: one White shall all yovr credit break.

With the career of Sir Thomas White and others like him, the urban milieu came at last into respectability. The commemoration of his achievements seems part of a broader, if related, effort whereby the benevolent qualities of mercantile endeavour might be appreciated, not just on the local scene, but more widely and broadly by the writers and publicists of the day. It indicates some of the contemporary vocabulary of public celebration; both helped establish the merchant and townsman as worthy subjects for such discourse.

CHAPTER 5

Henry Manship: Constructing the Civic Memory in Great Yarmouth

In the year 1619, after a lifetime of residence and many years of careful work, Henry Manship of Great Yarmouth completed a long and weighty manuscript history of his native town.[1] Though this sort of endeavour had not yet become a common pastime amongst intellectually precocious civic boosters as it would later do, Manship was not alone in undertaking something of the sort in the early seventeenth century. The writing of civic chronicles had been established in England for a long time, and more sophisticated notions of historical writing associated with the Continental Renaissance had begun to have their impact in England in the sixteenth century. Following John Stow's magnificent *Survey of London*,[2] first published in 1598, and a few contemporary provincial histories like John Hooker's well-known work on Exeter (c. 1575),[3] English town histories started to appear with greater frequency towards the beginning of the seventeenth century.[4]

Manship's work remains far less familiar to us than either of those classics of the genre by Stow or Hooker. It describes a town which was more modest in size and farther from the centre of national life than either London or Exeter. The work itself lay unpublished until a local Yarmouth antiquary, Charles John Palmer, made it available in a limited edition of 1854. Until that time it remained little known outside of Great Yarmouth or its County of Norfolk. Since then, the original manuscript has been lost, and no new edition has been possible.

Given those conditions of obscurity, one may well wonder why Manship's *History* should command our attention now. But as we have seen elsewhere in these pages, the unheralded events and people of an age often convey the tenor of the times just as usefully as the great and famous. This is precisely the promise of Manship and his *History*. Both the author and his work have been about as 'unheralded' in the scholarly literature as they could be, and yet the work itself proves a remarkable—and remarkably revealing—document.

It rewards our consideration in three ways. First, it proves an impressively sophisticated intellectual and literary achievement for its time, suggesting that even seemingly isolated provincial towns like Great Yarmouth were not beyond the wider intellectual currents of the age. Second, it is striking that it could have been written by a local man of no particular distinction, and whose formal education began and ended with the town's grammar school. And finally, its themes and perspectives reveal some keen insights into the political goals of historical writing in that age: goals shared by town and nation alike.

One might well expect early and serious town histories to have been undertaken first in towns of great rank, or wealth, or sophistication, or those in close contact with the intellectual world of London or the Continent. This was not always the case. London, of course, well in a class of its own as England's only metropolis, had its Stow and others. But of the five greatest English towns after London at that time, Bristol and Exeter seem well enough served by local historians of the same era, especially by Robert Ricart and John Hooker respectively. Yet Newcastle, York, and, surprisingly, Norwich did not fare as well.

Yarmouth may have been England's greatest herring port, but neither in its size, sophistication, nor importance could it rival any of those great provincial centres. Somewhat isolated landwards by the desolation of the Norfolk Broads, its main contact with the rest of the realm came by river from Norwich and by sea. Yet these links served it well. In providing an outlet to the sea for Norwich, Yarmouth's importance came to increase during the course of the sixteenth century with the growing prominence and prosperity of that larger city. Where its value to the economic and political life of the nation had once been largely confined to the six or so weeks of the herring season (between Michaelmas, September 29, and Martinmas, November 10), its role had broadened considerably by Manship's time. Fishermen, fish merchants, and others continued to come from all over the North Sea/Baltic region to its annual Herring Fair as they had always done. Now Dutch Calvinist refugees,[5] and merchants of all description, came as well and at all times of the year, both to Yarmouth itself and on their way to and from Norwich.

When not swollen in these few weeks by the seasonal throngs of fishermen, mariners, and herring workers—coopers, salters, packers, carters, and so forth—Yarmouth's normal population reached several thousand souls. All of them were at least nominal parishioners at the single (though admittedly very large) parish church of St. Nicholas. Though it boasted a grammar school, founded in 1551, to educate the sons of local freemen, it is difficult to say how much intellectual contact Yarmouth had with the rest of the realm.

Odd as it may seem, it would not be too much of a stretch to count the herring fishery as an important factor in Yarmouth's tradition of historical writing. History does seem to have followed herring because of the peculiar jurisdictional position of the town in regard to its fisheries. From the earliest days of the Herring Fair in the thirteenth century, Yarmouth's jurisdiction was continually challenged by several rival authorities. These included the neighbouring port of Lowestoft, the Court of the Admiralty, and especially the Barons of the Cinque Ports, representing the interests of the several fishing communities in Sussex and Kent which composed that unique administrative entity. Though by and large Yarmouth had succeeded pretty well through the years in defending its position, it had frequently to do so by litigation. The key to success in that arena was the ability to establish its case through persuasive and written documentation.

In this long-standing necessity Yarmouth's experience may have been fuller than that of most other towns, but the essential need to preserve a written record of a borough's rights and privileges applied to virtually all such communities. In the litigious ethos of the sixteenth century, it was becoming more essential all the time.

In these circumstances Manship's magnificent effort was not the first response to the need of a written record. That laurel goes to a chronicle of local events said to have been compiled by the Benedictine monks of the local priory in days long past, and which was still consulted in Manship's time.[6] There were also at least two early efforts to compile some record of Yarmouth's rights to the fishery and of its periodic necessity to repair its haven, and one effort of a more literary nature to describe both fishery and town.

The first of these was a 'Book of Charters' compiled by the prominent townsman Thomas Damet in about 1580.[7] At the time he wrote this, Damet was still in the early summer of a successful career in the ruling inner circle of the town which lasted into the next century. He had already served as town clerk (1568–73) and alderman. These posts had taught him at first hand the value of having the written record close by for use in litigation. In the course of his labours on the town's behalf he had searched what he described as 'our writings and ancient rolls . . . and the rolls in the Tower of London' stretching back to the time of Edward III. His 'Book of Charters' may be more of a codification than a 'history' in the narrative sense. Still, it performed an important service by mustering the relevant sources for defending the town's rights to the herring fishery. And, as we now know, it did not lay to rest Damet's desire to compile a useful record of Yarmouth's past.

His next effort has had a curious history of its own, and one which the modern archivist and historian of Great Yarmouth has unravelled. The manuscript, entitled 'Greate Yermouthe. A Book of the Foundacion and Antiquitye of the saide towne and of diverse Specialle Matters concerninge the Same', had long been attributed to none other than the father of our historian Henry Manship. This had certainly been the assumption of its Victorian editor, Charles John Palmer, who published it locally in the year 1847, and of others both before and since. But notwithstanding the disappearance of the manuscript itself shortly after Palmer's edition,

Mr. Paul Rutledge, in an essay of 1965, cast serious doubt on the elder Manship's authorship. Rutledge's counterproposal of Thomas Damet as the author received definitive support when the manuscript itself reappeared a few years later.[8] What has always been known as the elder Manship's work is actually the summation of Thomas Damet's historical efforts, written in two parts between 1594 and 1599.

The literary approach to the subject of Yarmouth history also lies well out of the ordinary, for it came from the disgraced writer Thomas Nashe.[9] Nashe's effort to escape his enemies in London, and to find some source of income, led him in 1599 to Yarmouth, where he appears to have been warmly received. In gratitude for this, and perhaps in the hope of a stipend, he turned his pen to the history and description of the town. Employing Damet's work as well as some other sources, he produced his 'Lenten Stuffe'. This curious contribution to late Elizabethan literature provides an interesting appreciation of the community.

This brings us to Henry Manship the younger and, as it turns out, the sole historian of his family. Like Damet, Manship seems to have lived his entire life in Yarmouth, but with little of Damet's distinction or personal reputation. His father, a merchant and ship owner rather than a man of letters,[10] had been elected a Freeman in 1550 and had served in several minor and middling offices. The elder's greatest contribution to the town had been his role in securing the services of a prominent Dutch engineer to help restore the channel of the town's harbour, following one of its periodic siltings-up. Beyond that he left little mark, save for a reputation as a dishonest and quarrelsome man.[11] In the end his decision to send his son and namesake to be educated in the local grammar school may be his most important act.[12]

Following at least partway in his father's footsteps, Manship the younger engaged in some overseas trade. But this was probably secondary to other occupational activities. Despite the lack of evidence of any additional formal schooling, he considered himself at least a notary and perhaps a lawyer, and seems thus to have been accepted by his contemporaries. From time to time he served the Borough as one of its four attorneys (only a town facing as much litigation as Yarmouth would have four attorneys!), as town clerk (1579–85), and sometimes as its agent at Westminster. He inherited little in the way of material resources from his father, who died in modest circumstances,[13] but he does seem to have inherited the paternal penchant for irascibility and petty dishonesty. The elder Manship had been caught evading duties on salt in 1564 and falsifying custom's accounts in 1565.[14] The younger Manship had a very promising appointment as a local customs official cancelled in 1585 when it was discovered that he, too, had evaded customs duties in his time.[15] He tells us himself that he was 'estranged' from town business regarding the harbour over the nine years before completing his work, which would be from about 1610.[16] And in 1616, on what would be his final mission on the town's behalf, Manship fell into disgrace again for borrowing money in the town's name without authorization.[17]

His petty dishonesty and irascibility seem reflected in a lifetime of fractious relations with some of the leading lights of the Borough, as a result of which Manship fell continually in and out of favor.[18] In this general surliness, Thomas Damet—whose high esteem in the eyes of most of the townsmen contrasted markedly with Manship's far less salubrious reputation—came in for special attention. Damet's success seems to have rankled Manship throughout his life. As the two must have come into very frequent contact for a good many years in a community of just a few thousand souls, the rivalry between them must have formed something of a cleavage point in local affairs. In 1604 the feud came to a head. Manship seems to have engaged in a public shouting match in which he called Damet and his colleague John Wheeler, both just returned from representing the Borough in the Parliament of 1604, 'sheep' and 'dunces'. In response, the Borough assembly dismissed Manship from his burgess-ship.

Neither Manship's tenuous relationship with his neighbours nor his particularly quarrelsome relationship with Damet can have been irrelevant to his great undertaking. He seems likely to have seen the project as a means of regaining favour. It was a tactic well employed by many mercurial literary and political figures of the time, including Nashe and even the great Sir Francis Bacon. Part of his aim must also have included the hope of a monetary reward for his labours. And no small part may have been played by his effort to outdo his rival Damet at the business of writing a successful history. Though he could hardly ignore the earlier work in writing his own, he missed few opportunities to point out Damet's errors.

Yet however much a scoundrel Manship may have been, and however petty and self-serving some of his motives may seem, we cannot deny his achievement. His *History of Great Yarmouth* is not only a far larger work than Damet's, but far greater as well: more extensive, more intellectually engaging, and certainly more enduring. It proves far more than a mere compilation of evidence to be used in defense of rights and privileges. It offers thoughtful reflection on its subject and from time to time offers views of a highly polemical nature. It rests on a surprisingly thorough and critical reading of the sources, and is informed by purposes, attitudes, and outlooks which are highly revealing of the author and his age. Though its subject may have been a glorified herring port of a few thousand people, it is no exaggeration to see Manship's *History* as a significant milestone in the writing of a conceptually advanced and relatively sophisticated local history.

This recognition begs several questions. It leads us to wonder at some of the deeper motivations behind the undertaking, and at the ideas expressed in it. It promises to tell us about Yarmouth itself, and also about the need of contemporary governing authorities, in town no less than nation, for a relevant and legitimizing history.

Although Manship did not undertake his masterwork until he was well along in years, we can say that in one sense he had worked towards it all his life. Aside from business trips to London, Norwich, and elsewhere, and perhaps a few trading voyages to nearby Continental ports,[19] we have no indication that he ever resided anywhere else but in Yarmouth. For much of his adult years he served the government and the freemen of the community in numerous capacities.

In addition to all this, Manship had undertaken a project seven years earlier, in 1612, which was highly unusual for the time and which proved essential to the larger project. In that year he formed and led a committee of aldermen and common councillors to retrieve, describe, and reorganize the town's very considerable accumulation of official documents.[20] Though this may not strike us today as either a difficult or unusual task, it proved quite the opposite at the time. The fact is that Yarmouth's records, like those of many contemporary towns, lay in daunting disarray. They were to be found, if at all, in several different places, not only in Yarmouth itself but also at London, Westminster, and probably Norwich. Only once had they been even partially calendared: by Thomas Damet, ironically enough, some years earlier. Yet this task had overwhelmed Damet's energies. As Manship well knew from his own experience, it still proved very difficult to locate the appropriate records and to marshal them on the town's behalf when Yarmouth needed to defend its interests in court.

In describing the work of the committee in the preface to its final report, Manship put the need this way:

Forasmuch as many [of] the charters, evidences and writings, which doo apperteyne to the said towne, hath of longe tyme been remayninge in the custody of sondry p[er]sons, who have been imployed in the business of that Township: by meanes whereof sondry of them been myssing,[21] wherof the Towne at their greate costs and chardge, hath been enforced to take exemplifications aswell out of his Ma[jes]ty's Records reymaininge at West[minster] as also out of the Tower of London and other places. . . . For Reformacion thereof and to theend that every one of the Com[mon]e assembly, and every other good and well affected Townsmen may be further instructed with knowledge, whereby they may bee better able to doo more good to the estate of this Township in future time. . . . [Manship proposed that the Assembly] appoint these persons . . . to be present with him to effect the busynes.

On 12 June, 1612, a regular meeting of the common council and bailiffs approved the proposed undertaking and appointed a committee of six aldermen and seven common councillors to serve under Manship's direction. The committee held its first meeting on Monday, 22 June, 1612, and began the methodical retrieval, listing, description, and re-filing of all the relevant documents it could locate. Over a span of some eight weeks and in no less than twenty-three meetings it carried out this task with impressive diligence. In the last of these meetings, on 13 August, the committee devised a filing system in the town 'hutch', dividing this large cabinet into three parts for the purpose. Members then mandated Manship to draw up a final report and description of their common labours. This he did, though at a much more relaxed pace, calling the committee into its twenty-fourth and final session on 20 January, 1613, so that the members (none of whom aside from Manship actually attended every meeting) could subscribe their names at the bottom for presentation to the town assembly.[22]

Even at a time when many towns were recognizing more than ever before the importance of methodical record keeping,[23] few took quite this much care with their records. But in addition to the undoubted benefit which this achievement conveyed to the Borough, the project provided Manship himself with a virtual graduate training in the historical sources for the great opus which lay ahead. It is no surprise that Manship's *History*, completed seven years later, is as thoroughly researched and thoughtfully composed as any other contemporary work of its type.

Personal motives aside, Manship's approach to the history of his town could well be explained, as his preface suggests, in purely practical terms: the need for the town's records—and thus a narrative explanation of their place and meaning—to be well organized, well understood, and readily available for the town's defense in litigation. But this seems an insufficient explanation. After all, Thomas Damet's work had already provided at least some of this, albeit on a more limited scale, and Manship's own committee of 1612 had done much more. When we turn to a careful reading of the *History* itself, Manship's critical approach and the full scope of his polemical inclinations become more evident.[24]

The first point to make about the work is that, unlike the conventional chronicle, it does not have a strictly chronological scheme; it is not, in fact, a pure narrative at all. It does, however, begin with the question of the town's origins, and here the reader discovers the first of the elements of Manship's work which sets it apart from most previous and much contemporaneous civic history: Manship rejects the temptation to follow the traditions of, for example, Geoffrey of Monmouth,[25] in accepting what we would consider a mythological past for his town. In this he departs from a long and pervasive tendency which explained the foundation of many communities, London not the least of them, by the acts of pseudo-historical and legendary figures: Lud of London, Ebrauk of York, Bevis the Giant of Southampton, Bladud of Bath, and so forth.

Rejecting any such contrivance, Manship merely offers the rational view that '. . . few Cities or Towns in England do know their first foundations',[26] and then laconically attributes Yarmouth's origins first to the settlement of early Saxon kings and then, more permanently, to people who came there to fish for herring.[27] This patent unwillingness to prefer the authority of tradition over documentary evidence runs right through the work. It extends even to criticism of such respected contemporary writers as John Speed and William Camden for their sometimes casual or inaccurate use of sources.[28]

Having put Yarmouth's origins behind him, Manship sets out on a somewhat random, if very considerable, journey from one to another of the central themes in Yarmouth's past and present affairs. Though he treats each theme historically, placing particular issues in a chronological sequence and always exhibiting a well-developed sense of cause and effect, his cannot be termed a tightly organized discussion. Nevertheless, one by one, Manship takes up the crucial issues: the origins and authority of Yarmouth's government; the history of its ecclesiastical and fraternal institutions; the development of its harbour (vulnerable to silting and a frequent cause of local concern); its relations with the Cinque Ports or the rival port of Lowestoft over legal jurisdiction in the herring fishery, and of the fishery itself; and so forth. Drawing on his un-

paralleled knowledge of local records, Manship constantly situ-
ates these discussions in the appropriate constitutional context.

Other issues come up for prolonged discussion as well. Manship displays keen interest in the town's natural and built environment, including its river and coastline, its defenses, the town
common and market, its quay and harbour, its parish church of St.
Nicholas, and some of its other buildings. Despite his care with the
written record, his history certainly becomes more finely detailed
the closer Manship gets to the period of contemporary experience.
Here he had a greater abundance of records from which to work,
and he could more readily draw on oral recollection instead, both
his own and those of some of his contemporary townspeople.

But once we have followed our author through these narrative
passages, observing Yarmouth's origins and historical development and physical characteristics as we go along, we see that there
is still more to the work than this. A more didactic agenda begins
to appear, in which Manship employs some elements of the narrative to illustrate his visions of political authority and civic behaviour.

This, too, is informed by wide reading, but reading of a different sort. We should be cautious in awarding to Manship full
status as a humanist historian in the Renaissance vein, for many
of his sources were by his time the common coin of a good grammar school education. Yet he does cite and make intelligent use of
a number of classical writers in developing and defending his
ideas. They include Thucydides, Pliny, Horace, Virgil, Seneca,
Ovid, Sophocles, Aristotle, and Demosthenes. Perhaps more interesting are the references to such contemporary English sources
as Speed and Camden, Raphael Holinshed, John Leland, Thomas
Nashe, and (on the subject of Kett's Rising and its failure) Alexander Neville. We are especially surprised to find his use of Cardinal Gaspar Contarini's history of the Venetian Republic, which
had been translated and published in English for the first time in
1598.[29] How extraordinary that an obscure man like Manship,
whose formal education ended with the local grammar school
and who never seems to have dwelled for long outside Great

Yarmouth, should have availed himself of such a long shelf of writers!

Informed by this strikingly broad reading, Manship gradually develops several distinctive themes for his readers. They include a strong expression of local pride; an emphasis on the virtues of civic amity; a plea for deference towards the governing authorities; and a cogent discourse on the force of law and the powers of magistracy both in making and enforcing it. Taken together, they reveal the author's intellect and his perspective. In addition, they show that, by choosing what to write about and what not to write about, an historian like Manship could shape a common vision of the past. Let us look at these themes in turn.

A discussion of civic pride must be prefaced by the reminder that the general moral reputation of towns and cities in the ambient English culture had always been mixed at best. Dominated by traditional views of London, England's largest urban complex and thus its most familiar urban experience, urban life had conventionally been seen as licentious, sordid, unwholesome, and dangerous. Certainly, in a society where the virtues of agrarian society—from the presumption of aristocratic and chivalric values at the top to the moral integrity of the sturdy yeoman at the bottom—presented the dominant model for civil behaviour, the urban scene stood outside the mainstream of what was familiar and acceptable. Not much before the Elizabethan era did these negative stereotypes began to yield to other, more positive, views of urban life and people. Only then did the classical notion of the city as a potentially civilizing force begin to gain credence; only then did the merchant and at least some other urban types begin to gain broad respectability.[30]

This reputational transition is most familiar as it applied to London. Historical works like Stow's *Survey*, other prose works like Richard Johnson's *Nine Worthies of London*,[31] and the recognition of such 'merchant heroes' as Sir Thomas Gresham and (as we saw in the previous chapter) Sir Thomas White, illustrate this well. But Manship's *History* demonstrates a comparable reputational transition unfolding in the lesser as well as the greater urban areas of the realm.

If Manship's efforts were not a genuine labour of love, and of admiration for the civilizing potential of his native town, he certainly must have had his tongue in cheek when he extolled Yarmouth's virtues as he did. Thus we read his prayer to '. . . my most sweet beloved native town of Yarmouth', in which he rejoices, 'from the bottom of my heart that it has such a spacious haven, so strong a navy, and is so strong and valorous town'. Larding his praise with citations from Thucydides and Pliny, and also from the Henrician traveller and writer John Leland, he finds its people civil and courteous to strangers, its site at the confluence of river and sea both pleasant and commodious, its fishing most plentiful, and its foreign trade famous. He ends by noting that 'it [may] be said of Yarmouth, as Thucydides did of Athens, that it was the Greece of Greece or . . . the quintessence of Greece, so Yarmouth, of all the coast towns of England, may be said to be the very quintessence of England'.[32]

Some pages further on Manship turns to the importance of civic amity and thus, implicitly, to another important cultural transition of the age. On one side of this transition lay a civic culture which had emerged over the course of a millennium, hand in hand with the practices, doctrines, and institutions of the traditional pre-Reformation Church. Civic authorities at all levels, from crown to town, had come to depend on those forms to uphold their own authority, to mediate disputes, and generally to maintain harmony and order in their communities. Civic amity had been a central goal of that tradition. On the other side of that transition lay civic bodies now devoid of those traditional supports, and which were thus compelled to devise new ones in their place to serve the same civic ends. The maintenance of that civic amity hung in the balance.

Manship exhibits a keen awareness of that shift. While he himself had clearly abandoned the Old Faith, he nevertheless understood and still appreciated some of its value to the civic weal. He looks back with fond nostalgia on the work of the old Trinity Guild, dissolved along with all other religious guilds and fraternities in the 1540s, and to its annual guild feast held in the guildhall on Trinity Sunday. At that feast, he continued, 'all private quarrels and emulations were heard and ended, to the Glory of God and mutual love amongst neighbours; for which cause, in the primitive time of the church, such Guilds and Fraternities were by the ecclesiastical laws ordained'.[33]

But he no sooner acknowledges the benefits of that now defunct usage than he recognizes its counterpart in his own time:

... if laudable and praiseworthy is the bond of amity and friendship amongst mere natural men, then, how much more especially is that which is amongst christians, who be tied by the strongest bond of faith and religion; but above all amongst those christians which be of one fraternity, bound and linked together by solemn oath for performance, as those be that are chosen into the society of Common Council at Yarmouth.[34]

With that conclusion, Manship takes the potential for civic amity once realized through the ritual of the old fraternity, and gives it over to the civic body of the Borough council instead. The foundation is still religious, (indeed, as he tells us, there is still even a conciliatory feast!),[35] but authority has now been focused on the Word, and on those who preach it; on the law and those who administer it: 'Thou art ... a little island, and yet, by God's help, invincible. Be thou well assured if thou hear the word of the Lord, delivered by his ministers from heaven, and wilt be ruled thereby. ... the Lord will prefer thee far above other towns; he will be thy shield and buckler'.[36]

In distinctly Calvinistic terms (and notwithstanding the irony of expressing these views when he had been such a troublesome man himself!), he recognizes man's natural tendency toward evil, and the importance of the magistrates' administration of the law in thwarting those inclinations. Quoting, as he tells us, from Aristotle, Manship offers the thought that 'Laws be the bounds of the city, foundations of liberty, and fountain of equity, for that in them do consist the very mind, soul and council of the city'.[37] He continues by defending the importance of the magistrate to the well-ordered commonwealth, especially so that he might promulgate and enforce the law. After all, he concludes, '. . . the force of law doth not consist in the outward letter, but in the execution of them by the magistrate'.[38]

Taken by themselves these sentiments fit easily enough with other Puritan-inspired political views of the time.[39] But Manship goes even further than most others when he then tells us that 'a good magistrate is as well a law unto himself as unto others' and (citing Cicero) that 'a magistrate is speaking law'.[40] This is nothing less than a spirited and stirring defense of the Puritan oligarchy which had come to govern in Manship's Yarmouth, and a fervent entreaty to defer to it.[41] In Manship's view, the legitimacy of oligarchic rule derived not from any delegation by the freemanry so much as from above, from both God and King.[42] Though he makes little actual use of them, his thoughts surely suggest the metaphors of the 'City of God' and the 'New Jerusalem'. He would have felt right at home with the Pilgrim fathers as they went about founding their theocracy on the coast of New England just two years later.

Our concluding thoughts must be devoted to placing Manship in a wider historiographical context. We have already noted in at least general terms where the work seems to fit in the long continuum of historical writing. In its critical use of both primary and secondary sources, and in its interpretive character, *The History of Great Yarmouth* certainly looks forward rather than backwards. In this respect it exceeds even the better known history of Exeter by Manship's approximate contemporary John Vowell, *alias* Hooker (1527–1601). But in addition, we might usefully consider two other questions. How shall we evaluate Manship's *History* in the context of the Yarmouth of his own age, and what might it tell us about the political culture of English towns in general in that era?

Notwithstanding his critical scholarship and his philosophical moments, Manship could not have ignored the outlook and requirements of his immediate surroundings. His work must of course be considered a document of its time and place, written in close familiarity and general sympathy with the ruling element of his town, and in the light of its political, economic, and social circumstances at that time.

Though we may be tempted to think of Manship's Yarmouth as the isolated backwater which its map coordinates would suggest, its role as a port allowed it to overcome such isolation. In addition, its history during Manship's time proves studded with economic, social, and political concerns of very substantial weight. The memory of Kett's Rebellion of 1549, which climaxed in neighbouring Norwich and in which the rebels destroyed part of Yarmouth's harbour, remained vivid throughout the period as a reminder of the perils of civic unrest. Age-old disputes over jurisdiction in the herring fishery, carried on against the burghers of Lowestoft, the Cinque Ports, and even the aggressive Dutch; the continual burdens of dredging the harbour;[43] and interruptions in the supply of salt essential for preserving herring; all imperilled the town's economy.[44] The annual influx of migratory herring workers, and of foreign fishermen and mariners who flocked to its shores, when added to the general inflation, poverty, and threat of unrest which predominated in England at this time, threatened equally to undermine the social order. And finally, deepening divisions between Puritan and non-Puritan factions amongst the Borough's freemanry, which would erupt spectacularly just a few years after Manship put down his pen, had already begun to form.[45]

All these factors gave rise to the need for effective government, for a faithful and obedient citizenry, and—above all—for the sort of vivid civic consciousness and loyalty required to support those conditions. Manship had a clear sense of what the content of that civic consciousness should be. Part of this was his vision of oligarchic rule, but not necessarily one which bore the negative connotations the word holds for us. His vision of the just society had much more in common with what Aristotle called 'aristocracy', the rule by the few but with the interests of the whole in mind.

Now that such mediatory institutions as the old guilds had been removed, the task of insuring amity amongst the townspeople had to be performed in other ways. Manship's solution was to encourage a greater compliance with the local magistrates, who would rule justly as God's vicars, entrusted with the care of His people. His *History* must certainly be seen as an effort to use the past as a means of legitimizing the prevailing distribution of power in his own time.

Another part of this consciousness lay in a more positive view of urban life. In contrast to many others of his and earlier times, he saw this not as corrupting and dangerous but rather as a potentially liberating and civilizing experience. We must read his references to Athens, and his use of Contarini's *History of Venice*, as invocations of urban ideals from the historic past. Clearly he is more interested here in the positive qualities of the urban milieu in and of itself, and of the possibility of claiming those virtues for Yarmouth, than he is in sermonizing about man's moral perfectibility from any particular doctrinal position.

A final part of Manship's concept of civic consciousness lies in his vision of Yarmouth's past, and in his use of its historical experiences to create an authoritative account of that vision. Like all written histories, Manship's is a work of memory, and of its reconstruction, and of its preservation in a particular form. And like all written histories, it is necessarily a selective construct. There are simply too many facts at hand, and too many ways in which each may be remembered, to be able to recount them all, or in all ways. The historian must inevitably decide which ones to recall, and how to recall them. When the ultimate selection is written down, it becomes fixed in time, often 'forever'. The very act of writing down what is remembered, and thus preserving it, imparts a certain authority. It is taken to be the 'real' memory unless and until it is successfully challenged.

In Manship's time such historical reconstructions were especially important, for he lived soon after the effective obliteration of many forms of collective memory upon which communities like his depended. These were associated with the practices and beliefs of the Old Faith. They included mnemonic associations with patron saints, with ecclesiastical buildings, with masses for the departed souls of local citizens, and with material objects like stained glass and church furnishings and religious statuary. All of this and more had become part of the community's consciousness over time, provided a collective memory for generations of its inhabitants, and formed the basis of local loyalty and identity. The destruction of nearly all these devices, and the memories which they invoked, threatened to undermine these foundations, and thus to uproot and destabilize the community. In order to prevent that outcome, such elements had to be replaced, and a new identity thus forged in place of the old. Whether Manship and others like him understood his task in precisely these terms or not, they assuredly worked very effectively towards that end. This labour produced a revised version of Yarmouth's past. It justified the civic oligarchy of his time with ideas and experiences which were not drawn from traditional Catholicism. It pointedly recalled certain memories which were supportive of this end, so that, for example, its careful and lengthy treatment of Kett's Rebellion of 1549 (which he saw as 'hindering the building of Jerusalem')[46] allowed Manship to show the dangers of popular unrest. By the same token, he overlooked (and thus *dis*remembered) other events of comparable magnitude when they ran counter to his vision. The failure of judgement on the part of Yarmouth's government in preferring Jane Grey over Mary Tudor in 1553, an incident of which Manship must have been aware but does not mention, provides a fine example of such disremembering.

It is odd that Manship's *History* was not published in his own time. There are some indications that he fell out of favour with the town's leaders upon completing the work, and that they refused to pay for its publication.[47] At his death in 1625 he is said to have been a poor man, unappreciated and unrewarded.[48] Yet his *History* seems always to have been well known in local circles and to have remained so. It stood up well in preserving a particular version of Yarmouth's past. It undoubtedly helped in the construction of a new and refashioned civic consciousness for the community. It afforded a sense of civic pride and both extolled and explained the nature of good citizenship. In broader terms both it and other contemporary works of the same sort articulated an urban identity which was not based on aristocratic influences imported from the countryside or on metropolitan influences drawn from London, but one which was home grown and deeply rooted in the provincial urban experience. The extensive use which Yarmouth's subsequent historians made of Manship's work, which they knew very thoroughly even in its unpublished form, provides its surest validation.[49]

CHAPTER 6

Henry Hardware and the Face of Puritan Reform in Chester

Thanks to the colourful and dramatic nature of his actions as Mayor of Chester, revealed especially in the pages of Lawrence Clopper's *Records of Early English Drama* volume on that City, Henry Hardware has become a familiar example of Puritan-inspired destruction of traditional festivities.[1] It was Hardware, after all, who '. . . caused the Gyanntes in the Mydsomer show to be put downe & broken and not to goe, The devill in his fethers . . . he put Awaye, and the Cuppes and Cannes. And dragon and naked boyes. . . . he caused the bull Ringe to be taken upp. And the Leave Lookers were restrayned, for sending wine, According to the Anciente use and Custome of this Cittye'.[2]

But Hardware's curtailment of these festivities, and his destruction of the ceremonial costumes and objects associated with them, have thus far been the whole extent of his fifteen minutes of fame. After that both he himself and his iconoclasm disappear from our view, as if he had spoken his lines and exited stage-left forever. This is something of a shame, because much more lies here than meets the eye. The timing and civic context of Hardware's famous actions helps us better to understand this oft-cited example of Puritan moralism. Indeed, the full story suggests a more subtle perspective on Puritan moral reform, and on Puritanism itself, in the urban context.

So just who was this man with the amusingly appropriate name, the mayor who banned the traditional ceremonial figures of the giant and the naked boys, the dragon and the devil in feathers, and who banned the provision of wine for the occasion? For that matter, who was he not? Just when *did* he so disrupt the traditional Midsummer festivities? And why did he take such a drastic and, at least with many of his fellow Cestrians, unpopular step? Once we solve these little mysteries the story and its implications become much more meaningful.

The conventional modern account takes for granted that Hardware served as Mayor of Chester three times, in 1559–60, 1575–76, and again in 1599–1600,[3] though this would have made a very old man of him when he came to take his oath of office for the last time. Sure enough, the many mayors' lists with which Chester is so bountifully blessed (save for one or two which are a year off in their reckoning!) do all have 'Henry Hardware' as Mayor in those years.[4] That assumption has also encouraged speculation about which of Hardware's terms saw the destructive actions for which we remember him. Clopper's inclination has been to place them in 1575 or 1600; Patrick Collinson rather loosely considers Hardware to have been active 'by the early seventeenth century'.[5]

The question of dating his actions proves the easiest to resolve, at least in somewhat less speculative a manner than exists at present. One of the several descriptions of Hardware disrupting the Midsummer festivities also notes that it was Hardware who 'firste tooke ye toole from the sergents'.[6] (This is to say that he took the responsibility for collecting market tolls ['ye toole'] from the hands of the serjeants, presumably to consolidate them under his own more direct control.) The two references come virtually in the same breath or—as loose a grammatical concept as this remained in contemporary usage—virtually in the same sentence. We must thus assume that the two reforms came in the same year. And one source at least dates this administrative reorganization to the mayoral term of 1599–1600.[7] It seems most likely that Hardware's destruction of the giant and other figures came at the same time. Finally, a reference in another of Chester's antiquarian histories to putting the giant down at Midsummer places that event itself in the 1599–1600 mayoral year (in which Midsummer would have come on 24 June, 1600) to clinch the point.[8]

This is not the only part of the conventional story of Hardware to falter before close scrutiny. One's suspicions must be raised as well by the fact that the standard heraldic visitation for the County of Cheshire, carried out in 1613, shows Mayor Hardware to have served in 1559–60 and 1575–76, but says nothing of 1599–1600.[9] Can the herald have missed this last term, especially for a year so close in time to his own visitation? And secondly, the only will for 'Henry Hardware' listed in the most obvious source for wills of prominent people—the files of the Prerogative Court of Canterbury—was proven in the same year as the herald's visitation of 1613. Assuming that one would have had to be at least thirty-five years of age before becoming mayor of such a substantial provincial centre as Chester, a mayor of 1559 would have been at least seventy-five in 1599 and at least eighty-nine in 1613. The mystery deepens when we realize that the relatives mentioned in the will of 1613 are not the same as those whom the herald documented for the Mayor of 1559–60 and 1575–76. But when we locate the writer of that 1613 will on the family tree reconstructed by the herald's visitation, the fog begins to lift. The relations named in the 1613 will show the testator to be, not the early Elizabethan Mayor at all, but his grandson. In addition, the reconstructed genealogy shows a third Henry Hardware in between. We have, then, Henry Hardware I, the early Elizabethan Mayor who served in 1559–60 and 1575–76; his son Henry Hardware II; and *his* son in turn, Henry III, the testator of 1613.

But this revelation merely begs another mystery. Which of these three Henry Hardwares served as mayor in 1599, and undertook the iconoclastic actions of that year? Probably not Henry Hardware III who, as it turns out, only first married in 1607 and left a three-year-old child at his death in 1613.[10] He would clearly have been too young in 1599–1600 to take the mayoralty in a city with such a relatively large population (around four thousand in 1600)[11] and as lengthy a wait for high office as Chester. In addition—and one savours the irony—amongst the bequests in his will he notes two musical instruments, a viol and a bandora, and a pair of red silk stockings: not the sort of possessions we would expect from the man whose Puritan convictions led him to break up the giant in the Midsummer Show![12] These suspicions are confirmed by the classic historian of Chester, George Ormerod, who notes that this Henry was only baptised in January of 1587.[13]

And the Mayor of 1599 was just as clearly not Henry I, as has been assumed. Several indications point to his probable death some years before that time. For one, we know that when a list was made in the year 1590 of those paying a special tax in the City, Mrs. Anne Hardware, and not her husband, the former Mayor, was listed as the householder.[14] Had he still been alive in 1590 the list would have had his name rather than hers. Even before this, Henry I may have retired from city life to the village of Little Mouldsworth, seven miles northeast of Chester. We find him listed there, as 'Henry Hardware, gent.', in a visitation of 1580.[15] And finally, as Ormerod confirms, he turns out to have been married by 1560 and to have died in the Chester Parish of Tarvin in 1584.[16] In listing him as Mayor in only 1559–60 and 1575–76, the herald of 1613 was not at all making a careless omission: he had done his job with complete accuracy! Henry I was probably born in the 1520s and died in 1584. Especially in the absence of any surviving will, we have no particular indication of any Puritan sentiment on his part.

By process of elimination, then, the Mayor who disrupted the Midsummer Show in 1599–1600 was the second Henry Hardware, serving in his only mayoral year. His will proves to have been dated and witnessed on 7 December, 1607, and to have been proven on 28 February, 1608,[17] with the date of death lying somewhere in between. He describes himself in this document as living at Little Mouldsworth; it contained the estate of Peele to which he retired.[18]

Now that we have unravelled the identity of the 'right' Henry Hardware, at least a few details of his life fall into place. He proves to have been born in 1561, the only son amongst the six surviving children of his father, Henry Hardware I, and his mother, Anne Gee. Anne, too, came from a prominent local family, her father Henry Gee (d. 1579) having served a successful and eventful mayoralty in both 1533 and 1539. Sometime around 1580,

Henry Hardware II, 'our Henry', married Elizabeth Aldcrofte of Mouldsworth, the probable origin of the family's presence in the parish of Little Mouldsworth and another link to the ruling elite of Chester City. Most of their five children seem to have been born in the 1580s.

In January of 1583, the same year as his daughter Anne's birth, our Henry became a freeman of Chester, as a merchant.[19] Eight years later, in 1591, he had his first crack at civic office when he was elected a member of the common council of the City, also known as The Forty.[20] But much to our surprise, Henry forfeited that honour by refusing to take his oath of office. When the City Assembly voted to fine him the princely sum of £20 he proved even more obstinate, refusing either to take the oath or pay the fine.[21] The Assembly, that ruling body made up of the aldermen and The Forty, took great offense at such a brazen act by a young freeman of just thirty years. Its members nullified his election and barred him from their midst.[22]

But if Henry proved to be a stubborn man—firm, self-confident, and true to his own principles—he must also have become an important one. Despite his obstinacy, the Assembly gave him a second chance at high office by electing Hardware four years later, and not—ironically—to the lesser and larger council of The Forty, but as one of the eight aldermen of the City.[23] Without knowing more about the political realities of late-Elizabethan Chester, we can only conclude for the moment that Hardware had somehow become too important a figure, or that his personal qualities had become too valuable, to keep him out. The fact that he was selected as Mayor just four years later, at the still somewhat tender age of thirty-eight, bears out this impression. We will return to this interesting question of his rapid political rise in due time.

Beyond his service in those offices, it is hard to know much about Hardware's personal life or even his business. His will offers a few clues, though disappointingly few, and it is impossible to know whether all the details it reveals would have applied to him at the time of his mayoralty or would have accrued in the seven or eight years thereafter, in his retirement to Peele Hall. Still, we do know him for a wealthy man, leaving Peele Hall and its lands in Little Mouldsworth, two watermills, and a windmill just to his wife, Elizabeth. To his first son and namesake he left lands in Cheshire, including his other property at Bromborough and his stone house in Chester, plus lands in Flintshire as well. He left eight hundred marks to be divided between two of his daughters, with a third daughter to be provided for by arrangement with her father-in-law—presumably the balance of a dowry. Save for a library of books, his personal possessions proved unexceptional: they consisted largely of furnishings, two gilt bowls, and a damask suit of clothes.[24]

One has the impression here of a somewhat colourless but hard-working man perched at his death on the threshold between the urban elite and the minor county gentry. Indeed, his son and namesake crossed that threshold just months after Henry's death when he received a grant of arms from the College of Heralds.[25] One further impression bears heavily on his career and his reputation. It derives from his testamentary formula, whereby he left his soul to Almighty God and his body 'to the earth whence it came', with his burial to be carried out 'as befits a Christian member of Christ's Church'. Such formulae were often written by an attending clergyman, but the spartan simplicity of Hardware's fully supports his reputation as a pious and righteous man to the end. He no doubt was, as the chronicler confirms, '. . . a godlye ouer zealous man' with 'a verye worshippfull and A plentifull howse'.[26]

These meagre details of Hardware's life provide at least some context for the year of his mayoralty, a year which ran from his election, the Friday after St. Denis's Day (9 October) 1599, to the election of his successor a year later.

But for a fuller and more revealing picture, we must now look at Chester itself at that time, and thus of the immediate circumstances surrounding Hardware's actions against the Midsummer festivities. It seems useful, too, to see what we can learn about other aspects of Hardware's mayoralty. Most important, we need to see what that information might suggest about the kind of moral reform, most likely of a puritan nature, which Hardware brought to Chester in his mayoral year.

Hardware's term came at a perilous time. For both Chester and the nation as a whole, the period from the defeat of the Spanish Armada in 1588 to the death of Elizabeth in 1603 constituted the most difficult period of the sixteenth century. Nothing would match it until the outbreak of the Civil Wars more than a generation later. Against the background of an aging Queen whose successor remained undetermined, court politics reached a crescendo of factional strife with the revolt of the earl of Essex against the Queen's authority and, implicitly, against the influence of the Cecil faction. War with Spain, prolonged rather than concluded by the great naval 'victory' of 1588, extended by 1594 to the Spanish-supported Irish Revolt. Three successive harvest failures from 1594 through 1596 placed almost unprecedented strains on the economy and the price of food, and thus on fears of instability. Religious tensions, in which the fear of Catholic recusants on the one hand and the activities of Puritan radicals on the other tightly squeezed the via media of the Elizabethan Church, also reached new extremes and brought an intensified government response.

Though Chester lay on the opposite end of the realm from London and Westminster, Cestrians escaped none of these pressures; some in fact were experienced more keenly there than almost anywhere else. Since 1594 Chester had served as one of the chief ports of embarkation for troops en route to the war provoked by O'Neill's Rebellion in Ireland. The central government's effort to send troops and supplies to Ireland placed extraordinary demands on Cestrians and their governments alike.

In addition, the City's merchant community, to which Hardware certainly belonged, had problems of its own. Though it may have made some money out of supplying troops during the wars, most such profits were cancelled out by the disruption of normal trade. Many Chester merchants had their ships confiscated by pirates off St. Malo in 1598 or 1599. In response, they tried to imprison some French merchants as pawns for the return of their goods. But when Secretary Walsingham ordered them to release their hostages, they were compelled to seek alternative forms of compensation. In response to their petition, a panel of three privy councillors, Sir Thomas Egerton, The earl of Nottingham, and Sir John Fortescue, accepted the validity of their hardship, found them greatly impoverished, and urged the Queen to extend a license to import calfskins as an appropriate compensation for their losses.[27] At least some of these events need to be examined more closely to allow us to see what Hardware stepped into on his election in October 1599.

As recorded by Chester chroniclers, the buildup of troops through Chester began in 1594 and reached substantial proportions by the following year. Some 2,700 men passed through the City in the mayoral year of 1595/96, 1,500 in 1596/97, 4,200 (or, by one account, 9,900!)[28] in 1597/98, and 6,300 in 1598/99. In Hardware's year the pace continued. Eight hundred troops came through in mid-February, 3,000 more on the first of March, another 2,130 in mid-July, and a final 800 in September, making 6,700 troops in all. With them, of course, came their supplies and ordnance, carts and horses, and the ships and sailors it took to transport them. And more often than not it took several weeks for these large contingents to pass through. They had to wait until their supplies caught up with them and for favorable winds to sail. That meant, for example, that the 2,600 troops who assembled by the end of February 1599 waited three weeks before sailing in late March,[29] and 800 foot soldiers who sailed in late September had actually arrived in Chester itself on 21 August, cooling their heels, consuming food and taking up lodging, chasing local women and brawling with the inhabitants and amongst themselves, before departing five weeks later![30]

As one might imagine, and even with Privy Council support, the task of billeting these troops stretched the resources of the Cestrians almost beyond endurance. Chester's own population has been estimated at no more than 4,000 or so in these years,[31] which means that Cestrians were sometimes feeding and housing something on the order of two and a half times the usual number of people for the duration of the war. Even though they were able to spread some of this burden to the surrounding villages, including Bougham, Christleton, Rowton Newton, and others (Hardware's predecessor on one occasion even succeeded in sending a thousand off to Liverpool),[32] the City found itself severely stretched.

And as if these numbers alone didn't make things bad enough, the three failed harvests of 1594, 1595, and 1596 rocketed food prices to unprecedented levels. When the price of wheat in Chester hit 28 shillings a bushel early in 1596, one chronicler called it 'more deare than in the memorie of man', but by late April of the same year it soared to 41 shillings a bushel.[33] Conditions did not improve, and 1597 saw one of the gravest dearths of the century widespread throughout the entire realm.[34] Only in 1598 did a better harvest moderate grain prices somewhat. Wheat drifted down to 11 shillings a bushel by the summer of 1599 and must have been at near normal levels at Hardware's accession in early October.[35] Yet the experience of such high prices can hardly have made Cestrians any more tolerant of the strangers in their midst, and there can have been little novelty in having them about in the sixth year of their presence. Soldiers being what they were in those years— and many of those sent off to Ireland were conscripts and vagrants impressed into service—the civil order came under constant pressure.

Even before the Irish wars broke out Cestrians, like citizens of some other towns, had been obliged to keep certain arms at their homes against fears of crime and more systematic unrest.[36] But after the arrival of soldiers in 1594 the public order deteriorated rapidly. The first mayor to contend with this new turn of events, in 1594, ordered a gibbet erected near the High Cross as a warning to brawling soldiers.[37] This was repeated by Mayor Thomas Fletcher in 1598 when the soldiers 'weare verye quarrelsome'.[38]

In addition, along with the burdens of feeding, housing, and generally suffering this unwanted presence, Cestrians came in these years more than ever under the watchful eye of the central government at Westminster. Like most towns, Chester had always found itself hard-pressed to assert its independence from the multiple authorities ringed around it. Against the claims of the bishop and diocese, the County Palatine of Chester and its officials, and the central government as represented primarily by Queen, court, and council, Chester struggled to run its own affairs as much as its charters allowed. This entailed such battles as the one against the earl of Derby, as Chamberlain of the County Palatine, and of Sir Francis Walsingham to secure an important local office for their man Peter Proby.[39] It meant constantly trying to keep the Privy Council and others running the war effort aware of Chester's interests and the burdens of its residents.

These efforts required that Chester lived up to its obligations to entertain, at considerable expense, the great figures of state who came through the City in connection with the war effort. In the mayoralty of Hardware's immediate predecessor, Richard Raborne, the earls of Essex, Rutland, Southampton, and Kildaire came through Chester, along with some thirty knights, and various captains and other worthies. The Mayor and aldermen met them at the city gates on their arrival, banqueted them at the civic hall known as The Pentice, and bestowed gifts upon them as well. Essex received a gold cup worth £10; others received less valuable gifts according to their status.[40] The funds for these gifts were raised by subscription amongst the members of the City Assembly (comprising the Council of Forty, the eight aldermen, sheriffs, recorder, town clerk, and mayor) rather than by the normal revenues of the city. Yet they did add up, and the members of the ruling elite found themselves shelling out with some frequency for such occasions.

The business of being a good host in wartime also extended to less happy occasions. It included staging the funerals and burial of dignitaries killed in the war, whose bodies were returned to England by way of Chester. Thus, for example, the funeral of Sir Thomas Egerton, son of the Lord Keeper of the Great Seal, Knight of the Shire for Cheshire and long friend to the City, was held with appropriate pomp and circumstance on 27 September, 1599, hardly a fortnight before Hardware's election as Mayor.[41]

This then forms the scene which greeted Hardware at his election in early October of that year. As an alderman and member of the Assembly for the previous four years he must surely have known what he was getting into. And those members of the City's elite who selected him knew what they were getting in him, a point to which we will shortly return. From what we can reconstruct about Hardware's term in office, he brought a no-nonsense approach to all the City's problems, even at the considerable risk of alienating some of his fellow townsmen.

From his first recorded meeting of the City Assembly as Mayor, held on 29 October, 1599, he set out to assert greater control over various aspects of City government. He induced the Assembly to approve the addition of two auditors to the two who were already in place, thus allowing him to place his own men in that sensitive post. In his next session, on 9 November, he ordered each of the eight aldermen to survey their wards at least once a month. He succeeded in getting assembly approval for a ban on butchers and hucksters opening their shops on the Sabbath. He induced them to approve honourary freeman's status for Richard Vaughan, bishop of Chester, perhaps intending to add the bishop's clout to his own in City affairs.[42]

In his third meeting, held in mid-December, he took further steps to reform local government and bring order to the City. He had the assembly crack down on corrupt practices by the City serjeants and 'leave lookers' (market inspectors), who were known to be accepting bribes. He had it disband journeymen's brotherhoods which threatened to undermine the interests of the guild masters, and he induced it to award the valuable office of the Pentice clerkship to a local man, Ellis Williams, against the efforts of several privy councillors to prefer their own candidate for the post.[43] And in the last session before Christmas, as we have noted above, he took the controversial step of taking over from the City serjeants the lucrative collection of the toll on corn sold in the marketplace, which he intended to use for his own official expenses and for paying to maintain the market.[44]

As if waiting for him to settle into his post and establish his authority by such means as these, the month of January 1600[45] brought with it a string of events to which he had to react. In the middle of the month the River Dee froze over for the first time in several winters and remained frozen for five or six days on end. The event was rare enough to have provoked much merriment amongst the townspeople, and especially those still too young to have seen such a thing before. Many citizens walked and frolicked on the frozen river. Amongst them were a group of youths who got up a game of football on the ice and, '. . . not remembering to keep the sabbath day, so yt among divers yt hardly escaped, three young men fell through the Ise and were drowned'.[46] Still others are said to have fallen through but '. . . fell in an[d] gate out and escaped out of daunger'.[47] This tragedy, taking place on the Sabbath Day, 27 January, 1600, no doubt caused great grief throughout the community. Many will have taken it as an object lesson in the need to observe the Fourth Commandment, and Hardware undoubtedly seized the opportunity to make just that point. It may well have had the same effect, if to a lesser extent, as the 'fire from Heaven' which would level parts of Dorchester a few years later.[48]

Shortly after these tragic events, on Thursday, 14 February, Lord Mountjoy, Lord Deputy for Ireland, came to the City with several other dignitaries and military commanders, along with 800 foot soldiers bound for Ireland. On the following Sunday Hardware entertained Mountjoy and other officers at a lavish banquet. Two days after that, on the 19th, he saw the Lord Deputy pass on by sea to Ireland with many of his troops.[49]

But if townsmen sighed with relief at their departure, they would not have done so for long. The first of March brought 2,800 more foot soldiers and 200 horse. They stayed on for eight weeks, until the end of April. It was not a pleasant time for the Cestrians. As several of the chroniclers noted, the year was also very notable for an especially foreboding portent. For the first time since 1516, and the last time again for several decades, Black Monday—the Monday after Easter—coincided with the New Year day of 25 March.[50] These portents could well have applied to the City's role as unwilling host. Soldiers fought constantly amongst themselves and menaced the citizenry. One may well imagine friction and even violence between soldiers and townspeople, and townspeople both fighting back and appealing to their Mayor for protection and redress. At roughly the same time that Hardware entertained Mountjoy at a banquet, the quarrelling of the soldiers 'caused the cittizens often tymes to Rise'. Hardware responded by reverting to the tactics of his predecessors in having 'a Gallose [gallows] set up at the heighe crosse',[51] as a warning to those who would break the peace. Some soldiers were arrested by the local constables or citizens and 'some of them had theire eares nayled to peeces of tymber at the high crosse'.[52]

Throughout this period Hardware acted almost as a factotum of the Privy Council in the government's war effort in Ireland. His letters, sent rapidly to Westminster by the elaborate post system in place since the early 1590s, and now preserved in the Salisbury Manuscripts and elsewhere, show the full range of his activities. They have him constantly informing the councillors of news from Ireland, arranging for the provision of transport ships, commenting on the state of troops billeted in his City, organizing the provision of certain military supplies or clothing to those unprepared for battle, and even coordinating the effort to prevent desertion before embarkation.[53]

As Hardware undoubtedly knew, the citizens also needed to be watched closely if the peace were to be kept in these circumstances. In addition to frequent urgings that the aldermen carry out monthly surveys of their wards, and the crackdown on official corruption by the serjeants and 'leave lookers', Hardware's administration seemed determined to stamp out the efforts of some Cestrians to profit illicitly from the hordes of soldiers in their midst. Those who ran bawdy houses, or played games on the Sabbath, or ran gaming houses found themselves closely watched, and Hardware's government cracked down hard on those who sold ale without license. No fewer than 124 local people were fined for breaking the assize of ale in the July Sessions alone, with another 15 fined for breaking the assize of beer.[54] This astonishing record of convictions at the July Sessions covered the period including Midsummer.

That Hardware took these steps out of necessity is obvious. What is less obvious is that he did so in the face of considerable risk to himself, mostly from the press and menace of the 'visitors' in their midst: '. . . the Cittye so full of gents & strangers . . . all about', but also partly, perhaps, from irate citizens. Some no doubt objected to his breach of ancient custom, by banning the traditional festivities and also by cracking down on what many saw as transgressions against the civil order: '. . . he ruled so ell yeat he gate greate yll will Amongst the Commons for Appoosinge hymselfe Againste some Companyes orders and agaynste oulde customes of this Citye'.[55]

Others no doubt feared he was doing too little, blamed him for their constant inconvenience, and urged him on ever more strenuously to the task of bringing order out of chaos. Several of the chroniclers refer to him approvingly as a 'godly and zealous man'.[56] In any event, his unpopularity with 'the commons' cannot be denied, and not very long into his mayoral year he 'commanded 4 freemen out of every ward daly to wayte on hym wth halberes by reason of [the] multitud of souldiers . . .', and perhaps out of fear of the townsmen as well.[57]

Hardware's willingness to stand up to these pressures suggests why a City Assembly offended by Hardware's refusal to take his oath of office in 1591 and willing to expel him at that time came to forgive and readmit him four years later, and to elevate him to its highest post four years after that. In 1591 all had seemed well with the world in Chester, but by 1595 a crisis of public order lay at hand, and by 1599 the City found itself, if anything, in even deeper distress. In those circumstances the City's ruling elite needed a much stronger hand than it might otherwise have wanted—or been willing to tolerate. The tenor of the times demanded a man of Hardware's strength and resolve, even one so recently spurned for his obstinacy, in the hope that he would have the steel to see the City through. And if 'he gate greate yll will Amongst the

Commons', which we can hardly doubt, his forceful actions must have found favor with those of the City elite who brought him in.

It may well be that Hardware's rule, authoritarian and evidently strongly Puritan, serves as a metaphor for the place of Puritan reform itself in towns and cities throughout the land. Not that many faced the scourge of such a sustained military presence as did Chester. But these were very difficult times for many provincial towns and, indeed, the realm at large, with the burdens of unrest created by high grain prices, frequent plague, and the effects of war on several fronts widely experienced. Under these circumstances, forceful government, and a system of beliefs which justified forceful government, must have seemed ever more attractive to those with the greatest stake in local affairs. It is times like these which brought the Henry Hardwares to power, and times like these which made their Puritan convictions most welcome to many ruling elites throughout the realm. Puritanism has most often been approached as a chapter in the history of religious ideas, and investigated by a methodical reading of its apologists and theologians. These are valid approaches. But in the urban context it must also be seen as a cultural construct, and as an effective vehicle for civic order and discipline.[58] For the ruling elites of many contemporary towns, and especially for those as beleaguered as Chester in the 1590s, these features proved irresistibly attractive.

In this additional context, Hardware's assault on the traditional Midsummer Show may be seen as a decisive symbol of cultural transformation. Contrary to one's initial impression, he did not so much abolish the Midsummer festivities entirely (which would have been an even more unpopular and disruptive act and which would have lost a chance for using a traditionally ceremonial occasion in a didactic manner) as change its content and meaning. He may have 'put down' the giant and the naked boys, the devil in feathers and the dragon, but at the same time he inserted a new figure in the same procession in their place. In the words of the contemporary account, he 'caused a man in complet Armor to goe before the show in their steed'.[59] The significance of this change, symbolically akin to the erection of a gibbet near the guildhall a few years before, should not be underestimated.

In former times celebrations like the Midsummer Show had been prime occasions for asserting the harmony and coherence of late-Medieval civic society.[60] They entailed mediation amongst the sundry participating crafts and guilds to determine the order of procession and the conduct of the day. They served as ritual occasions to recognize and honour the fame of the community, and to display it, through the form of the festivities themselves, to the multitudes who flocked to observe them. They often included opportunities for disparate elements of the local society literally to break bread together and thus renew their fellowship. Yet however much such occasions had been employed to foster harmony in former times, some of them could very well have worked to the opposite effect under the circumstances of the 1590s. Not only did communities like Chester then face unprecedented stresses, but much of the former doctrinal meaning which underlay and gave life to such festivities had fallen into abeyance with the triumph of Protestantism by that time.

In the end, Hardware did not entirely abandon the Midsummer Show as, indeed, some other towns had already done. He merely directed it (as some others had also done elsewhere)[61] to different ends by changing its symbolic vocabulary. The man in armor presented as stark a symbol of the City's might, and of its resolve to maintain public order by use of that might, as could be devised. It held no ambiguity for either soldier or civilian. Under his guiding hand Chester converted traditional festivities to new and civic purposes.

Swaddon the Swindler and Pulman the 'Thief-Taker': Crime and Variations in the Great Metropolis

Were this a film rather than an essay, it would not open on an urban scene at all, but onto a weary horseman on a backcountry road, head bent into the swirling snow, making his way from Warwickshire towards Woodstock. Both by calendar and weather, this 28th day of December 1605 certainly qualified as 'in the bleak midwinter'. Anyone who had chanced to pass him would have noted the horseman's haste and determination. Once at Woodstock, he later related, he 'was enforced to lodge because my mare was tyred and Yt snowed fast and was night & [I] was not able to travaile further'.[1] This tired rider was Ralph Handes, steward of the Warwickshire gentleman and one-time MP Sir Thomas Temple. He was pursuing a mission on Temple's behalf which was both difficult and very dangerous.

It seems that Temple had been swindled by three men, John Selman (also known as 'Selby'); William Matthews (also known as 'Wright' and 'John Jones'); and Robert Swaddon (also known, sooner or later, as 'Captain Roberts', 'Captain Swanne', 'Webb', and 'Robert Johnson'). This trio had managed to forge Temple's signature and personal seal, and then used those identity cards of the day on a bogus obligation for a loan from one of Temple's acquaintances, the vintner and merchant Thomas Farrington of Broad Street, London. Having dealt with Temple many times before and knowing his signature, Farrington handed over the 'loan' of £120 without hesitation. Handes's mission was nothing less than to find and apprehend the swindlers in the large, complex, and potentially dangerous world of the London demi-monde.

In the end they led him a merry chase, which Handes recorded in detail in the itemized list of expenses he submitted to his master, Sir Thomas Temple. Handes's mission lasted ten weeks, spent mostly in and around the seamier parts of London and its suburbs. Though Handes met with only limited success, he gained a hard introduction to several types of contemporary criminal activity, and to the possibilities for anonymity, afforded in London at that time. Fortunately for us, Handes kept careful note of his adventures. Added to further documentation emanating from the courts of London and the County of Middlesex, his experience tells us a great deal about a subject which has been relatively neglected for this early period: crime in the metropolis.[2]

All three of those whom Handes sought to capture provide valuable insights. Selman and Matthews turn out to be petty criminals, clearly subordinate to Swaddon, indistinguishable from the vast majority of those who cluttered the dockets of London and Middlesex courts at that time. They will figure only tangentially in our story. Swaddon proves much the most interesting of the trio. He represents the more sophisticated criminal, preying on the merchant community of which he himself had been an integral part. His career reveals the vulnerability of normal commercial activity on the one hand and the possibilities for fraud on the other.

In addition to Swaddon, a great deal may also be learned from one other shady character who quickly gets bound up in Handes's adventure. This is John Pulman, who presented himself to Handes within days of his arrival as someone who could lead him to the other three. But Pulman turned out to be neither quite what Handes took him for, nor a conventional criminal of the Matthews or Selman type. He, too, will be worth our scrutiny. Finally, there is a geographic element to the story. Both Swaddon and Pulman, briefly serving as adversaries in Handes's hunt, lead us to those more marginal areas of the City which conveniently sheltered illicit activities. They allow us to see why London could retain its reputation for shady dealings at the same time that, thanks to people like Sir Thomas White, its image grew more positive in other respects.

Swaddon

The first thing which sets Swaddon apart from most other criminals is his background. In contrast to those who were his accomplices in the bilking of Sir Thomas Temple, and to almost all the other shadowy characters whom Handes would encounter in his quest, Swaddon seems to have come from a privileged home, and to have turned to crime out of choice rather than necessity. He appears to have been born around 1570 or shortly thereafter,[3] one of the six children, four sons and two daughters, of William Swaddon, a prominent clothier and timber merchant of Calne, in Wiltshire.[4] Nothing of what can be determined of Swaddon's family background offers the merest hint that it would lead to a criminal career. The elder Swaddon seems to have been something of a pillar of his small community. Calne records show him frequently to have served in local office, either representing the borough in its legal business at Westminster, or serving as a local collector of rents and taxes.[5] In 1576 he had been assessed for the subsidy at the second highest rate of anyone in Calne.[6]

Save of course for Robert himself, respectability seems to have been universal in the younger generation of Swaddons as well. The oldest of William's sons, and his namesake, took a Doctorate of Divinity at Oxford and ended his days as Archdeacon of Worcester. He left a small charitable bequest to the Borough of Calne on his death in 1624.[7] Robert's other two brothers, Thomas and Philip, remained in the Calne area, serving the Borough, as their father had done, in numerous useful capacities: steward, constable, collector of rents, and so forth.[8] Neither achieved the fame of William, or the notoriety of Robert.

But there are suggestions in the surviving wills of the two Williams, elder and younger, that the Swaddon family may have had its tensions. The paterfamilias left generous bequests within his means to Thomas and Philip, but did little for William and Robert. William still smouldered about this slight when it came time to write his own will.[9] Robert received from his father the offensively small sum of £10, at the discretion of his executor: a suggestion that perhaps by 1602, when he wrote his last will, the senior Swaddon had come to despair of Robert's amounting to much.[10]

And, indeed, by 1602 there might already have been good reason to harbour such doubts. William the Elder does seem to have been willing to undertake the considerable initiative and expense of apprenticing young Robert very nicely with a prominent Londoner, the Grocer and merchant Richard Sheppard, probably by the mid or late 1580s. Sheppard led Robert Swaddon to some interesting connections. Sheppard's daughter Elizabeth had married Lionel Cranfield, the future earl of Middlesex and the grandson of another very prominent Londoner, William Cranfield of the Mercer's Company. Young Lionel also served as Sheppard's apprentice, working alongside Swaddon on a number of occasions and obviously remaining in close touch with him. By the early 1590s, though he cannot have been much older than twenty, we find Robert Swaddon acting on Sheppard's behalf in collecting money owed him, and running similarly important errands.[11] By July 1594, Robert collected a sum of no less than £1,390 for Sheppard,[12] and by the following year he was sending substantial sums overseas on his master's behalf.[13]

These transactions show Swaddon to have risen quickly in Sheppard's regard, to have been given considerable responsibility, and to have learned the business of international trade in clothes and other items pretty well. It is possible that he may even have travelled abroad on Sheppard's business. This extensive experience should have provided Robert the firm foundation for a solid career, one which would have kept him in the company of the Cranfields, the Sheppards, and their ilk, and one which would sustain his contacts with foreign merchants as well.

But here a discordant note creeps into what can be reconstructed of Swaddon's early career. It suggests that Swaddon had been up to other, less respectable, activities in these years as well, living beyond his means and running up debts. In March or April 1596, Swaddon fled Sheppard's household, taking with him £300 of his master's money to Ireland. Sheppard asked the Privy Council to have him pursued by the Lord Deputy of Ireland, explaining that, not only had Swaddon absconded with that substantial sum, but that Sheppard had already lent £250 more to Swaddon. Sheppard had also given Swaddon an additional £250 to settle debts which Swaddon had run up.[14] We can hardly wonder that, in June of the same year, in a letter to his grandson Lionel, Old William Cranfield wrote that he 'had lost much in the last two or three years by Sweden's [a variant spelling of 'Swaddon's'] ill dealing'.[15]

This dramatic action on Swaddon's part should have earned him permanent disgrace and disbarment from the merchant community of London, and certainly from Sheppard's employment. But the merchant community, and the City itself, had become sufficiently large by that time so that he could return to it and still find opportunity. Somehow Swaddon was able to wriggle out of his dilemma and regain at least something of his former position. By April 1600, he was back dealing in the international cloth trade on his own, though it is noted that his stock was said not to be very saleable according to the fashions of the day.[16] As this and later evidence bears out, Swaddon may have disgraced himself with Sheppard and the Cranfields, but he somehow managed to keep the contacts he had made while in that job.

Still, at least some of his unsavoury reputation must have travelled with him and hampered his business efforts. It probably limited his opportunities for honest profit, and he was undoubtedly not making enough to support the penchant for fast living which poor Sheppard had learned about to his sorrow. Within a year or so we pick up Swaddon's trail again, not in the archives documenting commerce, but in rather those recording crime. This brings us closer to Handes the horseman, but not all the way there yet, for by the time Swaddon bilked Handes's master, Sir Thomas Temple, he had practiced his deceits on others.

One such victim, perhaps amongst others, was the Norwich merchant and alderman John Pettus. Working from the Norwich end, Pettus had built up a lucrative business over the years by buying up the local cloths called 'Norwich stuffs'. These he sent to his brother William in London, who sold them in that more lucrative market. In most years John shipped his goods every week, and William sent him back the substantial sums of money which were his share of the proceeds. The two were in constant communication on virtually a weekly basis, and had been for many years.

This was, of course, just the sort of business which was repeated hundreds of times weekly in transactions between factors in the metropolis and merchants from all parts of the realm. As London grew at breathtaking rates in these very decades, voraciously consuming resources from the realm over to supply its market, this proved a more common and lucrative form of trading than ever. But because business methods had not yet evolved to keep pace with the requirements of such transactions, such arrangements lay open to all sorts of mishaps: accidental and contrived, natural and manmade. Messages and money alike, even if the latter came in the form of bonds and letters of credit, had still to be privately carried by hand from one party to the other, exposed to the perils of the road as they went. And although such activities are extremely difficult to describe in any systematic manner, it is certainly arguable that such transactions—'these devellishe and accustommed practize(s)', as Pettus described them—fell prey quite easily and often to criminal activity. Well trained in the methods of commerce and well known to many of those who were engaged in wholesale trade, Robert Swaddon knew this well. By the opening years of the new century he strove to make his living accordingly.

In approaching the Pettus operation, in April 1603, Swaddon first gathered two accomplices, Thomas Llewellyn and William Matthews, and then all three assumed aliases under which to operate their scam. Llewellyn assumed the equally Welsh name of 'John Jones'; Matthews became 'John Strange', and Swaddon became 'Swanne' (perhaps reminiscent of 'The Swan' Inn in his native Calne).[17] They first approached William Pettus in London, showing him a forged letter from a Sir Henry Baynton, and working up a ruse about a runaway maid servant of Baynton's who had presumably fled to one of the Pettuses.[18] When William Pettus, predictably enough, knew of no such servant, they got him to write a letter to his brother John Pettus in Norwich to make a similar enquiry. The purpose of the scheme, of course, had nothing to do with the maid-servant, who had never existed, but with getting a letter that would have William Pettus's signature and seal. William Pettus inadvertently helped by including in his letter some business details as well: these would be familiar to John Pettus, and add credibility to the swindlers' story. The trio took William's letter, forged the signature and seal—evidently relying on a shady seal-maker who was readily enough available in a city the size of London[19]—added the business details, and worked them all into a bogus request from William for £100. John Pettus, in turn, paid the £100 to messengers whom he assumed had been sent by his brother. He, too, added a business letter with his own signature and seal in his response to William. The swindlers forged this in the same manner, and used it to secure the sum of £200 from William Pettus under similarly false pretences.[20]

Of course it did not take long for the Pettus brothers to discover the truth, and somehow to learn of the swindlers' identities. John Pettus made all these accusations in a bill of complaint in the Court of Star Chamber, dated 17 March, 1604, causing the attorney general to issue a subpoena for Swaddon and his accomplices to appear.[21] The suspects failed to do so. Eventually they were arrested by the sheriff of London and, failing to provide sureties (i.e., guarantors) for their appearance, were committed (on 28 January, 1605) to the London prison known as the Wood Street Compter.[22]

Throughout the term of his imprisonment and the opening stages of the case in the Court of Star Chamber, Swaddon steadfastly refused to cooperate. He refused to appear in court when required to do so; he refused to respond to the charges against him. As it happened, one of the keepers of the Compter was Martin Llewellyn, a relative of Swaddon's accomplice Thomas Llewellyn. Eventually, the Llewellyns conspired to arrange a gaol-break, in which Swaddon and his friends appeared to have sawn through one of the wooden window bars to their cell and let themselves out the window and down to the ground with a towel. This they accomplished on 14 June, 1605, making good their escape from the Compter and apparently disappearing into London.[23]

Oddly enough there are some suggestions that even at that time Swaddon may still have tried to resume his life in the world of wholesale trade. But his reputation had begun to catch up with him. Lionel Cranfield was amongst those who spread the word about Swaddon, and it seems not to have surprised those who learned of it. Cranfield's associate Francis Ottley responded to the news, writing from abroad at Middlesburgh, with the conviction 'that the gallows will be his end, and pity that he should be spared that cannot take warning by the action committed by him here'.[24] Obviously Swaddon had tried some of his tricks abroad as well.

Six months later Swaddon and his accomplices—John Selman taking Llewellyn's place along with Matthews—marked Sir Thomas Temple as the object of a similar scheme. As we have noted above, they forged Temple's signature and seal in an effort to extract money from the London vintner Thomas Farrington, with whom Temple frequently conducted business. In order to get a copy of Temple's signature to begin with, they forged a letter to Temple from his friend Sir Henry Baynton, who appears for the second time as an innocent bystander in Swaddon's schemes. They intercepted Temple's reply, duly signed and sealed. This they used as a basis for forging Temple's name in a request for a loan from Farrington. Farrington released to them the loan, for £120, on 21 December, 1605. It took Temple and Farrington only a week to realize they had been duped, and Temple swiftly sent Handes on his mission to find the swindlers.

Over the course of ten weeks the chase led Handes through the inns and alehouses, highways and back alleys, gaming houses and tenements of London and Middlesex. It brought him in touch with a cast of characters worthy of Dickens at the height of his powers. In the end he met only partial success: two of the accomplices were eventually captured, but Swaddon himself escaped.

Pulman

This leads us to Pulman, to whom Handes was referred by two employees of the Marshalsea Prison as one who might help him track down Swaddon and his men.[25] For reasons which Handes probably never fully recognized, Pulman became Handes's companion in arms in chasing down Swaddon and his friends. His story proves every bit as revealing and important as Swaddon's. Not only are his activities well documented in the court records of the day, but those same records also reveal the world in which he operated. It makes an interesting contrast to Swaddon's more white collar approach to earning a dishonest living.

An extensive and scholarly case has been made for London's being well and closely governed, and thus (especially in contrast with its suburbs) relatively stable and law-abiding in the period at hand.[26] Others have argued for quite the opposite picture, in which both the suburbs and City itself remained plagued by crisis and instability, and in which its suburbs especially proved only partially governable.[27] It is true that most of the suburban areas outside the walls of London were governed somewhat differently than most of those inside the walls. And, like suburban areas elsewhere, both then and now, these areas hosted a higher proportion of single people and migrants rather than established families, more occupational instability, more single occupancy dwelling units, and a much looser social and moral character in general. But pockets of wealth and poverty could be found in all areas of the metropolis. In addition, whether under the regular governing structures of the City itself or not, all areas came under the legal and administrative jurisdiction of recognized authorities: none of them were completely liminal in the administrative sense or lawless in the social or legal sense.[28] Above all, the astonishing population growth of the era produced a density of urban population previously unknown in London or elsewhere in the realm. That density made government in any of its areas a challenging task. In consequence, those who sought the metropolis for its anonymity could find it in almost any part. Those who sought to hide from the authorities—whether the Five Members of the House of Commons hiding from Charles I in 1641 or a common thief hiding from the JPs at almost any time—could often do so with perfect impunity.

Pulman obviously knew this very well, and as we learn more about his activities the reasons for this knowledge become clear. Between the years 1605 and 1617 his name appears nearly seventy times in the court records of Middlesex and the City of London.[29] Variously described as a yeoman, a 'horse-corser' (i.e., horse-trader or dealer), and 'hackiman' (i.e., hackneyman or coachman), Pulman lived in several places within a radius of a few hundred yards in the large western parish of St. Sepulchre, taking in much of Clerkenwell, Smithfield, and Newgate: he is variously described as living in Cow Cross, Cock Lane, and St. John Street. Ironically, all of those short streets were very close by both the Castle Inn on St. John Street, where the Middlesex Sessions were conventionally held, and Newgate Prison. But more important for Pulman's 'career', most were also just beyond the Ward of Farringdon Without, and thus outside the administrative jurisdiction of the ward system. The maintenance of law and order in this area fell largely to the Middlesex JPs, a group which had every reason to feel overwhelmed in pursuit of the task before them in this era.

There are a few instances, early in his 'career', in which Pulman himself engaged in illicit activity. On one occasion he was bound over to keep the peace towards someone whom he had threatened.[30] He was accused once of receiving stolen goods,[31] and twice of theft.[32] One of the latter accusations, for stealing a silver cup from a local tavern, led to an indictment and a brief period in gaol.[33]

But Pulman's real source of income seems to have derived from the myriad opportunities for legitimate (or at least quasi-legitimate) profit provided by the legal maze of the metropolis in all its complex and overlapping legal jurisdictions. In the usual system of the day, when someone was accused of a misdemeanor, both that person (the defendant) and his or her accuser (the plaintiff) would be examined by a JP. If the accusation seemed to him to have merit, and neither mediation nor summary conviction seemed to him appropriate, the JP would bind over the accused (and sometimes the plaintiff as well) by recognizance, so as to ensure his or her appearance before a grand jury and his or her peaceful demeanor in the meantime. The recognizance served as a bond, usually for the substantial sum of £40, payable to the Crown in case the defendant defaulted on its conditions. If the grand jury then found the likelihood of guilt, a further recognizance could be demanded to ensure appearance before the Court of Quarter Sessions itself. [34] In addition to the £40 bond which had to be posted against the appearance of the appropriate party, two sureties, each posting a £20 bond, had also usually to be found. If the conditions of the recognizance were not kept, that is if the defendant failed to keep the peace until his court hearing or failed to turn up at the hearing, the bond became forfeited to the Crown. If sureties could not be found the JP could either send the accused directly to prison, there to linger in considerable duress and great expense until the next meeting of the Sessions,[35] or (less frequently) have him punished summarily even before the next Sessions.[36]

Those defendants who were well established in a local area or who had family nearby might easily find sureties. Friends or relatives would be anxious to keep them from the hardship, expense, and indignity of prison until brought to trial. But in the relatively impersonal world of London, and especially in those parts (and at those times) where social ties were weak and well-to-do relatives in short supply, sureties could be hard to find. To add to the challenge, defendants had only a short time to come up with such guarantors (merely a few hours in the latter decades of the seventeenth century), and the quest had usually to be carried out while the suspect remained in custody. Even given ample time, the poorest, the most recently arrived, or the more socially marginal defendants might not know potential sureties who would meet the requirements of personal solvency and respectability.[37]

This desperate but common plight created an opportunity for those looking to profit from the misfortune of others. As a result, at least in the environs of London, the role of standing surety seems to have become something of a profession by this period. Some, perfect strangers to the accused, made a regular living by standing surety for a fee or some other consideration, thus anticipating the role of the modern bail bondsman.

Pulman also understood this urgent need very well. He stood surety no fewer than thirty times between May 1605, when his name first appears in that capacity in the Middlesex Sessions records, and his death in September 1617.[38] Most of his clients were poor people who lived close by, in or around Clerkenwell. They included people like Elizabeth Cover, also of Cow Cross, accused of receiving stolen goods;[39] the spinster Mary Vargus of St. Sepulchre's, accused of felony;[40] or the coachman William Bennett of St. Sepulchre's, bound to keep the peace towards his wife.[41] A few of these people, like Bennett, drew upon Pulman's services more than once. Though none of them appear to be related to him, some may have known him personally before they required his services. A very few may even have known him well enough to have drawn upon his friendship in asking his help as a guarantor without compensation. But it is unlikely that Pulman had as many relatives or close friends as this. It seems certain that most went to him because neither they nor their closest friends and relatives, if such there were, were sufficiently respectable or solvent to be accepted as sureties. (Indeed, it is something of a surprise that Pulman himself was so considered, though the evidence here is plain enough.) For most of these clients, Pulman served on only one occasion.

In addition to this local clientele, some who resorted to Pulman's services came from outside the metropolis altogether. These included people like William Hill, a yeoman of Bristol, who appears to have been involved in a brawl,[42] or John Grey of Reading, who stood accused of cheating with false dice and then knifing his victim when called to account.[43] It is extremely unlikely that they knew Pulman beforehand, and it leads us to ask how they came to his attention.

All things considered, we may infer that, just as Ralph Handes had learned of Pulman through two keepers of the Marshalsea, Pulman enjoyed the frequent cooperation of lower-level court officials or employees in steering such clients his way. No doubt he compensated them for doing so. This is all the more likely when we consider that, when indicted wrongdoers had sudden need of a surety, they were already under arrest and in the custody of such officials. Finally, Newgate Prison was within a few hundred yards of all of Pulman's known residences throughout this period: he was never far to seek. (Then, as now, the three secrets to success in business were location, location, location!)

Because at least two sureties were required for each case, we find that Pulman often joined with others in providing this 'professional' service. These associates usually came from the same neighborhood, were of his same social and economic position, and were sometimes just as likely to have been involved on both sides of the law. Some of them collaborated with Pulman on more than one occasion, suggesting a marked degree of cooperation in such activities amongst a circumscribed group of men in and around Clerkenwell (and, presumably, similar groups in other parts of the metropolis as well).

By a very curious coincidence, one of Pulman's one-time associates in serving as surety turns out to have been John Selman. Just a few months before Swaddon, Matthews, and Selman bilked Sir Thomas Temple, Selman himself had joined with Pulman as a surety for a James Heyes, a fustian-maker of Southwark in Surrey, and almost certainly a stranger to them both.[44] We will return to the implications of this interesting collaboration in a few moments.

But Pulman had more than one form of livelihood in and about the law, and he did more than hang about in ale-houses waiting for people in need of a surety to beat a pathway to his door. He also sought business in a pro-active manner. On nine occasions he served as witness against those accused of some crime,[45] and on another four occasions the Sessions records refer to him as a 'prosecutor' of suspects or, in other words, an accuser.[46] He appears on three occasions on Gaol Delivery Rolls as having charge of conducting convicted felons to prison (perhaps serving, formally or informally, as a deputy constable).[47] On five more occasions he received custody of those who had been accused or indicted, presumably also for the purpose of conducting them to gaol.[48] And on one occasion he was bound over himself—two of his frequent associates serving as his own sureties—for releasing thieves entrusted to his care.[49]

What exactly may we make of these recorded activities? Clearly Pulman became so familiar with the working of the local court systems and its procedures on the one hand, and with the shady nooks and dark alleys of the metropolis on the other, that he was able to sniff out several sorts of regular opportunities for profit. It seems certain that he kept abreast of criminal activities in his own particular neighborhood, and that he was well acquainted with a wide circle of men and women who operated on both sides of the law. He, himself, had crossed that threshold from time to time, though it is mostly his legitimate activities which were most frequently recorded.

Though in theory a constable might well have taken part in the investigation of a crime and in the apprehension of the accused, in reality some constables did more, and had time to do more, than others.[50] That left a void in the system. In practical terms the victim himself was often left to identify and locate the suspect and to rev up the machinery of prosecution.[51] That same void, in turn, encouraged men like Pulman who were able to serve such victims, presumably receiving a fee from them if he brought in suspects and perhaps one from the perpetrators if he did not. In this private prosecutorial, do-it-yourself, stage in England's legal system, the services of men like Pulman almost certainly went to the highest bidder. He had no hesitation in facilitating the prosecution of those who refused, or were unable, to pay him for looking the other way when crimes came to his attention.

In this way he served as prosecutor for several suspects who were subsequently convicted and sometimes, as with the highway robber 'Sweetface Will' and his accomplices, even sent to their death.[52] On the other hand, he sometimes seems to have let others go: he was once caught doing so and found himself bound over in consequence.[53] Sometimes, too, he would stand surety for their appearance if the price were right. In some instances he may have collected fees from both victim, for helping in the apprehension, and perpetrator, for standing surety, in the same case.

Though the term itself would not gain common parlance for nearly another century, Pulman in fact operated as a professional 'thief-taker'.[54] Along with his occasional collaborator William Elder, he was so described in a record of the London Sessions: *'Johi Pullman et Williamo Elder de poia pred[ictus] Thieftakers'*.[55] The fact that he came to Handes's attention for his presumed ability to track down Swaddon, Matthews, and Selman attests to his local reputation in that role.

In the context of this dubious career, it is thus not surprising that Pulman should have come to Handes's attention, or that he should have accompanied Handes in his quest. And those who recommended him to Handes were not entirely misleading an innocent from the provinces. Pulman's skills at.locating and apprehending criminal suspects were indeed well developed and available to all who might require and could afford them. Handes recognized those skills and paid well for them: his accounts record frequent payments for Pulman's services, and for his expenses, and several times Pulman put Handes up in his own home.

And, to an extent, Handes got what he paid for. In late February of 1606 Pulman led Handes to Matthews in Islington, and together they were able to find three constables to arrest him.[56] Eventually Pulman and Handes encountered another confederate of Swaddon's at Uxbridge, and after a violent skirmish, in which Pulman was injured, they managed to capture him as well.[57] But despite Pulman's and Handes's efforts to track them down over a period of nearly ten weeks, they never apprehended Swaddon or Selman.

Knowing what we know (and what Ralph Handes almost certainly did *not* know) about the earlier collaboration between Selman and Pulman, perhaps this should not surprise us. It is possible that in the few months since their collaboration as co-sureties in a Sessions case in May of 1605, Pulman and Selman had come to a falling out. Yet it seems even more probable that they remained friends, and in collusion, over the entire course of Handes's chase. This raises the strong possibility that Pulman was in fact cleverly steering Handes *away* from Selman—and Swaddon—(if not the less fortunate Matthews) during the entire time he was getting paid for finding them. In fact, considering that Selman and Pulman lived within the same neighborhood and parish, seemed to travel in the same circles,[58] and had recently collaborated in 'business', it strains the imagination to believe that Pulman was being at all honest with Handes in appearing to help him track Selman down. It also raises the possibility that Swaddon had bought Pulman off to the same effect.

Pulman's tenuous role in Swaddon's story thus comes to an end. His career as a thief-taker continued as we have seen virtually to the end of his life, and his death is recorded, in the parish register of St. Sepulchre's, in September of 1617.[59] But Swaddon lived to fight, and to cozen, another day (or, to be accurate, quite a few more days!). It is to his story we must now return.

Swaddon Again

Having escaped Handes's grasp as effectively as he had earlier escaped from the Wood Street Compter, Swaddon made a point of laying low. Handes himself gave up on ever finding him, which was just as well. When Handes finally left London for Warwickshire in mid-March, he left a warrant for Swaddon's arrest with a Buckinghamshire JP, but this was probably a wild guess as to Swaddon's location rather than the result of confirmed knowledge of his presence in that county. Given his share of the money he had received from Temple and his earlier experiences on the Continent, it is even possible that Swaddon fled abroad for a time. But before too long he resumed his former residence. This turned out to be William George's inn or lodgings in the Parish of St. Saviour's, Southwark—also outside the twenty-six wards of the City—where he appears to have lived more or less continuously since about 1603.[60]

Before very long at all, he had picked up where he left off as a 'cozener'. By February 1608, he had developed the technique of securing funds from unsuspecting merchants through forged bills of exchange, and he used this ruse to cheat a number of merchants in provincial towns who had factors or agents working in London.

The technique is well illustrated by his swindle of two Cambridge merchants, Nathanial Craddock and William Brett, and their London factor, Frances Marten of Lombard Street. It is spelled out in fine detail in the Star Chamber case of 1610 in which Swaddon's former landlord and probable partner in crime, William George, sued both Swaddon and his victims for blackmail and libel.[61]

Swaddon and George rode up together to Cambridge in February 1608 and made their way to the Sign of the Dolphin, an inn well frequented by that city's merchants. There Swaddon introduced himself as 'Robert Johnson', and claimed that he and George (also provided with a pseudonym) were London merchants travelling on business. He expressed his fears of carrying great sums of money on those journeys, and asked if the innkeeper knew of any local merchant who would enter into a bond agreement with Swaddon to avoid this risk. Before he left London on his next trip he would pay to the London agent of any such merchant a sum of £80, and the agent would give him a receipt or bill of exchange for that sum. Swaddon would then journey to Cambridge to conduct his business without having to carry that amount of cash with him, and would collect his £80 back from the Cambridge merchant upon presentation of the agent's bill.

Speaking for his partner Brett as well, Nathanial Craddock, a prominent Cambridge mercer, agreed to such an arrangement. He agreed that 'Johnson' would pay £80 in London to Craddock's agent, Frances Marten of Lombard Street, who was also a mercer. Marten would give a bill of exchange to 'Johnson', who would redeem it a few days later from Craddock and Brett in Cambridge. As Craddock later testified in a related court case, he had frequently engaged in such agreements as a matter of convenience between fellow merchants,[62] and in fact (though this is hard to imagine) it is nowhere indicated that he expected to profit from providing 'Johnson' such a service. Sure enough, at the appointed time a week or so later, 'Johnson' showed up at the Dolphin as arranged, presented the bill of exchange from Marten, and received his £80. This he split with William George. But the bill from Marten had of course been forged, and Swaddon had never paid his

£80 to Marten as agreed. As Craddock and Marten discovered shortly thereafter, they had been 'cozened'.

From Cambridge, George rode with Swaddon to receive similar sums on the strength of other forged bills. Thus they successfully bilked a Mr. Noble of Newark-upon-Trent of £50 against one forged bill, and would have bilked a Mr. Peacock of Huntingdon of £40 on yet another forged bill if Peacock—who perhaps smelled a rat and stayed away—had kept his pre-arranged meeting with Swaddon at the Christopher Inn in that town.

As with the earlier bilking of Sir Thomas Temple, it never took very long for the victims of these ruses to discover that they had been cheated. Swaddon must have known that on each occasion he had but limited time in which to get away, and we may well doubt that he ever unsaddled his horse for long. But he seems to have been reasonably confident that at the conclusion of these business trips, he could always retreat safely into the alleys and byways of the great metropolis, and that he could rely on the obscurity of George's inn in Southwark so as to lay low when he had to. Of course if he had always been confirmed in that confidence we would know a little less of his escapades: what we do know comes from court cases in which the full details of his ruses lay revealed.

On at least two occasions we know him to have been caught and imprisoned: first, as we have seen, following his cozening of John Pettus early in 1605, and then again roughly a year after Ralph Handes gave up his chase and returned to Warwickshire in March 1606. Though we do not know the precise circumstances of this second period of incarceration, it appears to have been prompted by a writ of arrest from the Lord Chief Justice himself, on charges of cozening. Once again Swaddon found himself locked into the Wood Street Compter. Word of his imprisonment soon got around amongst his victims, and several of them later reported visiting him there and seeking to get their money back.[63] And once again he escaped, this time fleeing abroad to Cologne.

It was from Cologne, probably in the spring of 1610, that Swaddon, already known to have swindled Craddock and Brett, wrote them to apologize for his actions. He did so because they had discovered his whereabouts and he feared they would come after him. In this missive, Swaddon advised that they could retrieve their £80 from his erstwhile accomplice William George, who owed Swaddon his share of £40 and more. And Swaddon provided Craddock and Brett enough details about George's part in the ruse to allow them to blackmail George into yielding up his share. Finding it easier to ride to London than travel to Cologne, Craddock and Brett then rode in from Cambridge and confronted George. But when faced with this threat, and Swaddon's letter, George sued all three of them, and Francis Marten besides, for libel and blackmail, giving us the court cases from which a lot of our information derives.[64]

Crime and Variations in the Metropolis

There is yet one more central character in this story, though a character of a different kind: this is the great metropolis itself. It is time to ask what these picaresque tales have to tell us about illicit activities in the setting of England's only true metropolis, and about related matters as well. Certainly they speak eloquently of the great anonymity which such a large urban centre afforded. Those caught up in the tangled net of the court system here often had by necessity to rely on the services of strangers to set themselves free. In almost any other community in the realm, they might well have been able to rely on family and intimate friends close at hand. This is not by any means to say that there were no networks or associations amongst groups of individuals, as defined by neighborhood, parish boundaries, frequenting of similar taverns and inns, and other spatial factors. Such networks certainly seem to have existed amongst people like John Pulman and his many associates in the business of standing surety, both for one another on what was presumably a friendly basis, and for strangers on what was almost certainly a pecuniary basis. This is the most likely conclusion to be drawn even from the impressionistic reading of the records of the Middlesex and London courts, where one finds the same combinations of names repeated with more than coincidental frequency. Nevertheless, these were networks of an impersonal, even professional, sort, and they were more necessary in London than elsewhere.

The prevailing scholarly view of London criminal behaviour at this time holds that criminals did not organize in gangs or other such formal and enduring associations as much as was once thought.[65] But the extensive record of the Sessions rolls from both the County of Middlesex and the City of London does show the existence of at least some forms of collaborative activity in the period at hand. These factors are well exemplified by John Pulman's varied 'career' in and around the law, and by the light shed by his activities in the behaviour of those around him. The resulting picture does not approximate either the contemporary literary descriptions of London criminal organization,[66] or the extent of criminal organization which has been well documented for a somewhat later period.[67] Yet it does suggest a large pool of petty and part-time criminals of various sorts who formed constantly shifting alliances to carry out their illicit activities.

It also suggests that, given the large area of London's sprawl and its great and rapidly growing density of population, one could confidently hide out from the authorities for considerable periods of time. Swaddon counted on being able to return to London after each of his swindles and blending inconspicuously into the vast and complex streetscape of the metropolis while his pursuers searched for him in vain. He could also forge new alliances in that same environment with men like John Selman, William Matthews, and William George, for his next escapade.

Swaddon's career in particular also tells us something about the centrality of London to merchant networks elsewhere in the realm and on the Continent. Thanks to his early training in mercantile affairs, he found it easy to locate the London agents of provincial merchants or manufacturers who would be vulnerable to his blandishments. He understood the business practices of the day, including the commercial intercourse between London and the rest of the country, and the operation of letters of exchange. He had come to know, and to know about, many individual merchants as well. He obviously spoke well and convincingly enough to pass as the merchant he had started out to be. These skills allowed him to use London as the 'head office' for his schemes. And when those schemes failed, the same skills also offered him a quick and ready opportunity to flee abroad without attracting the attention of the authorities.

Swaddon's career also tells us one more useful thing about urban-based activities. The business methods of the day were still sadly underdeveloped in relation to the volume, scope, and relative integration of commercial ties in the urban network of the time. Swaddon's experience speaks to the contemporary difficulties of transporting cash, arranging credit, or transferring wealth amongst merchants operating in different parts of the realm. It also suggests the very considerable extent to which merchants like Craddock and Marten necessarily still relied on interpersonal trust, and how vulnerable such reliance could be. Provincial merchants tried to do their London business through relatives, as demonstrated by the brothers Pettus, or through close friends. But this was not always possible to arrange. When personal connections broke down, the cracks in the system become obvious at once. Men like Swaddon knew them well. As is well known, London had become even more essential to the economic life of the nation than ever, but until the nation's legal system and its business methods caught up with the realities of contemporary commerce, the City would also be a perilous place in which to carry out that business. And as with many elements of England's urban communities, this was much more the case with London than any other town or city.

Neither the ruses of Swaddon nor those of Pulman seem particularly common forms of criminal or quasi-criminal activity in other English towns and cities of the time, which were simply too small. But they seem common enough in London. They exemplify the vulnerabilities of both the legal and the commercial practices of the day, and they remind us that the metropolis served activities which were both licit and laudable on the one hand, and quite the opposite on the other.

CHAPTER 8

Joyce Jefferies and the Possibilities of Spinsterhood in Hereford

The demi-monde of Swaddon the swindler and especially of Pulman the thief-taker, explored in the last chapter, show that, at least in a city like London, there could indeed well be 'worlds within worlds'. Their experience makes one wonder whether such circles might be found in smaller cities as well, and amongst people whose common associations were more legitimate in nature. It also makes one wonder how cut off such smaller groupings might be from the mainstream of society. The professional and personal activities of the Hereford spinster Joyce Jefferies lend interesting insights to all these questions.

One thing which seems certain about spinsters in early modern England is that they remain pretty shadowy figures. Given the strength of the imperative for women at this time to marry, spinsters were not all that common, and we have far fewer sources for their lives than, for example, we do for widows. Yet there are nevertheless assumptions about the subject which seem widely shared. In his recent literary source collection entitled *The Cultural Identity of Seventeenth Century Woman* [sic], Norman Keeble sums up the literary perspective on the subject as well as anyone when he tells us that while 'a widow enjoyed some status (for an exemplary widowhood . . .) and some independence; . . . an unmarried woman was an anomaly with no defined role or position'. '"Old maid"', he continues, 'was a name of scorn'.[1]

Of course, fashionable literary themes of a particular era don't necessarily offer a completely accurate perspective on contemporary attitudes. But social historians have widely shared this theme as well. Miriam Slater, for example, has concluded that 'continued spinsterhood was viewed as a form of social derogation. Spinsterhood condemned one to a life of peripheral existence; it was a functionless role played out at the margins of other people's lives. ... The single life was a despised condition'.[2]

Others, including Mary Prior and Barbara Todd, have lined up more or less behind this position, with Prior adding the challenging assertion that the single woman remained largely isolated even from the support of other women. Linda Woodbridge takes issue with this view of women isolated from each other, emphasizing close ties of friendship amongst women and how they tended to rely on one another during times of crisis, but she sees this as merely one more reason for which men resented them.[3] And Frances Dolan reminds us that single women of this period, living outside male protection or control, were suspected of crimes, including witchcraft, with disproportionate frequency.[4] Finally, of course, it is well known that women in general and single women in particular would normally have been debarred from most of the more visible aspects of urban society: the freemanry (under most circumstances), office holding, many traditional rituals (which were guild-based), and so forth.

Only a few doubts have been voiced about the tradition that widows and especially spinsters of this era lingered on the periphery. Amy Erickson has interjected an early note of caution based on what she considers to be slender evidence. She finds inconclusive the view that spinsters lacked support networks of other women, and suggests that under some circumstances they may have maintained a measure of independence even when living in someone else's household, as so many of them did.[5] And Amy Froide has described the operation of complex economic networks made up of women in the provincial port of Southampton, challenging several prevailing views of single women in particular.[6]

These more optimistic assessments at least raise the possibility that the life of the spinster in a specific community might extend beyond dependence on others and isolation from the mainstream. This possibility is so strongly supported by the life of one such spinster in particular that it seemed valuable to relate her experiences, even if they flow over our putative cutoff date of 1640 by eight years. The woman in question is Joyce Jefferies, who lived in and around the cathedral city of Hereford from sometime in the mid-Elizabethan period to her death in 1648. We are privileged to know about Joyce Jefferies because she left us a richly detailed diary of her financial transactions, covering the last ten years of her life.[7] Divided into receipts from her activity as a moneylender for the first twenty-two folios and expenditures in her personal life for a further forty-eight folios,[8] this record may be read as an autobiographical document. Such sources are exceedingly rare for any sort of person in this era, and this is virtually unique for a spinster.[9] The manuscript has been utilized by several Hereford antiquarians in summarizing what it reveals of the life of its author,[10] but it has enjoyed very little extended examination in modern historical scholarship.[11]

Jefferies's activities bear at least three themes which seem germane to our interests. All of them serve both to introduce the woman herself and to allow her experiences to expand our understanding of the provincial urban economic and social life around her. The first theme is that, far from being a marginal dependent, Jefferies carried on a successful business as a moneylender, which, as is well known, was not an uncommon activity for single women of means. Though little can be added here to the economic analysis of Jefferies's money-lending activities which has recently been published,[12] that phase of her life still seems the obvious place to begin in exploring her wider role in the society of Hereford and its hinterland. It will allow us to see how her business contributed both to her own place amongst a wide circle of friends and relatives on the one hand and to the capital supply of Hereford and its surrounding area on the other.

The second theme is that, far from being scorned as an 'old maid' and being debarred even from the attractions of female company, Jefferies moved easily and regularly in a number of social and family circles, showing no need to linger about the periphery of any of them. She enjoyed a rich and varied social life in and around the City of Hereford: one notable for the prominent part played in it by other women, and one notable, too, for demonstrating how women could after all find a niche in the provincial urban milieu.

And we have a third theme in the observation that, far from being isolated either socially or culturally from the world beyond her community and her family, Jefferies seems to have had some interest in the wider world, extending to politics, religion, and material culture. Her experiences here support the suggestion that even provincial townspeople who played no role at all in the formal political process were still not cut off from wider circles or concerns prior to the Civil War.

Just who was this woman, wealthy enough to have kept up a lively business in lending money and to have owned several houses, but who never married? How did she get to the state we find her in at the beginning of that document? Let us begin at the beginning, by summarizing what can be reconstructed of Jefferies's life before the 'Diary' begins in April of 1638.

The key to Jefferies's financial position in later life lay in her family connections, and in a peculiar set of circumstances which made her the legatee of several relatives' bequests. As indicated in a herald's visitation of 1634, she was the only child produced by the second marriage of her father, Henry Jefferies of Home Castle in the parish of Clifton-upon-Teme, Worcestershire, and the second of three marriages of her mother, Anne, widow of Johannes Coningsby of the parish of Nene Solars, Shropshire.[13] As an earlier visitation, carried out in 1569, shows her parents' marriage not yet having produced any children by that year, we surmise that Joyce was born shortly thereafter, most likely about 1570.[14] And we know that she died between April and November in the year 1650.[15]

Her father's connections gave her an important circle of relatives and friends, and (though Henry Jefferies's will has not survived) he seems also to have left Joyce a substantial legacy.[16] Yet it was Joyce's mother's side which seemed to do more for her. By her first marriage, to Johannes Coningsby (d. 1567) of Nene Solars, Anne Jefferies had a daughter and a son, Katherine and Humphrey Coningsby, who remained very close to Joyce Jefferies as long as they lived.[17] Though her two subsequent marriages gave her further connections to regional gentility and left her a 'lady', it is not clear if Joyce's mother became a wealthy woman. She left only modest amounts in her will of 1616, a year before her death.[18]

Joyce's half-brother Humphrey Coningsby, born in 1567, was something of a scholar and acquired a reputation as a traveller and travel writer. He never married, and died abroad in 1610. But he did become reasonably wealthy, and in his will he named Joyce, 'that beste doth know my mynde', as his executrix. This may have been an unusual choice, but it shows both his closeness to her and his respect for her administrative abilities. He requested that she erect a tomb to his memory, for which he left a substantial sum.[19] The half-siblings must indeed have been close, for he also noted that, in composing his last will and testament, he rested 'assured havinge ever found her lovyinge to me and iust to all'.

She did not let him down, either in supervising the erection of the tomb or in carrying out his other bequests. When her illustrious cousin Sir Thomas Coningsby (1550–1625)[20] drew up his will a few years later, and despite the many powerful and well-educated people with whom he was associated, he also named Joyce an executrix. As that document itself tells us, he did so particularly 'for the late proofe of her constant perseveration in manefesting the trust of the like kind reposed in her by my cousin her brother'.[21] Joyce obviously inspired trust, even in very important men, and even in the most consequential of administrative matters.

In addition to the trust they showed in her abilities, Humphrey and then Sir Thomas left her well fixed. Humphrey left her an annuity of a hundred marks, to be paid in two equal annual installments, plus his interest in houses and gardens 'within five miles of London' and moveable goods 'wheresoever'. His full sister Katherine received slightly less, and the bulk of his money went to his mother, who would outlive him by seven years before passing on in 1617.[22]

Sir Thomas, merely a cousin, left Joyce his deceased wife's linen and £10 a year from rents on some rural property. But this meagre monetary legacy was far outweighed in its importance to Jefferies by the hospitality he appears to have extended to her after the death of her mother in 1617: between her mother's death in 1617 and Thomas's in 1625, Joyce Jefferies almost certainly lived in the latter's household.[23] These years of residence would not only have polished her social skills and enhanced her education but they would have exposed her to a wide circle of influential families throughout the surrounding counties of Herefordshire, Worcestershire, Shropshire, and Breconshire, where Thomas held extensive lands and influence. When she came to live on her own after Thomas's death, these connections came to serve as the basis for her money-lending activities throughout those areas.

Until we can pick up the threads of her life through her account book from May 1638, we face large gaps in what we know of Joyce Jefferies's adult life. Still, we do know that she inherited modest sums from her mother and her cousin Sir Thomas Coningsby, an annuity of 100 marks annually from her half-brother Humphrey, and, if John Webb is to be believed, a lump sum of 200 marks from her father. Some property accrued to her as well, at least from her half-brother and cousin, and she would have been spared many of the usual household expenses by living with family well into middle age.

We know that Joyce had established residence in the City of Hereford by 1634, for she appears as a plaintiff in a suit of debt tried in the mayor's court in that year.[24] Most likely, following the death of her cousin and benefactor, she found it more convenient to live in an urban centre than in the countryside, especially an urban centre which lay at the centre of a wide circle of friends and relations scattered throughout the surrounding region.

By 1638 and probably much earlier, Joyce Jefferies lived in a house in Widmarsh (now Widemarsh) Street owned by John Fletcher, for which she paid £3 twice a year. She continued to live there even after Fletcher's death in March of 1642, paying rent to his widow instead.[25] But this modest rental seems more of a clue to her thrifty nature than an indication of her actual circumstances.

As we will see in a moment, she was at this time in a very sound financial state indeed.

Other aspects of her life begin to come through to us as well in these years, and one begins to feel an acquaintance which is personal and direct. Though Joyce may have moved to Hereford, presumably after Cousin Thomas's death, she did not thereby begin to live alone. Her goddaughter and distant cousin Eliza Acton lived with her until her marriage in 1643. Joyce supported her until then and provided a dowry of £800—a very substantial sum—on the occasion.[26] She had already retained the services of Matthias Rufford as a manservant and general dogsbody, paying him 20s a quarter for his services.[27] He would also serve as her coachman and her bill collector (though she sometimes had another coachman), and he remained with her for the rest of her life.[28] In addition, she employed up to three maidservants at any one time, for whom she provided clothes, shoes, and pocket money, along with both a cook and a cook's maid.

In November 1640, Joyce bought a house and garden on Widmarsh Street in Hereford, outside the North Gate of the City, from another spinster, Elizabeth Gollding, though it is not clear when or even if she actually went to live there.[29] By the autumn of 1642 fear of the approaching parliamentary troops forced her to flee from the city. She paid to have some of her goods removed to safety before departing herself on September 21. This must have been a traumatic event at the time, and it certainly proved pivotal in determining how and where she would spend most of the rest of her days. From that time on she lived in intermittent exile from Hereford, sometimes fearing for her life, and staying at the homes of a series of relatives who took her in.[30] Too proud to be dependent, and well enough off not to have to be entirely beholden, she paid her way as she went, and kept Rufford and some of her household with her.

Clearly Joyce did not expect her exile from Hereford to be permanent, and indeed, the parliamentary troops who entered the City on September 30 left again shortly thereafter.[31] She remained in the region and she kept up her dealings with Hereford merchants, crafts people, and friends as best she could, sending Rufford or her servants to run her errands. In March of 1643 she hired the mason Anthony Alldridge to build her a new house in Hereford, lending him money for his start-up expenses (which, as she records, 'he will never pay').[32] Still, and despite the surrender of the City to parliamentary troops on 24 April, 1643,[33] he did complete the house. Feeling confident again about her safety, she came back to Hereford 'to my newe house' in April of 1644 and resumed her membership in the parish of All Hallows by paying her tithe to the vicar a month later.[34] By that time she had three household servants in addition to Rufford, her maids and her cook, making a substantial household for a single woman.[35] But the entire move took a long time, and she did not make her final rental payment on her former home in Fletcher's house, on the same street, until September 1644.[36] Even so she seems not to have stayed in the new house for long, and we find her moving on yet again later in April 1644, to stay with relatives in Horncastle through the summer.

In May of 1645, at the beginning of a summer which saw Hereford hotly contested by both parliamentary and royalist armies, Jefferies received a last rental payment from her tenant Maud Prichard. The house which she rented to Maud, and possibly some of her other properties, were pulled down later that year, probably as part of the City's defenses against further attack.[37] At this critical time she made the difficult decision to sell off as much of her Hereford property as possible against the prospect of loss or destruction. This included a furnace (which may have been a kiln for brick-making),[38] and several properties in Widmarsh Street outside the North Gate. These stood in the line of defenses which the City was trying to erect against the threat of invasion, and, as she tells us, 'I was constrained to sell them or have them burned againste [the coming of] the Earl of Leven'. They included the new house Alldridge had so recently constructed for her, which went for £50 to 'Young Mr. Holmes', a Hereford mercer, and four other properties consisting of individual rooms or suites of rooms in other buildings, which brought in an additional £21 15s.[39] This having somehow been accomplished, Joyce wisely departed again to stay with relatives in Horncastle during what turned out to be the unsuccessful two-month siege of the city by a Scottish force loyal to the Parliament, taking up July and August.[40] Eventually, and after what must have been her strenuous protests, the County Committee agreed in November 1647 to reimburse her for some of her losses, though it is not clear that they ever fulfilled that promise.[41]

In the winter of 1647–48 the entries in Joyce's accounts become thinner, though she still wrote them out herself, and it is clear that she had grown ill. One of the last entries, in March of 1648, records her care by Nurse Nott. But this elderly patient, probably nearing eighty years of age, remained optimistic to the end. The very last entry of all records a payment of ten pence to mend her shoes.[42]

By following the account of Joyce's expenditures in isolation, we forget that through these difficult years she remained an active, methodical, and successful business woman, lending money which brought her over £500 income in some years, leasing lands and raising produce which brought her in still more, and keeping detailed account of the whole. The range, scope, and type of her financial transactions tell us not only about her own life but also about the flow of capital in and out of a provincial city like Hereford at a time when capital tended to be in short supply and there were still no banks operating, even in a rudimentary sense.

It was not unusual for a single woman who could afford it to engage in money-lending activities in pre-industrial times.[43] They provided an obvious means of making a living when so many other paths were barred. The legal status of unmarried women allowed them more than the usual reversionary interest in their estates: more commonly than other women, they held the freedom to dispose of property which, by the very dint of their inheritance, had reverted to them. In addition, the fact that they were unattached also gave them a great deal more economic freedom than most other women and many men. And finally, they often had legacies with which to invest.[44]

Jefferies's financial diary doesn't tell us everything we would like to know about this phase of her activities. It is not a conventional account book, with expenditures and receipts methodically recorded. Nor does it indicate the balance of cash on hand at the beginning of the book or—though it does offer yearly totals of outlay and income—at any point throughout, making it impossible to assess Jefferies's wealth in cash at any time. But it does yield a methodical and sequential list of transactions in the order of when the interest on each loan came in as payment. It tells us the name and (often) the residential location of the borrower, along with the principal, term, interest, and due date of the interest. Some transactions offer additional information regarding the occupation of the borrower, the agent or intermediary involved, the form of payment (stock or cash), or the type and circumstances of the loan. In addition to conventional loans, it records some mortgages; rental payments on her estates at Bradward, Warton, and Free Town; both sales and purchases of land (though not necessarily as investments), livestock, or moveable goods; and the regular receipt of annuities paid in to her from the estates of her benefactors.

And it also begins in the middle of her money-lending career, with many loans already outstanding (and almost certainly recorded in an earlier book or books which have not survived). From the very first pages of this document it is clear that by 1638, and almost certainly for some time before then, Jefferies lent money on a substantial scale. She received income of several hundred pounds a year in the early years recorded by the 'Diary' (see Table 3). This derived from interest (the largest share), rent money, her annuities, and some proceeds from sales of produce or other goods.

TABLE 3

Annual Income Received by Joyce Jefferies and Recorded Annually by Her on St. Mary's Day Eve, 1638–1646 (to the nearest pound)

1637–38	£543	1642–43	£383
1638–39	£658	1643–44	£264
1639–40	£443	1644–45	£320
1640–41	£528	1645–46	£366
1641–42	£525	1646–47	[incomplete]

These figures do not include the repayment of principal on any of the loans, which would, of course, have made for much larger sums. Principal on loans due in 1639–40 amounted to £5,890, though this was probably her best year. Although not all of the loans accounting for this total would have been made in the same year, it suggests that she was lending close to £6,000 a year in her best years, mostly at the 8 percent rate of interest which was permissible by statute after 1624. After about 1642 her interest income on loans declined, and we must assume that the war cut deeply into her business.

The 'Diary' reveals the identity of Jefferies's borrowers, and at least hints at how she came to link up with those borrowers and how she felt about lending to them. Our first inclination is to anticipate a high level of lending to members of her family. Other studies of money-lending in peasant or village society at this and earlier times emphasize ties of kinship in such transactions,[45] and the unusual complexity of Jefferies's network of family connections made this an even greater likelihood in her case. But the 'Diary' tells us that although kinship played some part to be sure, it was not as important as we might expect. Even if we count her cousin Fitzwilliam Coningsby amongst the borrowers—and he did sometimes borrow from the annuity which he administered from his father's estate for Joyce Jefferies—we still find only about 10 percent of Jefferies's 148 borrowers to be related to her, as compared with the 40 percent of loans to kin in, for example, B. A. Holderness's study of traditional money-lending patterns elsewhere.[46]

Kinship does, however, seem to have been important in an indirect sense. Many of those who borrowed from Jefferies, if not related directly to her, turn out often to be related to each other. Genealogical investigation[47] has turned up no fewer than forty (27 percent) of the known 148 borrowers who were related to other borrowers (the actual percentage is undoubtedly higher). A similarly substantial, if not precisely calculable, number were neighbours to each other. Many borrowers obviously passed on word of Jefferies's services to their relatives, and no doubt also to their friends, tenants, neighbours, and even servants.

Similar ties appear amongst friends and neighbours of Jefferies herself. A considerable number of those to whom Jefferies lent monies turn up again in the second part of the 'Diary' as people with whom she dealt in other economic and social relationships, most of them from within a region of fifteen or so miles. Many seem to have counted as friends and neighbours, others as sellers of commodities or services upon whom she relied. A few even lent money in turn to her, thus echoing the sort of reciprocity in financial dealings which seems to have been so common in the later Middle Ages.[48] Again, even if not tightly bound, as in Holderness's sample, by actual kinship or immediate physical proximity to the lender, personal ties seem important. In sum, Jefferies's relationships to many of her borrowers still exhibit some of the characteristics of what might be called a 'face to face' capital market.

To carry this theme further, we must also ask whether Jefferies's clients lived near her own home base in Hereford or not, whether they were town or country dwellers, and whether they would have followed occupations specific to one or the other of those milieux. The evidence which may be drawn upon in this regard is only partial: of 148 identified borrowers, only 108 may be classified by place of residence and, even if we count 'gentleman' and 'yeomen' as occupations, only 59 may be identified by occupation. Still, these numbers are sufficient to suggest general conclusions.

Though Jefferies lent to people as far away as London, most of her operations were still confined to the area in and around Herefordshire. The dispersal of her loans by distance, based on the 108 borrowers whose county of residence has been identified out of the total number of borrowers (148), may be described as follows:

TABLE 4

Distances of Jefferies's Borrowers from Hereford

1–4 miles	48	44.4%
5–9 miles	11	10.2%
10–14 miles	29	26.9%
15+ miles	20	18.6%
TOTALS	108	100.0% (rounded)

Though there is an obvious predominance of neighbourhood borrowers, as might be expected, in and around Hereford itself, a surprisingly large proportion, nearly half, came from ten miles or more away, nearly a fifth from more than fifteen miles, and 4 borrowers came from London. This makes a marked contrast with the prevailing medieval pattern of very much more local borrowing, but is similar to what has been found in Elizabethan Devon.[49] In addition, 45, or 41.7 percent, of the borrowers whose exact place of residence is known may be considered urban dwellers, not only in Hereford itself but also such neighbouring towns as Bromyard, Leominster, and Worcester.[50] This suggests that towns served as sources of credit for one another as well as for their rural hinterlands.

When we turn to occupations, we find a wide and representative range of urban occupations amongst the whole: no fewer than fifteen in all, craftsmen, artisans, professionals, and merchants amongst them.[51] In addition to these occupations identified amongst the known urban dwellers, 22 were identified by a civic office (nine mayors or aldermen of Hereford, two bailiffs of Leominster, three JPs, and five sheriffs for Herefordshire, two MPs for the City of Hereford, and a subsidy collector). Two more were identified as 'gildsmen', also of Hereford, and 2 as vicars. Of non-urban dwellers, 22 may be identified as 'gentlemen' or the wives of gentlemen, and 1 as a yeoman. Clearly Jefferies lent money to those who resided in both urban and agrarian areas, to representatives of a wide range of occupations, to those of the 'better sort' as well as to those of the 'middling' and 'lesser', and to a number of the ruling elite of the city and county. Again her lending activities served to connect people of diverse descriptions, this time in occupational and social terms as well as geographic locations.[52]

From this we may safely conclude that many of Jefferies's clients would seem to have fit into the two overlapping social milieux to which she herself belonged: the complex network of country gentry in Herefordshire and nearby parts of neighbouring counties, and the middle and upper rungs of urban society in Hereford and, to a certain extent, the neighbouring provincial towns of Leominster, Bromyard, and Worcester. Many members of each network would likely have known each other personally or by reputation, and would have been known to Jefferies in the same manner. Thanks to the contemporary dynamics of geographic and social mobility, many, too, would have been familiar with members of other circles. As Craig Muldrew has observed for King's Lynn, reputation still seems to have been important. 'Credit' still meant trust. There are still vivid signs, then, of traditional networks surviving in Jefferies's lending activities, and there are very strong indications that gender was no bar to earning confidence even in matters of considerable importance.

Finally, how sharp a business woman does Jefferies appear to be? Did she adopt a strictly 'modern' attitude which would have offered the same terms of interest to friend and stranger alike? Did she always exact the maximum permissible rate of interest? And how did she react to those in arrears or in default? The answers to these questions may give us some idea of how much she thought of borrowing in the traditional manner—that is, as something of a social obligation to those around her. To what extent, in contrast, might she have thought of it strictly in terms of a mature capitalist outlook?[53]

As one might have guessed, the results are mixed. Rates of interest in Jefferies's loans stand in sharp contrast to the worst excesses of the age.[54] Obviously she did not hesitate to exact interest, and thus saw these activities as more than simply helping friends, neighbours, and family. On the other hand, her rates were far from excessive and remained largely within a few percentage points of the statutory mean of 8 percent. One explanation for this modest return undoubtedly had to do with risk. As Jefferies tended to lend to those whom she knew, if not at first then at least at second hand, the risk and thus the desired rate of interest could be less. Whatever the explanation, the perspective exhibited by this characteristic lies roughly midway between the traditional moral economy on the one hand and the strictly-for-profit strategy, which represented the wave of the future, on the other. It also suggests a conservative approach which worked to avoid any possibility of being sued (or, for that matter, suing) in regard to excessive rates.

Perhaps more remarkably (and notwithstanding her decision to liquefy her assets by selling off her property at the time), it shows her avoiding the opportunities for profiteering even in the midst of civil war. It is easy to anticipate that loans extended in a time and place of war would bear increased risks, and that, rationally speaking, much higher returns on interest could thus have been demanded. Yet Jefferies continued to lend at the same relatively modest rates of interest.

In addition, Jefferies sometimes forgave borrowers the principal or at least the interest on loans which they could not pay; she sometimes forgave the estate of those who had died in her debt. Interestingly, several of these loans had been made to widows (Mrs. Sybil Weeks, Mrs. Jane [or Janet] Higgins on two occasions, Mrs. Barghill of 'the Bovine'—presumably a public house or inn—and Mrs. Francis Hereford), and we will return to this consideration below. These provide further indication that her intentions in extending loans fell short of the consistently 'rational' pursuit of profit.[55] Fewer than a quarter of the interest payments on Jefferies's loans came in on time, and less than 60 percent came in within a month of due. Yet only once did Jefferies go to litigation over overdue interest, and only once over a defaulted loan.

In sum, Jefferies's lending activities in nearly every way fall midway between the moral economy of a traditional, pre-industrial society on the one hand and an impersonal, highly capitalistic model on the other. While still essentially regional and to a degree even community centred, the geographic scope of Jefferies's lending shows that she (and perhaps others like her) was at least beginning to lend to distant borrowers, to whom she was connected by both local acquaintances and professional brokers. Such borrowers may be seen as 'clients' in the modern sense. If they sometimes came to Jefferies's attention through local connections, their financial relationship with her could hardly be described as personal or community based. Her ties with them affirm one way in which the metropolis of London in the early seventeenth century was beginning to draw regularly on resources through the far parts of the realm. Thanks to people like Jefferies, provincial towns like Hereford began to serve as sources of credit both for their own residents and those in the surrounding hinterland. These activities had already come to mark an important point of interchange between town and country;[56] they anticipated regional banking networks of a more formal nature within the century to come. On a more personal level, they certainly affirm that the life of the spinster need by no means be marginal to the rest of society.

The second part of the 'Diary', which records expenditures, shows Jefferies to be fully engaged in her social as well as in her professional life. Here we observe her close and altruistic interaction with friends, employees, and kin, and her centrality to several social milieux in and around the City of Hereford. A detailed examination of these activities also suggests that Jefferies's social life may have been most extensively carried on with other women: relations, friends, servants, and those with whom she sustained commercial connections.

The heart of Jefferies's social world consisted of both her own household—even when it was absorbed, in exile, into that of her hosts—and her extended family. She seems constantly attentive to her servants, especially the women amongst them, and to those servants of the household hosting her at any given time. She retained an obviously close interest in her several godchildren, at least two of them called 'Joyce' after her, her nieces as well as nephews, and her cousins. The chief amongst the relatives in her life was clearly her goddaughter and companion Eliza Acton, whose dowry of £800 she provided at her marriage, and who seems to have lacked for no material possession with which Jefferies could provide her before that time.

In these overlapping circles Jefferies appears not only as a devoted relative or friend but also as a supportive one. Aside from Eliza Acton, the most frequent and obvious recipient of this constant largesse, Jefferies rented a house for her cousin Jane Gorton and paid for Jane's funeral in the spring of 1643. She sent lavish gifts to her cousin John Jefferies and his wife in Ypres and her cousin Sybil Warren in Antwerp. She gave generously to several nephews and nieces going to London or elsewhere to serve apprenticeships. No child could be born into the family without Joyce giving handsomely to the midwife and the nurse at the christening, even if she herself could not usually attend the event. Many of her poorer female relations had their medical care, such as it may have been, paid for by Jefferies. When maid-servants left her service they did so with generous gifts, and if they left to get married, as several of them did, so much the more lavish were her contributions.

Some of Jefferies's social activities must be classed as acts of charity. She gave habitually small gifts of either money or pieces of clothing or adornments to a surprisingly large number of people, most of them women. Some of them were strangers, like the old women she met in a nearby field, or the local youth going up to Oxford and short of funds, on whose behalf the local vicar successfully solicited Jefferies's support. Some were probably the sort of local unfortunates known to all and supported by the goodness of many. Additional gifts went to her servants, for whom she seems to have provided ample material comforts and also such perks as spending money to go to the fair. And some recipients were the servants of friends or those in whose households she stayed in her years of exile from Hereford. Those who visited her went away with gifts as well, all of this being normal enough practice for the day. A number of servants and local workers of both genders received gifts at New Year's—celebrated in January rather than late March—and this, too, was as it should have been. But a great many gifts were bestowed throughout the year without obvious occasion or reason other than Jefferies's own concern to help out and to be remembered. A great many of these went to her female relatives, some of them no doubt in straitened circumstances, some obviously not.

And when Jefferies needed help herself, it seems to have been her female friends and relatives who came to her aid as much as the men: a pattern widely observed as well in literary portrayals of the period.[57] Her first refuge after the fear of the parliamentary troops drove her from Hereford—'when I durst not be seen', as she tells us—was to the house of a Mrs. Carpender of Hinton; here she stayed for some ten weeks. Only later do we learn that there was a Mr. Carpender in residence as well: Jefferies's payments for board and her record of gratitude were to the wife. A few months later she had to hide out for a night 'for fear of soldiers', and did so at the house of Goodwife Stefans.

A further and very intriguing aspect of her complex social relations consists of Jefferies's commercial dealings with other women. It is difficult to escape the impression that Jefferies seems to have carried out a remarkable share of her domestic business, and perhaps preferred to do business, with women rather than men, at least to the limited extent to which this was possible in the mid-seventeenth century. As we would expect, many specialized items of clothing, or the cloth from which they were made, were supplied by women artisans. But in other respects women seem surprisingly prominent amongst those with whom Jefferies had dealings. Records of these transactions help us to identify, at least by name, other women like Jefferies who might also challenge our stereotypes. A number of Jefferies's loan clients, as noted above, were women themselves, most of them widows. When she herself borrowed money, which she did from time to time, she did so from women as often as from men. When Jefferies rented a house for her poorer cousin Jane Gorton, which she did steadily until Gorton's death in 1643, she rented it from another woman, the Widow Beedleston. While Jefferies tenanted some of her farmland from Brasenose College, she also let several acres of hay meadow from the Lady Poyntz and pasture from the widow Joanne Delahay. She bought her paper and ink from Mrs. Morgan, as well as sundry textiles from the London mercer Mrs. Eaton and the Leominster mercer Mary Stephens. She had her shoes mended by 'Holt's wife', and she purchased one of her Hereford properties from Elizabeth Gollding, a spinster like herself, whom she then took in as a tenant.

These business relationships almost suggest a sort of regional shadow economy composed of independent women, many of whom were undoubtedly as enterprising and financially self-reliant as Jefferies herself. It is an intriguing possibility, and one which flies directly in the face of the assumption, made by Mary Prior and others, that no such ties applied to spinsters.

Notwithstanding this interesting feminist theme to Jefferies's social and domestic activities, she seems to have felt both free and welcome to join in some of the mainstream aspects of Hereford society as well, most of which were of course dominated by men. She remained an active parishioner in All Saints (sometimes called All Hallows), Hereford, and paid annually a small sum to the wife of the parish clerk to 'dress' the seat which she rented there by the year.[58] She celebrated the election of the Mayor in 1638 with a gift, in return for which she enjoyed a dinner at his house, and repeated both aspects of the electoral celebration in subsequent years as well.[59] On several occasions she bought a Valentine gift or token for a gentleman friend.[60] She contributed towards the costs of providing music at a local play performance in 1639.[61] And, though it was hardly a social event, in the summer of 1642 she contributed towards shoring up the City's defenses against the threatened invasion of the parliamentary army.[62] In sum, if Jefferies's involvement in the life of Hereford and its milieu are any indication, a spinster of means might wish to associate closely with others of her sex, even to the point of forming virtual networks of social and economic activity. Yet she might do so without jeopardizing a simultaneous and considerable engagement with the wider society of her city and region.

Finally, the dimensions of that engagement extended to the life of the mind as well: Jefferies's life also runs counter to cultural and intellectual stereotypes of the spinster. She was certainly aware of the wider world of politics, history, and literature, of current events and of religion. Jefferies was probably an anti-Puritan and a royalist even before the parliamentary occupation of her city and the destruction of her house. (This reminds us that one need not be a Puritan in order to exhibit the characteristics of thrift and a methodical attention to business: qualities which, ironically, the ardent London Puritan and contemporary Nehemiah Wallington lacked in abundance!)[63] Jefferies lamented the death of Ben Jonson, and she bought pictures of Strafford and Archbishop Laud (though also of the decidedly non-Catholic William of Orange, Prince of Nassau, and his wife, Mary). Among the seventeen books whose purchase she recorded are one 'of the earl of Strafford's armament', two pamphlets (one of poems) on the death of Ben Jonson, two books by the anti-Puritan controversialist Joseph Hall (1574–1656), and one about the life 'and death untimely' of Mary Stuart. She bought two more works of religious and political controversy, *Little-Wit's Protestation to Defend Popery* in 1641,[64] and *The Scots Scouts Discoveries* in 1642;[65] three almanacs (George Wharton's *An Almanack*,[66] Thomas Gallen's *An Almanak*,[67] and William Lilly's *Anglicus*[68]); and a book on astrology entitled *Araniam*.[69] She also records the purchase of works on classical laws and histories by Herodotus, Justinian, and Quintus Curtius, and a popular English translation of Leonardo Lessius's *Hygiasticon*, a treatise on health and longevity.[70]

In view of these wide interests it is a shame we can know so little of her education. She would probably have had some private tutelage with her half-siblings Humphrey and Katherine Coningsby, and she must also have picked up a great deal from her presumed residence in Sir Thomas Coningsby's household.

We can be somewhat more certain about her domestic pursuits and habits. Keeping up with fashions of contemporary townspeople of middling or gentle status, she kept a caged pet thrush, and had a 'Cipress catt'.[71] She used spectacles, which she kept on a silver dish when not in use,[72] and she owned a diamond ring which, like her spectacles, she misplaced from time to time.[73]

What may we conclude of all this? On first sight (and even aside from its obvious importance as a record of financial dealings), Joyce Jefferies's financial 'Diary' promises a rare view of how a gentlewoman in a provincial center carried out her relations with others in her place and time. It shows her to be both part of the mainstream (though not of all aspects of that mainstream) and also part of a 'world' of other women within that mainstream.

Certainly this record makes us reconsider prevailing assumptions about spinsterhood, at least insofar as they might apply to one of Jefferies's means and class. It takes more than one brick to make a house, but if Jefferies may be taken as typical, their role may be far different than one has been led to expect. Jefferies engaged quite successfully in a remarkable diversity of economic activities, all of them very much in the mainstream. She not only remained self-supporting but served as a means of support for others. Even when she had to take refuge in the homes of relatives and friends she remained sufficiently independent to keep her own servants and coach with her, and to pay her way both literally and figuratively. Her activities also show her to be far from isolated from the society around her. Her records of money-lending affirm her business relationships with nearly 150 people, distributed over one Welsh and three West Midland counties plus London. Other parts of this document describe for us the several social and family circles in which she moved as a central figure.

At the same time, she also participated actively with other women over a broad social spectrum, from the county gentry at one end to household servants and the cobbler's wife at the other. The range and nature of those associations offer a window into a feminine world of complex, supportive, and intentional interaction. Such a connection extended far beyond Jefferies herself, and beyond even the mainstream of Hereford City, but to the entire region of the West Midlands and even to London.

Finally, of course, the range of Jefferies's interests dispel any lingering tendency to think of provincial towns as isolated backwaters. Neither she, nor the circles in which she travelled, nor the City of Hereford itself, was as culturally or intellectually isolated as one might be tempted to think. No less than Henry Manship's Great Yarmouth, Joyce Jefferies's Hereford was very much connected to the whole, town to nation. The coming of the Civil War, and of successive armies to Hereford itself, may have strengthened those connections, but they did not create them. They existed independently, and had long done so.

Glossary

Glossary

NB: The following terms are defined as employed in the text. Additional definitions, or definitions of non-technical terms, should be sought in a conventional dictionary.

advowson: The right to appoint a candidate to an ecclesiastical office.

alderman: Usually a member of the inner council of town government; in London the representative of one of the twenty-six wards.

altar screen: The screen behind the altar of a traditional Roman Catholic church.

betterment migration: Migration motivated by the desire to better one's lot rather than merely to seek subsistence.

chamberlain: A financial officer.

chantry: An endowment used to employ a priest to say masses for departed souls in traditional Roman Catholic practice. It also often supported a chapel for that purpose.

cozener: A cheater or defrauder.

cursus honorum: The informal but traditional sequence of civic offices which one followed in a career of civic service.

feoffee: A trustee, especially for a charitable or civic foundation.

freeman: One (either male or female) who has been admitted—usually by apprenticeship, patrimony, or inheritance—to full participatory rights in the economy, though not necessarily in the governance, of the borough.

freemanry: The collectivity of freemen.

freeman's fines: Fines or fees paid at admission to the freemanry.

Gray's Inn: One of the four inns of court (schools for training in the common law), all located in London.

guildhall: Prior to the Reformation, in most instances, the hall of a religious guild. After the Reformation, it often meant a town hall.

Hanseatic League: A league of trading states and cities on the Baltic and North Sea.

herald's visitation: An examination of genealogical connections carried out by a member of the College of Heralds in order to determine worthiness to bear a coat of arms.

journeyman: A skilled worker who had completed an apprenticeship but not set up his own business or craft.

lantern: Architecturally, a small, open-sided structure mounted atop a building usually for the purposes of providing a light or a clock.

liveryman: A member of one of the livery companies of London or, more generally, one who wears the livery of a particular lord or authority.

Martinmas: The Feast of St. Martin, November 11.

Midsummer Show: Traditional festivity held on June 24, usually including dramatic performances.

mortmain: A form of land-holding which permits alienation (sale, etc.) without penalty to the Crown, and thus highly desired by civic and ecclesiastical corporations.

obit: Usually a ceremony (often a Mass) performed to commemorate the soul of a deceased person in traditional Roman Catholicism.

Quarter Sessions: Meetings of the Justices of the Peace in each county held four times a year for purposes of adjudication and administration.

recusants: Those who refuse to conform to the official Church, especially applied to Roman Catholics.

reredos: An ornamental screen placed behind the altar of a pre-Reformation church, usually with rich carvings, niches for statutes of saints, and similar figures.

rood screen: The screen, often finely carved in wood or stone, separating the nave from the chancel of a traditional Roman Catholic church. So called because it supports the rood (or cross).

sessions: Quarter Sessions, or county-level courts, staffed by JPs, which met four times a year.

shambles: Meat or fish stalls, or the area of the market containing such stalls.

Star Chamber: A prerogative court with particular jurisdiction over crimes of violence or against the state.

subsistence migration: Migration from place to place within England motivated by the search for basic essentials of subsistence.

surety: A pledge or bond to guarantee the fulfilment of an obligation, or the person who has agreed to provide such a pledge on behalf of someone else.

yeoman: A freeholder who holds his own lands but is lower in status than a gentleman.

Abbreviations

C.P.R.	*Calendar of Patent Rolls*
D.N.B.	*Dictionary of National Biography*
Ec.H.R.	*Economic History Review*
J.B.S.	*Journal of British Studies*
Letters and Papers	*Letters and Papers, Foreign and Domestic, of the Reign of Henry VIII* (21 vols., 1862–1910)
P. and P.	*Past and Present*
P.R.O.	Public Record Office
R.E.E.D.	*Records of Early English Drama*
S.T.C.	*A Short-title Catalogue of Books printed in England, Scotland, and Ireland . . . , 1475-1640*, ed. A. W. Pollard and G. R. Redgrave (3 vols., 1926)
V.C.H.	*Victoria County History*

Notes

Introduction

1. Peter Clark and Paul Slack, eds., *Crisis and Order in English Towns, 1500–1700* (1972).

2. These included discussions of ceremony and citizenship by Charles Phythian-Adams, trade guilds in York by David Palliser, migration in Kentish towns by Clark, poverty by Slack, Civil War politics by A. M. Johnson, East London housing by Michael Power, Norwich as a provincial capital by Penelope Corfield, and London merchants in the 1690s by D. W. Jones.

3. Peter Clark and Paul Slack, *English Towns in Transition 1500–1700* (Oxford, 1976).

4. See esp. David Palliser, 'Urban Decay Revisited', in John A. F. Thompson, ed., *Towns and Townspeople in the Fifteenth Century* (1988), pp. 1–21; Palliser, 'A Crisis in English Towns? The Case of York, 1460–1640', *Northern History* 14 (1978), pp. 108–25; Alan Dyer, *Decline and Growth in English Towns, 1400–1640* (1991); and, more generally, Palliser, *The Age of Elizabeth, England under the Later Tudors, 1547–1603* (1983, 1992).

5. See esp. Marjorie K. McIntosh, *Controlling Misbehaviour in England, 1370–1600* (Cambridge, 1998).

6. Clark and Slack, *Crisis and Order*, pp. 21–23; and Robert Tittler, *The Reformation and the Towns in England, c. 1540–1560* (Oxford, 1998), chs. 7–10.

7. An essay which has proven seminal to this thematic development, published in Clark's and Slack's *Crisis and Order*, is Phythian-Adams's 'Ceremony and the Citizen: The Communal Year at Coventry, 1450–1550', pp. 57–85. Following in one way or another on that foray into the religious aspects of urban political culture are such landmark works as, e.g., Patrick Collinson, *The Religion of Protestants* (1982) and *Birthpangs of Protestant England* (1988); Paul Seaver, *Wallington's World: A Puritan Artisan in Seventeenth Century London* (Stanford, 1985); Susan Brigden, *London and the Reformation* (Oxford, 1989); David Underdown, *Fire from Heaven: Life in an English Town in the Seventeenth Century* (1992); and Patrick Collinson and John Craig, *The Reformation in English Towns, 1500–1640* (1998). In the

206 Notes to Introduction

same vein, see Muriel McClendon, *The Quiet Reformation* (Stanford, 1999); and Laquita Higgs, *Godliness and Governance in Tudor Colchester* (Ann Arbor, Mich., 1998). Though more heavily concerned with religion than with the urban scene, Eamon Duffy, *The Stripping of the Altars, Traditional Religion in England, 1400–1580* (New Haven and London, 1992), still bears enormous relevance to that context.

8. Again, Phythian-Adams's 'Ceremony and the Citizen' serves as something of a landmark work, along with Mervyn James, 'Ritual, Drama, and Social Body in the Late Medieval English Town', *P. and P.* 98 (February 1983), pp. 3–29. Representative works of more recent vintage include David Mills, 'Chester Ceremonial: Re-Creation and Recreation in the English Medieval Town', *Urban History Yearbook* 18 (1991), pp. 1–19; and David Harris Sacks, 'Celebrating Authority in Bristol, 1475–1640', in S. Zimmerman and R. F. E. Weissman, eds., *Urban Life in the Renaissance* (Newark, Del., 1989), pp. 187–223. Recent work has benefited very considerably by the publications of the Records of Early English Drama project, whose volumes provide ample raw material for such research.

9. E.g., Victor Morgan, 'The Norwich Guildhall Portraits: Images in Context', in Andrew Moore and Charlotte Crawley, eds., *Family and Friends: A Regional Study of British Portraiture* (1992), pp. 21–30; Robert Tittler, 'Civic Portraiture and Political Culture in English Provincial Towns, c. 1560–1640', *J.B.S.* 37, no. 3 (July 1998), pp. 306–29; and Tittler, *Architecture and Power: The Town Hall and the English Urban Community* (Oxford, 1991).

10. Alan Dyer, 'English Town Chronicles', *Local Historian* 12, no. 6 (1977), pp. 285–91; Peter Clark, 'Visions of the Urban Community: Antiquarians and the English City before 1800', in D. Fraser and A. Sutcliffe, eds., *The Pursuit of Urban History* (1983), pp. 105–24; Daniel Woolf, 'Genre into Artefact: The Decline of the English Chronicle in the Sixteenth Century', *Sixteenth Century Journal* 19, no. 3 (fall 1988), pp. 321–54; Woolf, '"The Common Voice": History, Folklore and Oral Tradition in Early Modern England', *P. and P.* 120 (August 1988), pp. 26–52; and Lawrence Manley, *Literature and Culture in Early Modern London* (Cambridge, 1995).

11. E.g., McIntosh's *Controlling Misbehaviour*, which, though not devoted exclusively to the urban scene, certainly sees a continuity in her titular subject over the putative medieval/early modern divide.

12. E.g., with reference to European urban history in general, Christopher Friedrichs, *The Early Modern City, 1450–1750* (1995).

13. This is emphasized especially in works like Phythian-Adams, 'Ceremony and the Citizen'; Margaret Aston, 'English Ruins and English History: The Dissolution and the Sense of the Past', *Journal of the Warburg and Courtauld Institutes* 36 (1973), pp. 231–55, and *England's Iconoclasts* (Oxford, 1988); Susan Brigden, 'Religion and Social Obligation in Early Six-

teenth Century London', *P. and P.* 103 (May 1984), pp. 67–112, and *London and the Reformation* (Oxford, 1989); Duffy, *The Stripping of the Altars.*

14. John Hatcher, *Plague, Population and the English Economy, 1348–1530* (1977), pp. 63–67, and 'Mortality in the Fifteenth Century, Some New Evidence', *Ec.H.R.*, 2d ser., 39, no. 1 (1986), pp. 19–38; B. Harvey, *Living and Dying in England, 1100–1540: The Monastic Experience* (Oxford, 1993), pp. 129, 144–45; Mark Bailey, 'Demographic Decline in Late Medieval England: Some Thoughts on Recent Research', *Ec.H.R.*, 2d ser., 49, no. 1 (February 1996), pp. 1–19. For a precise projection of population totals from 1541, see E. A. Wrigley and R. S. Schofield, *The Population History of England, 1541–1871: A Reconstruction* (1981, 1989), Table A3.1, pp. 528–29. This projects the total population in England as a whole as growing from 2,773,851 in 1541 to 4,109,981 in 1601 and then to 5,091,725 in 1641.

15. For population decline in Boston, see p. 43 below; for Coventry, see Charles Phythian-Adams, *Desolation of a City: Coventry and the Urban Crisis of the Late Middle Ages* (Cambridge, 1979), pp. 35–38, 64–66, 300–305, *passim*; for York, see Chris Galley, *The Demography of Early Modern Towns: York in the Sixteenth and Seventeenth Centuries* (Liverpool, 1998), pp. 33, *passim*; and Dyer, *Decline and Growth*, pp. 18–19; for Leicester, which claimed 235 decayed houses as late as 1587, see *V. C. H., Leicester* 4 (1959), pp. 63–64, and Mary Bateson, ed., *Records of the Borough of Leicester* 2 (Cambridge, 1905), p. 239. In general, see the list of towns with populations estimated to be in decline over the period 1377–1525 provided in Dyer, *Decline and Growth*, Appendix 3.

16. The question of whether early modern towns always had a 'natural' decrease in population—an excess of deaths over births—so that growth came only through net migration has vexed historical demographers for some time. The most recent contribution to this debate points to periods of natural population growth in the sixteenth century in such towns as Ipswich, Colchester, and Reading. See Allan Sharlin, 'Natural Decrease in Early Modern Cities: A Reconsideration', *P. and P.* 79 (1978), pp. 126–38; R. Finlay, 'Natural Decrease in Early Modern Cities', *P. and P.* 92 (1981), pp. 169–74; and, most recently, Galley, *The Demography of Early Modern Towns*, esp. pp. 18–19.

17. Aptly summarized in Dyer, *Decline and Growth*, pp. 9–10.

18. Donald Woodward, *Men at Work, Labourers and Building Craftsmen in the Towns of Northern England, 1450–1750* (Cambridge, 1995), p. 97; Paul Slack, *Poverty and Policy in Tudor and Stuart England* (1988), esp. ch. 3; A. L. Beier, *Masterless Men: The Vagrancy Problem in Tudor and Stuart England 1560–1640* (1985); and Peter Clark, 'The Migrant in Kentish Towns, 1580–1640', in Clark and Slack, *Crisis and Order*, pp. 117–63 and esp. p. 141. The fact that reports of vagrancy to local courts declined in these years seems more a reflection of the judicial level at which such cases were handled

than any decline in vagrancy itself. See McIntosh, *Controlling Misbehaviour*, pp. 88–89.

19. Galley, *The Demography of Early Modern Towns*, p. 33; Ronald M. Berger, *The Most Necessary Luxuries: The Mercer's Company of Coventry, 1550–1680* (University Park, Penn., 1993), pp. 69–72; Phythian-Adams, *Desolation of a City*, pp. 48–49; Dyer, *Decline and Growth*, pp. 20–21.

20. R. B. Wernham, *Before the Armada: The Emergence of the English Nation, 1485–1588* (1966), pp. 189–91; G. D. Ramsay, *The Queen's Merchants and the Revolt of the Netherlands* (Manchester, 1986), passim.

21. Sarah Rees Jones, 'Property, Tenure and Rents: Some Aspects of the Topography and Economy of Medieval York', Ph.D. diss., University of York, 1987, pp. 289–90. See also Colin Platt, *The English Medieval Town* (1976), p. 182; Stanford E. Lehmberg, *The Reformation of the Cathedrals: Cathedrals in English Society, 1485–1603* (Princeton, 1988), pp. 172–76.

22. The following is largely based on Robert Tittler, '"For the Re-edification of Townes": The Rebuilding Statutes of Henry VIII', *Albion* 22, no. 4 (winter 1990), pp. 591–605. In most respects it should be taken to supersede the more cautious and speculative discussion in Dyer, *Decline and Growth*, pp. 34–39, which, though published later, did not take account of the former work.

23. 26 Henry VIII, c. 8, 'An Act for the re-edifyinge of voyde groundes in the Citie of Norwich'; and 26 Henry VIII, c. 9, an act to the very same effect for the borough of King's Lynn. While the titles of several statutes going back to the 1470s also implied a concern for housing, these turn out to be more concerned with abandonment of farm buildings and agrarian dwellings than with urban housing; Tittler, 'For the "Re-edification of Townes"', p. 593.

24. 27 Henry VIII, c. 1, 'An Acte for Re-edifying of Diverse Towns in the Realm', listing seven towns; 32 Henry VIII, c. 18, 'An Act for the Re-Edification of Towns', listing thirty-six towns; 32 Henry VIII, c. 19, 'An Act for Re-edifying Townes Westward', listing twenty-one towns; 33 Henry VIII, c. 36, 'For the Repayringe of Canterbury, Stamford and Diverse other Townes', listing nine towns by name and all others under the jurisdiction of the Cinque Ports; and 33 Henry VIII, c. 4, 'An Acte Touchinge the Repayringe and Amendinge of Certyain decayed Houses', listing an additional twenty-five towns in England and Wales.

25. Tittler, 'For the "Re-edification of Townes"', pp. 601–3.

26. Wrigley and Schofield, *The Population History of England*, p. 402, and Figure 10.1, p. 403.

27. Ibid., pp. 638–42, and Table A9.2: 'A Real-Wage Index for England, 1500–1912'. Taking the year 1500 as the index base line of 1000, real wage levels fell by a third (to 663) by 1540–41, and by more than half (to an index figure of 451) by 1640–41. Real wage index levels were especially low

in the crisis decades of the 1550s (reaching a low of 371 in 1556–57) and the 1590s (an even lower level of 292 in 1596–97), though there were obvious recovery periods between those points.

28.   Alan Everitt, 'The Marketing of Agricultural Produce', in Joan Thirsk, ed., *The Agrarian History of England and Wales, 1500–1640* (Cambridge, 1967), pp. 502–6.

29.   Dyer, *Decline and Growth*, p. 46.

30.   McIntosh, *Controlling Misbehaviour*, passim.

31.   These are, in fact, two of the defining characteristics of urban society. For the others, see below, p. 19, and also the slightly different definitions provided in Clark and Slack, *Crisis and Order*, p. 4.

32.   Margaret Aston, 'English Ruins and English History: The Dissolution and the Sense of the Past', and *England's Iconoclasm: Laws against Images* (Oxford, 1988).

33.   Brigden, 'Religion and Social Obligation', p. 71. There were, of course, exceptions to this desired result. In practice, some such observances sometimes divided rather than bound members of the community. See Andrew D. Brown, *Popular Piety in Late Medieval England: The Diocese of Salisbury, 1250–1550* (Oxford, 1995), ch. 9. My thanks to Paul Seaver for bringing this to my attention.

34.   The vast literature on this includes the following: Phythian-Adams, 'Ceremony and the Citizen'; James, 'Ritual, Drama, and Social Body'; Susan Brigden, 'Religion and Social Obligation in Early Sixteenth Century London'; Duffy, *The Stripping of the Altars*, pt. 1; Ronald Hutton, *The Rise and Fall of Merry England: The Ritual Year 1400–1700* (Oxford, 1994), chs. 1–3, and *The Stations of the Sun: A History of the Ritual Year in Britain* (Oxford, 1996); David Harris Sacks, 'The Demise of the Martyrs: The Feasts of St. Clement and St. Katherine in Bristol, 1400–1600, *Social History* 11 (1986), pp. 141–69, and 'Celebrating Authority in Bristol, 1475–1640', in Susan Zimmerman and R. F. E. Weissman, eds., *Urban Life in the Renaissance* (Newark, Del., 1987), pp. 187–223; Muriel C. McClendon, 'A Moveable Feast: Saint George's Day Celebrations and Religious Change in Early Modern England', *J.B.S.* 38 (January 1999), pp. 1–27.

35.   Pierre Nora, 'Between Memory and History: *Les Lieux de Memoire'*, *Representations* 26 (spring 1989), pp. 7–25.

36.   Collinson, *Birthpangs of Protestant England*, p. ix.

37.   Underdown, *Fire from Heaven*, passim.

38.   McIntosh, *Controlling Misbehaviour*, passim.

39.   This has been argued especially in Margo Todd, *Christian Humanism and the Puritan Social Order* (Cambridge, 1987), ch. 5; and in Margaret Spufford, 'Puritanism and Social Control?' in Anthony Fletcher and John Stevenson, eds., *Order and Disorder in Early Modern England* (Cambridge, 1985), pp. 41–57, and has been held up to critical scrutiny in Paul Slack,

From Reformation to Improvement: Public Welfare in Early Modern England (Oxford, 1999), pp. 36–37.

40. See Chapter 6, below, and also Slack, *From Reformation to Improvement*, pp. 44–45.

41. These themes are developed at length in Tittler, *Architecture and Power*, esp. chap. 6; Tittler, *Reformation and the Towns*, chs. 11–14; and Tittler, 'Civic Portraiture and Political Culture'.

42. The phrase is Clark's and Slack's, *Crisis and Order*, p. 22.

43. This is loosely based on the definition given in Clark and Slack, *English Towns in Transition*, p. 5.

44. As almost all marketing centers were also 'towns' in our sense of the term, an approximate listing may be extrapolated from the list of markets in Everitt, 'The Marketing of Agricultural Produce', pp. 467–75. The populations of many of these have been compiled in Peter Clark and Jean Hosking, *Population Estimates of English Small Towns, 1550–1851* (rev. ed., Leicester, 1993).

45. A. E. Wrigley estimates that only ten towns had a population of five thousand or more c. 1520, but that this number doubled by c. 1600. Wrigley, 'Urban Growth and Agricultural Change: England and the Continent in the Early Modern Period', in R. Rotberg and T. K. Rabb, eds., *Population and Economy: Population and History from the Traditional to the Modern World* (Cambridge, 1986), pp. 126–27.

46. Wilfred Prest, *The Rise of the Barristers: A Social History of the English Bar, 1590–1640* (Oxford, 1986), pp. 142–43, 240–52; Tittler, *Reformation and the Towns*, pp. 223–29.

47. Calculated as ninety-seven statutes between 1509 and 1603 in Tittler, *The Reformation and the Towns*, p. 240, based on *Statutes of the Realm*, ed. A. Luders, T. E. Tomlins, and J. Raithby (11 vols., 1810–28), passim. The vast majority of these statutes came forth after 1536.

48. Tittler, *Reformation and the Towns*, ch. 5; and in Slack, *From Reformation to Improvement*, esp. ch. 1.

49. Bristol in 1373 and 1499; Norwich, 1404 and 1417; Newcastle, 1400 and 1589; and York, 1396 and 1607. Martin Weinbaum, *British Borough Charters, 1307–1660* (Cambridge, 1943), 'Analytical Index', pp. xxix–lv.

50. Wallace T. MacCaffrey, *Exeter, 1540–1640* (2d ed., Cambridge, Mass., 1975), p. 26.

51. Calculated in Tittler, *Reformation and the Towns*, p. 188, and Table 1, pp. 345–47.

52. Discussed in D. J. Lamburn, 'Politics and Religion in Sixteenth Century Beverley', Ph.D. diss., York University, 1991, p. 261.

53. Michael Faraday, *Ludlow, 1085–1660: A Social, Economic and Political History* (Chichester, 1991), pp. 25–36; Penry Williams, 'Government

and Politics in Ludlow, 1590–1642', *Transactions of the Shropshire Archaeological Society* 56 (1957–60), pp. 284–88.

54. Abingdon Corporation Order Book, Berkshire County Record Office MS. D/EP 7/84, fol. 20d.

55. Public Record Office (P.R.O.), STAC 5/23/37.

56. P.R.O., STAC 5/21/6; J. C. Roberts, 'The Parliamentary Representation of Devon and Dorset, 1559–1601', Master's thesis, London University, 1958, pp. 217–30.

57. Perhaps the best guide to the jurisdictions of London government is now to be found in Joseph P. Ward, *Metropolitan Communities: Trade Guilds, Identity, and Change in Early Modern London* (Stanford, Calif., 1997), ch. 1. See also Vanessa Harding, 'The Population of London, 1550–1700: A Review of the Published Evidence', *London Journal* 15 (1990), pp. 111–28; V. Pearl, *London and the Outbreak of the Puritan Revolution: City Government and National Politics* (Oxford, 1961), ch. 2; and Ian Archer, *The Pursuit of Stability: Social Relations in Elizabethan London* (Cambridge, 1991), ch. 2.

58. Vanessa Harding estimates these figures in a careful examination of published evidence to 1990; Harding, 'The Population of London', pp. 111–28, esp. Table 1.

59. A. L. Beier and Roger Finley, eds., *London: The Making of the Metropolis, 1500–1700* (London and New York, 1986), Figure 1, p. 3.

60. Clark and Slack estimated that between c. 1520 and 1603 Norwich grew from 12,000 to 15,000; Bristol from 10,000 to 12,000; York from 8,000 to 11,000; and Exeter from 8,000 to 9,000; while Salisbury (8,000 to 7,000) and Coventry (6,601 to 6,500) actually declined. Galley revises the 1600 figure for York to 12,000, while the other figures remain roughly accurate. Clark and Slack, *English Towns in Transition*, Table 1, p. 83; Galley, *The Demography of Early Modern Towns*, Table 1 1, p. 5.

61. See, for example, the commentary on London's being 'fouly bell'd with faithless husbands' in the ballad entitled 'An Amorrous Dialogue between John and his Mistress' (1572–76) in John S. Farmer, ed., *National Ballad and Song: Merry Songs and Ballads Prior to the Year AD 1800* (5 vols., London, 1897), vol. 2, pp. 65–69.

62. Ward, *Metropolitan Communities*, pp. 17–18.

63. Michael J. Power, 'The Urban Development of East London', Ph.D. diss., London University, 1971, passim.

64. John Stow, *A Survey of London* (1603 ed.), ed. C. L. Kingsford (2 vols., Oxford, 1908), vol. 1, p. 126.

65. Ibid., pp. 126–27.

66. Pearl, *London and the Outbreak*; Rappaport, *Worlds within Worlds: Structures of Life in Sixteenth Century London* (Cambridge, 1989); Archer, *Pursuit of Stability*; Ward, *Metropolitan Communities*, esp. chs. 1–2.

67. The phrase is Steve Rappaport's, *Worlds within Worlds: Structures of Life in Sixteenth Century London* (Cambridge, 1989).

Chapter 1: John Browne

1. The term has been prominently employed in Platt, *The English Medieval Town* (1976), p. 181.

2. W. G. Hoskins, 'English Provincial Towns in the Early Sixteenth Century', *Transactions of the Royal Historical Society*, 5th ser., 6 (1956), pp. 11–12. The point has been echoed in D. M. Palliser, *Tudor York* (Oxford, 1979), p. 265; and in Platt, *The English Medieval Town*, pp. 182–83.

3. The point is discussed at greater length in Tittler, *The Reformation and the Towns*, ch. 6.

4. W. G. Hoskins, *Local History in England* (1974), p. 176. Steven Rigby has preferred the even more impressive ranking of fifth, assigned by R. E. Glasscock in 1976; see Rigby, 'Boston and Grimsby in the Middle Ages: An Administrative Contrast', *Journal of Medieval History* 10, no. 1 (March 1984), p. 51; and Glasscock, 'England circa 1334', in H. C. Darby, ed., *A New Historical Geography of England before 1600* (Cambridge, 1976), p. 184.

5. The best summary of these two themes is Rigby, 'Boston and Grimsby', passim.

6. S. H. Rigby, '"Sore Decay" and "Fair Dwellings": Boston and Urban Decline in the Later Middle Ages', *Midland History* 10 (1985), esp. pp. 48–54.

7. Rigby, 'Boston and Urban Decline', p. 55, gives a higher figure, but Peter and Jennifer Clark, eds., *The Boston Assembly Minutes, 1545–1575* (Lincolnshire Record Society, 1987), p. x, offer a more reliable estimate based on a 1563 household survey yielding 471 households and reckoning 4.5 people per household.

8. Thirsk, *The Agrarian History of England and Wales*, pp. 32–33, 474. Customs records show that in the mid-sixteenth century Boston shipped substantial quantities of wool and lambskins, calfskins and cowhides (both showing the stock-rearing potential of the fens north of Boston); both hemp and rope (indicating a flourishing new industry); and coals trans-shipped from Newcastle en route to London.

9. Testimony regarding this local disaster may be found in the Defendants' Answer in the case of *Browne* vs. *Roberts and Wendon*, P.R.O., STAC 3/8/18.

10. Summarized in Rigby, 'Boston and Grimsby', pp. 57–60. See also *Huntwicke et al.* vs. *The Lord Mayor of London*, P.R.O., C1/1235/57; John F. Bailey, ed., *Transcriptions of the Minutes of the Corporation of Boston* (3 vols., Boston, 1980–83), pp. 113–14, 184, 193, 205, 209, 563, 564, 578, 598, passim.

11. See, for example, incidents of riot and similar behaviour described

in lawsuits earlier in the reign of Henry VIII: e.g., P.R.O., STAC 2/ 20/ 77 (c. 1529) etc.

12. *Letters and Papers*, 20, no. 1, p. 418.

13. Only the charge to the Commissioners by the Court of Requests to investigate the issue has survived. P.R.O., Req. 2/16/19 [1548].

14. *Letters and Papers* 20, no. 1, p. 418.

15. Ibid., pp. 424–26.

16. P.R.O., STAC 3/5/11 and STAC 3/8/18 (1547); G. A. J. Hodgett, 'The Dissolution of the Religious Houses in Lincolnshire . . .', *Lincolnshire Architectural and Archaeological Society* 4 (1951), pp. 83–99.

17. C.P.R., *Edward VI*, 4, p. 235; grant of 30 January, 1552.

18. Bailey, *Minutes of Boston*, pp. 9–13.

19. P.R.O., PROB 11/64/35.

20. A Patent Roll entry of 1559 lists him as 'John Browne . . . of Boston, . . . *alias* late of Brothertofte'; C.P.R., *Eliz.*, vol. 1, p. 161.

21. He is almost certainly the John Browne of West Deeping who received a share of lands in Boston by a patent of 1545: his earliest known acquisition. *Letters and Papers of Henry VIII*, 20, pt. 1, p. 418.

22. A John Browne of Lincolnshire had been admitted for legal training to Gray's Inn in 1548, though this is late for someone already engaged in litigation in 1547. Yet, as we will see, Browne was eventually employed as an attorney for the Borough and obviously knew a lot about the law. Joseph Foster, ed., *Register of Admissions to Gray's Inn, 1521–1889* (1889), p. 20.

23. This accusation is made in the Defendant's Response in the case of *Browne v. Roberts and Wendon*, c. 1547, P.R.O., STAC 3/Bundle 8/18. Browne did not deny it.

24. The precise relationship is not clear, though the two do not seem to be father and son and, judging by the considerable span of time between their deaths, there was probably a substantial age gap between them. They were most likely uncle and nephew. Thomas is mentioned as being a JP in the defendants' answer in the case of *Browne v. Roberts and Wendon*, P.R.O., STAC 3/bundle 8/18.

25. P.R.O., PROB 11/39/41.

26. P.R.O., STAC 3/Bundle 5/11, esp. plaintiff's certificate and the (sealed) Certificate of Commission directed to seven commissioners.

27. P.R.O., STAC 2/20/77, c. 1529.

28. Indenture of Gift from John Margery, Alderman of the Guild of St. Mary, to Nicholas Robertson, Mayor of Boston, and the burgesses thereof, 12 July, 1545; Boston Borough Archives, Lincolnshire Archives Office MS. 4.A.1.1/1; Bailey, *Minutes of Boston*, p. 2.

29. Browne writes of the Father, the Son, and the Holy Ghost, in whose name he had been baptized, and of his hope for redemption

through the death and passion of the Son of God. P.R.O., PROB 11/64/35, 2 October, 1578.

30. Bailey, *Minutes of Boston*, pp. xxi–ii.

31. P.R.O., STAC 3/Bundle 8/18.

32. The Lordship of the Honour of Richmond reverted to the Crown on the death of the last incumbent, Henry Fitzroy, in 1536.

33. P.R.O., S.P. 10/15/52, 27 November, 1552.

34. Bailey, *Minutes of Boston*, p. 18.

35. Ibid., p. 19.

36. The mature form of this legislation is expressed in the statutes 27 Henry VIII, c. 1 (1536); 32 Henry VIII, c. 18 (1540); 32 Henry VIII, c. 19 (1540); 33 Henry VIII, c. 36 (1542); 35 Henry VIII, c. 4 (1544). For a general discussion, see Tittler, 'For the "Re-edification of Townes"', pp. 591–605.

37. This was the property known as Tyle Green in the Skirbeck suburb; Bailey, *Minutes of Boston*, p. 23.

38. Bailey, *Minutes of Boston*, pp. 25–26 (14 and 20 January, 1556).

39. Ibid., pp. 28, 31, 32.

40. The mayor in question was William Wesenam, against whom Browne brought suit over conveyance of a pasture in the Court of Chancery at about the same time; P.R.O., C3/26/40.

41. C. W. Foster, ed., *Lincoln Episcopal Records in the Time of Thomas Cooper, Bishop of Lincoln, AD 1571–AD 1584* (Lincolnshire Record Society, 1912), vol. 2, p. 247.

42. Bailey, *Minutes of Boston*, pp. 233–34.

Chapter 2: John Pitt

1. Slack, *From Reformation to Improvement*, p. 71 and n. 71.

2. Tittler, 'For the "Re-edification of Townes"', pp. 591–605.

3. Tittler, *Architecture and Power*, pp. 10–17, and 'Late Medieval Urban Prosperity', *Ec.H.R.* 37, no. 4 (November 1984), pp. 553–54.

4. Calculated from Weinbaum, *British Borough Charters*, pp. xxix–lv.

5. Tittler, *Architecture and Power*, esp. ch. 2.

6. Ibid., ch. 3.

7. Martin C. Brown, 'Blandford in Elizabethan and Early Stuart Times', *Notes and Queries for Somerset and Dorset* 30 (1975), pp. 118–19.

8. E. L. Jones, S. Porter, and M. Turner, eds., *A Gazetteer of Urban Fire Disasters, 1500–1900*, Historical Geography Research Series 13 (Norwich, 1984), Table 3.

9. Wrigley and Schofield, *The Population History of England*, Table A3.1, p. 528.

10. Based on the Blandford Forum Chamberlain's Accounts, 1564–

1750, Dorset County Record Office MS. DC/BFB, passim. Hereafter referred to as Blandford, 'Accounts'.

11. Everitt, 'The Marketing of Agricultural Produce', pp. 4, 67–68, 470–71.

12. John Hutchins, *History and Antiquities of the County of Dorset* (2 vols., 1774), vol. 1, p. 75.

13. Everitt, 'The Marketing of Agricultural Produce', pp. 590–91.

14. Noted in Hutchins, *History of Dorset*, vol. 1, p. 78.

15. Based on an extensive analysis of Port Books for all the Dorset ports from 1565 to 1640, classed as E.190 in the Public Record Office. Some of this analysis is discussed and documented in Tittler, 'The Vitality of an Elizabethan Port: The Economy of Poole, c. 1500–1600', *Southern History* 7 (1985), pp. 95–118, and esp. Tables A-C.

16. Everitt, 'The Marketing of Agricultural Produce', p. 484.

17. K. J. Penn, *Historic Towns in Dorset*, Dorset Natural History and Archaeological Society Monograph Series, vol. 1 (Dorchester, 1980), p. 19; Hutchins, *History of Dorset*, vol. 1, pp. 75–78; Weinbaum, *British Borough Charters*, p. xxxii.

18. No text of the charter is known, but Hutchins summarizes the main points; Hutchins, *History of Dorset*, vol. 1, p. 78.

19. Penn, *Historic Towns in Dorset*, pp. 19–??; Hutchins, *History of Dorset*, vol. 1, pp. 78–81.

20. Blandford, 'Accounts'. These comprise the single surviving volume of Blandford's Chamberlains' Accounts, retrieved from loose papers in the Blandford Guildhall and bound in the seventeenth century, and now housed in the Dorset Record Office. Nearly all the other records of the town have been destroyed in one of the four destructive fires experienced in this particularly incendiary community between 1579 and 1731.

21. Ibid., fol. 11v.

22. John's will was dated 28 September, 1601, and was proven in February 1602. Family Records Centre, London, PROB 11/99/19. See also G. D. Squibb, ed., *The Visitation of Dorset, 1677* (London, 1977), pp. 55–56.

23. P.R.O., STAC 5/82/36 (undated).

24. C.P.R., *Elizabeth* IV (1566–69), item no. 1400; Blandford, 'Accounts', fols. 6r.

25. P.R.O., E.190/865/1; E.190/865/4; E.190/867/3; E.190/867/14; and E.190/867/16.

26. PROB 11/99/19; and T. L. Stoate, ed., *Dorset Tudor Subsidies Granted in 1523, 1543 and 1593* (Bristol, 1982), p. 9.

27. Hutchins, *History of Dorset*, vol. 1, p. 80.

28. Blandford, 'Accounts', fol. 2r, 7r, 9r; 4r–5r of 'reverse pagination'.

29. Ibid., fol. 9r; *R.E.E.D., Dorset*, Rosalind C. Hays and C. E. McGee, eds. (Toronto, 1999), p. 331.

30. Blandford, 'Accounts', fol. 7v.

31. Ibid., fol. 10r.

32. Ibid., fols. 1–5, reverse pagination.

33. For example, in renovating the old hall in 1583, Pitt and several others took turns feeding the labourers, and this sort of thing must have been done again on the new hall; ibid., fol. 7r.

34. See Tittler, *Architecture and Power*, Table 3, p. 52.

35. Bridport Borough Archives, Dorset Record Office MS. SC/BTB/M15/11, 1592–93.

36. Tittler, *Architecture and Power*, pp. 54–55.

37. Kevin Grady, 'The Provision of Public Buildings in the West Riding of Yorkshire, 1600–1840', Ph.D. diss., Leeds University, 1980, pp. 159–60; H. M. Colvin, *A History of Deddington, Oxfordshire* (1963), p. 6.

38. See the possibilities of terminology as discussed in Tittler, *Architecture and Power*, pp. 6–9.

39. 'A Plan of the Town of Blandford', drawn after the devastating fire of 1731 by the Surveyors of the Rebuilding, shows the layout of the town before that latest conflagration. The new plan of the marketplace cleared the site entirely, moving the hall to its present location, in the regular line of buildings facing south onto the marketplace rather than standing alone in it. This is reprinted in Royal Commission on Historical Monuments (England), *An Inventory of Historical Monuments in the County of Dorset*, vol. 3, *Central Dorset*, pt. 1 (1970), Plates 104 and 106 [hereafter referred to as *HM Central Dorset*]. See also the description in Hutchins, *History of Dorset* vol. 1, p. 78.

40. Royal Commission on Historical Monuments, *HM Central Dorset*, pt. 1, Plate 114.

41. Near contemporary examples from central Dorset include the Parish Church at Puddlehinton (fifteenth to sixteenth century); Sir Thomas Freke's Chapel at Melcombe Horsey (early seventeenth century); and the Manor House of Winterbourne Clenston (late sixteenth to early seventeenth century); Royal Commission on Historical Monuments, *HM Central Dorset*, pt. 2, Plates 184, 159, and 213.

42. The same combination of hillingstones and other roofing materials may be seen in 'The Old House' at Blandford (employing dating to about 1660) and other contemporary buildings in the area: e.g., the roof of Waterston House, Puddletown (1586). Royal Commission on Historical Monuments, *HM Central Dorset*, pt. 1 Plate 110, p. 26, and pt. 2, Plate 190, p. 226. The wall-stone came from Melbury, eight miles north of Blandford, which is known to have had quarries of Jurassic limestones that passed for marble. Yet there is no indication of any stone-working industry on site in Blandford which would have achieved a marble effect by polishing the surface. It remains hard to imagine that Blandford's tightly

stretched building budget could support such work. Alec Clifton-Taylor, *The Pattern of English Building* (1972), pp. 103; 184, n. 3.

43. For a discussion of the two basic types of town hall, see Tittler, *Architecture and Power*, pp. 25–32.

44. My thanks to Derek Keene, Steven Poole, and Darleen Wilson for their thoughts on this term.

45. *V.C.H., Gloucestershire* 11 (1976), p. 59.

46. For a fuller discussion of the incorporation of incarceratory or punitive facilities in civic halls, see Tittler, *Architecture and Power*, pp. 122–27.

47. Ibid., pp. 136–38, and n. 21, p. 138.

48. Tom Tribe and Philip Whatmoor, *Dorset Clocks and Clockmakers* (Oswestry, 1981), pp. 18–19. The first clockmaker mentioned in any Dorset records examined in this source was recorded in 1625; ibid., p. 21.

49. Hutchins, *History of Dorset*, vol. 1, p. 78.

50. See, for example, Jacques LeGoff, 'Au Moyen Age: Temps de l'eglise au temps du marchand', *Annales, SEC* (1960), pp. 417–33; S. De-Grazia, *Of Time, Work and Leisure* (New York, 1962); E. P. Thompson, 'Time, Work Discipline and Industrial Capitalism', *P. and P.* 38 (1967), pp. 56–98; and Gerald Moran, 'Conceptions of Time in Early Modern France: An Approach to the History of Collective Mentalities', *Sixteenth Century Journal* 24, no. 4 (1981), pp. 3–19.

51. Surrey County Record Office, MS. 2253/1/1. The spelling has been modernized.

52. Tribe and Whatmoor, *Dorset Clocks*, 38.

53. On the reception of Renaissance neo-classicism in England prior to Jones's work, see the collected essays in Lucy Gent, ed., *Albion's Classicism: The Visual Arts in Britain, 1550–1660* (New Haven and London, 1995).

54. *HM, Central Dorset*, pt. 2, Plate 190, p. 226.

55. Summarized in Tittler, 'The Building of Civic Halls in Dorset, c. 1560–1640', *Bulletin of the Institute of Historical Research* 58, no. 137 (May 1985), pp. 37–45.

56. Tittler, *Architecture and Power*, passim.

57. Hutchins, *History of Dorset*, vol. 1, p. 78.

58. PROB 11/99/19.

59. Hutchins, *History of Dorset*, vol. 1, p. 76.

Chapter 3: John and Joan Cooke

1. 'John and Joan Cooke'. Oil on panel, 32 x 29 3/4 inches. It is noted and reproduced in the catalogue, ed. by Brian Frith, for the exhibit entitled 'Twelve Portraits of Gloucester Benefactors', held at the Folk Life and Regimental Museum, Gloucester, 1972. It hung until 1892 in the Council Chamber of the old Tolsey, or guildhall, in Gloucester, and has hung since

in various local repositories before coming to rest in the Gloucester City Art Gallery.

2. Lawrence Stone, *The Crisis of the Aristocracy, 1558–1641* (Oxford, 1965), p. 712.

3. He reveals the place of his birth in his will, which was proven in 1528, and his approximate birth-date has been inferred from the known dates at which he came to various offices in the City. Family Record Centre, London, PROB 11/22/38.

4. Frith, *Twelve Portraits of Gloucester Benefactors* (Gloucester 1972), p. 9.

5. Martin Weinbaum, *British Borough Charters*, p. xxxviii.

6. John Arlott, ed., *John Speed's England, a Coloured Facsimile of the Maps and Text from the Theatre of the Empire of Greate Britaine, first edition, 1611* (1953), pt. 1, fols. 15–16.

7. M. D. Lobel, ed., *Historic Towns*, vol. 1, 'Gloucester' (Baltimore, n.d.), pp. 14 ff.

8. Ibid., p. 10.

9. Family Records Centre, PROB 11/22/38.

10. Ibid., PROB 11/31/4, 1 May, 36 Henry VIII.

11. W. K. Jordan, *Philanthropy in England, 1480–1660* (1959), Table 1, p. 368.

12. I am indebted to Dr. Joanna Woodall, Lecturer in Seventeenth Century Netherlandish Art at the Courtauld Institute, for these insights.

13. See Frith, *Twelve Portraits*, pp. 7, 10. The work seems almost certainly to have been commissioned by the City of Gloucester, most probably at about the same time as the other eleven 'Benefactors' portraits to which it bears strong stylistic resemblance.

14. The question of the likeness is raised and discussed by Frith, *Twelve Portraits*, p. 10.

15. Gloucester Borough Archives, Gloucester County Record Office MS. GBR B3/1, fol. 188v; Maureen Stanford, ed., *Ordinances of Bristol, 1506–1598* (Bristol Record Society Publications, vol. 61, 1990), p. 97.

16. John Earle, *Microcosmography, or a Piece of the World Discovered in Essays and Characters* (1628), ed. Edward Arber (1895), pp. 26–27.

17. Gary Shaw, *The Creation of a Community: The City of Wells in the Middle Ages* (Oxford, 1993), pp. 157, 198–99. I am grateful to Dr. Shaw for sharing his views on this with me.

18. W. S. Beck, *Gloves: Their Annals and Associations, a Chapter of Trade and Social History* (London, 1883; reprint, Detroit, 1969), pp. 189–97; R. Stewart-Brown, 'Notes on the Chester Hand or Glove', *Journal of the Architectural, Archaeological and Historic* (sic) *Society for Chester and North Wales*, n.s. 20 (1914), pp. 122–47; Totnes Borough Archives, Devon County Record Office, Exeter, MS. 1579/A/7/3; Joseph B. Gribble, ed., *Memorials*

of Barnstaple: A History of that Ancient Borough (Barnstaple, 1830), p. 292.

19. David Cressy, *Birth, Marriage and Death: Ritual, Religion, and the Life-Cycle in Tudor and Stuart England* (Oxford, 1997), pp. 263–66; Beck, *Gloves*, pp. 198–201. I am grateful to my colleague Dr. Shannon McSheffrey for confirming this usage in the late medieval period.

20. See, for example, Peter Clark, '"The Ramoth Gilead of the Good", Urban Change and Political Radicalism at Gloucester, 1540–1640', in Clark, A. G. R. Smith, and N. Tyacke, eds., *The English Commonwealth, 1547–1640* (Leicester, 1979), pp. 167–88.

21. This theme is pursued at greater length in Manley, *Literature and Culture*, esp. p. 15.

22. See, for example, Tittler, *Architecture and Power*.

23. See Tittler, *The Reformation and the Towns*, ch. 13, 'Corporate Rule and the Civic Memory'.

24. See esp. Collinson, *The Religion of Protestants*, ch. 4, and *Birthpangs of Protestant England*, ch. 2; Underdown, *Fire from Heaven*.

25. It is not absolutely clear what church this may be. The will speaks of burial in the Church of the Blessed Lady of the Cross on South Street. Even if we presume that 'South Street' meant 'South Gate Street', there does not seem to have been any such church. In fact, both Cookes are buried at St. Mary de Crypt, on South Gate Street, and one must infer that the Blessed Lady of the Cross was, of course, an alternate name for St. Mary. The alabaster table, a common bequest by wealthy parishioners prior to the Reformation, was earmarked for 'Christ Church', though that, too, is unidentified in the standard reconstruction of Gloucester's medieval street plan. Assuming that this lifelong resident of the area in and around Gloucester would have not so endowed Christchurch Cathedral, Canterbury, it, too, must be an alternate designation for one of the local churches. Family Record Centre, PROB. 11/22/38; Lobel, *Historic Towns*, vol. 1, 'Gloucester', pp. 14 ff.

26. See the complete list in Tittler, 'Civic Portraiture and Political Culture', Appendix, pp. 326–29.

27. Evidence has emerged only of one other double portrait of a civic worthy and his wife from this era. The Exeter City Council agreed in 1606 to pay for the portrait of Laurence Seldon and his wife 'to be sett upp in the Councell Cham[ber]', but the work seems not to have survived to the present day. Exeter Corporation Act Book no. 5, Devon Record Office, p. 172 (20 June, 3 James I). It is not clear if Seldon served as Mayor, but he was an important benefactor, and his wife would eventually leave a silver cup weighing fifty ounces in 1615. H. Lloyd Parry, *Exeter Guildhall and the Life Within* (1936), p. 163.

28. Virginia Tillyard, 'Civic Portraits Painted for or Donated to the Council Chamber of Norwich Guildhall before 1687 . . . ', Master's thesis,

Courtauld Institute, London University, 1978, p. 52. Percy was never a senior officer of the City, but rather a former priest who accepted the transition to the Rectory of a post-Reformation church. His was also a substantial benefactor, which earns him inclusion in our definition of civic portraiture.

29. Joan Tuckfield, Mayoress (which is to say, wife of the Mayor) and benefactress of Exeter, c. 1560, and Peter Read, soldier, benefactor and father of a mayor of Norwich, c. 1568; Lloyd Parry, *Exeter Guildhall*, p. 153; Tillyard, 'Civic Portraits', p. 45.

30. Joan Popley, d. 1572, benefactress of the City of Salisbury; Charles Haskins, *The Salisbury Corporation Pictures and Plate* (Salisbury, 1910), pp. 142–45.

31. An anonymous alderman of Bristol, painted in 1583 at 'aet. 62'; Richard Quick, ed., *Catalogue of the Second Loan Collection of Pictures . . . Held in the Bristol Art Gallery, 1905* (Bristol, 1905), no. 227.

32. Frith, *Twelve Portraits*, p. 5.

33. B. Cozens-Hardy and E. A. Kent, eds., *The Mayors of Norwich, 1403–1835* (Norwich, 1938), pp. 42, 48–49; Tillyard, 'Civic Portraits', pp. 21, 42–43, 45, 46; Andrew Moore and Charlotte Crawley, *Family and Friends: A Regional Survey of British Portraiture* (1992), pp. 24, 26–28, 196–97. A biographical sketch of Steward appears in S. T. Bindoff, ed., *The House of Commons, 1509–1558* (3 vols., 1982), vol. 3, pp. 383–85.

34. Margaret Statham, *Jankyn Smith and the Guildhall Feoffees* (Bury St. Edmunds, 1981), p. 3. Smith, who died in 1481, is considered the founder of the Guildhall Trust which provided the townsmen the few elements of self-rule permitted under abbatial lordship.

35. Quick, *Catalogue of Pictures*, no. 202.

36. Haskins, *Salisbury Pictures and Plate*, pp. 9–12.

37. See note 27, above.

Chapter 4: Sir Thomas White of London

1. Keith Wrightson, *English Society, 1580–1680* (1982), pp. 27–31; Richard Grassby, *The Business Community of Seventeenth Century England* (Cambridge, 1995), pp. 29–36.

2. Manley, *Literature and Culture*, ch. 2. See also John McVeagh, *Tradefull Merchants: The Portrayal of the Capitalist in Literature* (1981); and Alexander Leggatt, *Citizen Comedy in the Age of Shakespeare* (Toronto, 1973). I take the term 'merchant' in its broadest sense to include merchants, craftsmen, and others of the freemanry.

3. Laura Stevenson O'Connell, 'Anti-Entrepreneurial Attitudes in Elizabethan Sermons and Popular Literature', *Journal of British Studies* 15 (1976), pp. 2–20; Manley, *Literature and Culture*, pp. 113–17.

4. J. P. Cooper, 'Ideals of Gentility in Early Modern England', in Cooper, *Land, Men and Beliefs: Studies in Early-Modern History*, ed. G. E. Aylmer and J. S. Morrill (1983), pp. 59, 65–66; Laura Caroline Stevenson, *Praise and Paradox: Merchants and Craftsmen in Elizabethan Popular Literature* (Cambridge, 1984), pp. 79–81; Manley, *Literature and Culture*, passim.

5. See, for example, Leggatt, *Citizen Comedy*, pp. 4, 8–10, passim. Lawrence Manley suggests the emergence of a large-scale and widely based urban literary tradition emerging during this same era; Manley, *Literature and Culture*.

6. The following paragraphs are drawn from Stevenson, *Praise and Paradox;* and, more generally, Manley, *Literature and Culture.* On usury see Norman L. Jones, *God and the Moneylenders: Usury and Law in Early Modern England* (Oxford, 1989).

7. Cf., for example, Thomas Churchyard's 'Marchaunts that sails forrain countreys, and brynges home commodities and . . . doe utter their ware with regard of conscience and profite to the publike estate'; Thomas Churchyard, *A Generall Rehearsall of Warrs* (1579) as cited in Cooper, 'Ideals of Gentility', p. 59.

8. Leggatt, *Citizen Comedy*, esp. ch. 2.

9. Collinson, *Birthpangs of Protestant England*, pp. 28–32; Collinson, *The Religion of Protestants*, passim; Underdown, *Fire from Heaven.*

10. See esp. Paul Seaver, *The Puritan Lectureships: The Politics of Religious Dissent, 1560–1662* (Stanford, 1970).

11. A merchant tailor, to give the term its modern spelling, is defined by the OED as 'A tailor who supplies the materials from which his goods are made' and also, as in White's case, as a member of the London livery company of that name. Drapers and clothiers were manufacturers of woollen clothes. The prominent Bristol merchant John Smyth referred to White on at least two occasions as a draper; J. Angus and J. Vanes, eds., *The Ledger of John Smythe, 1538–1550*, Bristol Record Society Publications, no. 28 (1974), p. 111; and J. H. Bettey, ed., *Calendar of the Smyth Family of Ashton Court, 1548–1642*, Bristol Record Society Publications, no. 35 (1982), p. 3.

12. In addition to works about him in the sixteenth and seventeenth centuries which will be cited below, formative chapters have been devoted to him in a nineteenth-century history of the Merchant Taylors' Company, of which he served as master, and in a twentieth-century history of St. John's College, Oxford, of which he was the founder; in the *Dictionary of National Biography*, and even the antiquarian biography by C. M. Clode, *The Early History of the Guild of Merchant Taylors* (2 vols., London, 1888), vol. 2, chs. 10–12; W. H. Stevenson and H. E. Salter, *The Early History of St. Johns College Oxford* (Oxford Historical Society, vol. 2, 1939);

D.N.B., see White, Sir Thomas; A. Daly Briscoe, *A Marian Lord Mayor, Sir Thomas White* (Ipswich, 1982).

13. The *D.N.B.* and some other accounts have 1492, but Stevenson and Salter present convincing evidence for 1495. *Early History of St. Johns College*, p. 385.

14. Acton died in that year; Clode, *Early History*, vol. 2, 99.

15. Ibid.

16. G. D. Ramsay, *The City of London in International Politics at the Accession of Elizabeth Tudor* (Manchester, 1975), chs. 5–6.

17. Brian McClenaghan, *The Springs of Lavenham and the Suffolk Cloth Trade in the Sixteenth and Seventeenth Centuries* (Ipswich, 1924); G. D. Ramsay, *The Wiltshire Woollen Industry in the Sixteenth and Seventeenth Centuries* (2d ed., 1965), ch. 3.

18. Clode, *Early History*, vol. 2, p. 102; Ramsay, *City of London*, p. 40.

19. Clode, *Early History*, vol. 2, p. 100.

20. Ibid., p. 108.

21. *D.N.B.*; Mark Benbow, *Index to Aldermen of London* (unpublished manuscript in the possession of the Institute of Historical Research, London; 2 vols. [1992]), vol. 2, p. 516; Clode, *Early History*, pp. 102–3.

22. In 1534. Clode, *Early History*, p. 100.

23. *C.P.R., Mary*, vol. 2, pp. 322–23; and Stevenson and Salter, *Early History of St. Johns College*, ch. 1. Connections between the college and the Merchant Taylors' Company, both of which took St. John the Baptist as their patron saint, were very firm right from the College's start.

24. Campion (1540–81) made his mark early and emphatically at St. Johns College, where he took both his BA and MA before training abroad for the Jesuit Order; Stevenson and Salter, *Early History of St. Johns College*, pp. 386–90; *D.N.B.*, see Campion.

25. Clode, *Early History*, vol. 2, pp. 119–29.

26. Clode, *Early History*, vol. 2, pp. 133–35.

27. Coventry City R.O. MS. BA/D/A/1/7 (erroneously dated as 43 rather than 34 Henry VIII, the scribe having reversed the first two digits), *Letters and Papers, Henry VIII*, 17 (1900), item 556, no. 21. The actual purchase came to £1,378 10s; almost all the purchases were former priory lands.

28. Coventry City Record Office MS. BA/D/A/1/8, fol. 1.

29. Phythian-Adams, *Desolation of a City*; Berger, *The Most Necessary Luxuries*.

30. Coventry Record Office, BA/D/A/1/8, fol. 1, 6 July, 1551; Great Britain, House of Commons, Parliamentary Papers, *Reports of the Charity Commissioners* 28 (1834), pp. 172–74; Clode, *Early History*, vol. 2, p. 103; W. K. Jordan, *The Charities of London, 1480–1660* (London, 1960), p. 174.

31. In addition, after ten years of this scheme in Coventry, the City

corporation was to extend £20 each to two additional men, or £40 in all, again on a nine-year, interest-free loan. That, too, was to extend perpetually. And in addition to that, after another thirty years had transpired, £40 would be delivered in an interest-free loan to a single young man, again for nine years, and again in perpetuity.

32. By no means were all, or even most, recipients of this scheme cloth-makers in the conventional sense. In Leicester, for example, the first set of recipients included one weaver, but also an ironmonger, a shoe-maker, and a maker of bone lace. H. Stocks and W. H. Stevenson, eds., *Records of the Borough of Leicester, 1603–1688* (Cambridge, 1923), p. 101.

33. Coventry City R.O., BA/D/A/1/8, fols. 2–14. In the operation of this scheme the Merchant Taylors proved not to have been too efficient. It took them until 1695 to notice that, while Coventry continued to make payments based on a £70 annual value of the principal lands, the actual revenue produced thereby had expanded to £800 per annum! Coventry's government had been pocketing the difference between that sum and the original yield of £70. Coventry R.O. MS. BA/D/A/1/19.

34. Coventry City Record Office MS. BA/D/A/1/4 (the date has been torn off at the top of the manuscript and is not elsewhere given). It is this scheme which W. K. Jordan has somehow confused with a bequest to the Borough of Leicester; Jordan, *Charities of London*, p. 174.

35. Coventry City Record Office MS. BA/D/A/1/4 p. 2.

36. C.P.R., *Mary*, vol. 2, pp. 322–23, 1 May, 1555.

37. Clode, *Early History*, vol. 2, pp. 163, 166, 177, 182.

38. The plan is most conveniently described in the Charity Commissioners' Report on the scheme of 1822, as related to the House of Commons in the following year. Great Britain, House of Commons, Parliamentary Papers, *Report of the Charity Commissioners* 8 (1823), pp. 585–90. It, in turn, is based on the relevant documents held in Bristol. Unless indicated to the contrary, the following description derives from that report.

39. *Letters and Papers, Henry VIII*, 19, pt. 1 (1903), item 1035, par. 79, p. 626; D. M. Livock, ed., *City Chamberlains' Accounts in the Sixteenth and Seventeenth Centuries*, Bristol Record Society Publications, vol. 24 (1966), p. xviii.

40. *Reports of the Charity Commissioners* 8 (1823), p. 585.

41. Borough audits from at least 1561 record payments for borough officials to travel to London to confer with White about this and other matters. Bristol Records Office, Little Audit Book no. 7, MS. 04026, passim.

42. *Reports of the Charity Commissioners*, pp. 585–90.

43. I have used the text reprinted in John Vowell *alias* Hooker, *The Description of the Citie of Excester*, ed. W. J. Harte, J. W. Schopp, and H. Tapley-Soper (Devon and Cornwall Record Society, 1919), vol. 3, pp. 728–32.

44. As verified in an indenture between Chester and Bristol, signed on

St. Bartholomew's Day (August 24) of that year at the Merchant Taylors' Hall; Chester City Record Office MS. CHC/14/1.

45. Stevenson and Salter, *Early History of St. Johns College*, pp. 402–4.

46. 8 November, 1566, and codicil of 24 November, 1566; Family Records Centre, PROB 11/49/36.

47. These details about White's health have been drawn from the researches of Stevenson and Salter in White's correspondence with his college; *Early History of St. Johns College*, pp. 138–41. They correct earlier views expressed in the *D.N.B.*

48. Jordan, *Philanthropy in England*, p. 266.

49. See, for example, Thomas Wilson, *A Discourse on Usury*, ed. R. H. Tawney (1925), and Tawney's introduction, pp. 21–22; M. M. Postan, 'Credit in Medieval Trade', and 'Private Financial Instruments in Medieval England', in *Medieval Trade and Finance* (Cambridge, 1973); Elaine Clark, 'Debt Litigation in the Late Medieval English Vill', in J. A. Raftis, ed., *Pathways to Medieval Peasants* (Toronto, 1981), pp. 247–79; Jones, *God and the Moneylenders*; and M. K. McIntosh, 'Money-Lending on the Periphery of London, 1300–1600', *Albion* 20 (1988), pp. 560–64.

50. A statute of 1576 even attempted to prevent clothiers from buying more than twenty acres at a time in the West Country, so as not to intrude on the operation of sheep farming and grazing; 18 Eliz., c. 6, sec. iii. See also Grassby, *Business Community*, pp. 53–54.

51. The following paragraphs are based on B. E. Supple, *Commercial Crisis and Change in England, 1600–1642* (Cambridge, 1959), but they apply as much to the Tudor period as to the early Stuart.

52. Supple, *Commercial Crisis and Change*, p. 10.

53. Grassby, *Business Community*, pp. 65–66.

54. Grassby, *Business Community*, p. 83.

55. Berger, *The Most Necessary Luxuries*, p. 240.

56. Tittler, 'The Emergence of Urban Policy, 1536–1558', in Tittler and Jennifer Loach, eds., *The Mid-Tudor Polity, 1540–1560* (1980), pp. 74–93.

57. *Reports of the Charity Commissioners* 1 (1819), vol. 10, appendix, p. 243.

58. Norwich and King's Lynn had statutes devoted exclusively to themselves in turn, 26 Henry VIII, c. 8 and c. 9, respectively. Gloucester and Cambridge were listed in 27 Henry VIII, c. 1; Bristol, York, Canterbury, Worcester, Exeter, Salisbury, Southampton, Lincoln, Winchester, Oxford, Hereford, Bath, Ipswich, Colchester, and Newcastle were listed in 32 Henry VIII, c. 18; Cambridge, Derby, and Canterbury again on 33 Henry VIII, c. 36, and Chester and Shrewsbury again on 35 Henry VIII, c. 4.

59. 'It perhaps simplifies a process of social change far too much to say', he tells us, 'that men of the Middle Ages gave alms as an act of piety

while men of the sixteenth century gave, much more generously, under the dictate of social need'. Jordan, *Philanthropy in England*, p. 146.

60. I am grateful to Paul Seaver for this point. See also Paul Slack, 'Social Policy and the Constraints of Government, 1547–1558', in J. Loach and R. Tittler, *The Mid-Tudor Polity, c. 1540–1560* (1980), p. 109.

61. Susan Brigden, 'Religion and Social Obligation in Early Sixteenth Century London', *P. and P.* 103 (May 1984), pp. 77–86.

62. As represented esp. by Manley, *Literature and Culture*.

63. Material on Stow taken from the editor's introduction to *A Survey of London by John Stow*, ed. C. L. Kingsford (2 vols., Oxford, 1908), pp. vii–viii.

64. John Stow, *Summary of the Chronicles* (1565), Beinecke Library, Yale University, ref. DA 130/S376/1565, fol. 225v.

65. Ibid. (1573), Beinecke Library, Yale University, reference By7/51x, a work measuring only 2.5 x 4 inches in size and less than 300 pp. in length; *Chronicles of England* (1580), Beinecke 1987/303, in which Stow gets 47 lines; and Stow, *Summarie of the Chronicles* (1604), Beinecke By7/52b, in which he gets 3 pages and 150 lines out of 462 pages in all.

66. Including the funeral sermon preached by Campion as noted above, a c. 1610 life of White written in hexameters by Griffin Higgs of St. Johns College, and a substantial commemoration in John Taylor's College history of 1662, all cited in Stevenson and Salter, *Early History of St. Johns College*, pp. 382–83.

67. Richard Johnson, *Nine Worthies of London* (London, 1592), fol. D2, verso.

68. John Webster, *Monuments of Honor* (London, 1624), in F. C. Lucas, ed., *The Complete Works of John Webster* (6 vols., 1927), vol. 3, pp. 333–34. I am grateful to Lawrence Manley for pointing this reference out to me.

69. Tittler, 'Civic Portraiture and Political Culture', pp. 328–29; Edward Hasted, *The History and Topographical Survey of the County of Kent* (12 vols., Canterbury, 1797–1801), vol. 12, p. 642. M. G. Hobson and H. E. Salter, eds., *Oxford Council Acts, 1626–1665* (Oxford Historical Society Publications, vol. 92, 1933), p. 33; Stevenson and Salter, *Early History of St. Johns College*, p. 386; Stocks and W. H. Stevenson, *Records of Leicester*, vol. 3, pp. 162–63. I owe the Canterbury reference to my student, Laura McAlear, to whom I am grateful.

70. Stevenson and Salter, *Early History of St. Johns College*, p. 386.

71. Daniel Hipwell, 'Sir Thomas White, Lord Mayor of London', *Notes and Queries*, 8th ser., 2 (20 August, 1892), p. 145. My thanks to Mr. Jason McLinton for this reference.

Chapter 5: Henry Manship

1. Henry Manship, *The History of Great Yarmouth*, ed. Charles John Palmer (Great Yarmouth, 1854).

2. John Stow, *Survey of London* (1598, 2d ed., 1603), ed. C. L. Kingsford (2 vols., 1908).

3. Vowell *alias* Hooker, *The Description of the Citie of Excester.*

4. Aside from Robert Ricart, *The Maire of Bristowe is Kalendar* (c. 1484), ed. Lucy Toulmin Smith, Camden Society 5 (1872), which was remarkably precocious, and Hooker's well-known survey of Exeter, these include (amongst other works) David Rogers, 'The Breviary of Chester History' of 1609, partly transcribed in L. Clopper, ed., *Records of Early English Drama, Chester* (Toronto, 1979), pp. 232–54; and William Somner, *Antiquities of Canterbury* (1640).

5. Manship, *History*, p. 249.

6. Recounted in Paul Rutledge, 'Thomas Damet and the Historiography of Great Yarmouth', *Norfolk Archaeology* 33 (1965), pp. 124–25.

7. Ibid., p. 123; the document is now catalogued as MS. C18/4 in the Norfolk County Record Office.

8. Rutledge, 'Thomas Damet and the Historiography of Great Yarmouth', *Norfolk Archaeology* 34 (1969), pp. 332–34.

9. Thomas Nashe (1567–1601) was a popular pamphleteer and literary gadfly whose sharply satirical and even scandalous writings gained him numerous enemies in London and elsewhere.

10. In a survey of the port done in 1565 Henry Manship (the Elder) is listed as owning a thirty-ton ship named 'the Elizabeth'; P.R.O., SP 12/38/18.

11. Rutledge, 'Thomas Damet' (1965), pp. 121–22.

12. Manship, *History*, p. 45.

13. Rutledge, 'Thomas Damet' (1965), p. 121.

14. Ibid. N. J. Williams, *The Maritime Trade of the East Anglian Ports* (Oxford, 1988), p. 42, attributed these transgressions of 1565 and 1566 to the younger Manship.

15. Williams, *The Maritime Trade*, p. 42; *Draft Calendar of Patent Rolls, 27 Elizabeth. I, 1584–1585*, List and Index Society, vol. 241 (1990), p. 192.

16. Manship, *History*, p. 75.

17. Rutledge, 'Thomas Damet' (1965), p. 121; C. J. Palmer, ed., *The History of Great Yarmouth by Henry Manship* (1854), p. iii.

18. Manship, *History*, editor's introduction, p. iii.

19. Though he does appear to have been fined for evading customs as noted above, neither customs accounts, port books, nor other records identify him as a full-time member of Yarmouth's trading community.

20. The government of Great Yarmouth at the time had two bailiffs

serving jointly as senior governing officers, essentially filling the role performed by the mayor in other towns. It adopted a mayoral form of government in 1684. In addition to its bailiffs, its government rested with an aldermanic council of twenty-four and a common council of forty-eight, plus two chamberlains who kept accounts.

21. This seems an obvious dig at Damet.

22. The whole archival project is described in the opening pages of its ultimate result, the catalogue of Yarmouth's archives. A copy of this catalogue, made by Thomas Barber in 1763, may be found in the British Library as Add. MS. 23737, with Manship's preface on fols. 4r–5r.

23. On this theme see Tittler, *The Reformation and the Towns*, pp. 211–19; and also, for a parallel experience in London, Piers Cain, 'Robert Smith and the Reform of the Archives of the City of London, 1580–1623', *London Journal* 13 (1987–88), pp. 3–16.

24. My understanding and appreciation of Manship's thinking has benefited from conversations with my undergraduate student Mr. Chris Churchill.

25. Geoffrey of Monmouth's *Historia Regum Brittaniae*, or *History of the Kings of Britain*, completed in the year 1136, succeeded more than any other work in summarizing and perpetuating the mythology of Britain's foundation by Brutus after the Battle of Troy. In addition to providing many of the historical mythologies which became the commonplace of classic English literature, including the stories of Lear, of Cymbeline, and of the Arthurian legends, Geoffrey attributed the foundation of numerous British towns and cities to an imaginative assortment of Brutus's descendants and other mythological figures.

26. Manship, *History*, p. 20.

27. Ibid., pp. 19–20, 22–25.

28. E.g., ibid., p. 11. The fault he found with Speed's *Theatre* of 1611 is notwithstanding the fact that, as he tells us on the same page, he travelled fourteen miles each way to read it.

29. Gaspar Contarini, *The Commonwealth and Government of Venice* (S.T.C., 2d ed., no. 5642) cited in Manship, *History*, p. 25.

30. The fullest discussion of this transition as reflected especially in literature is Manley, *Literature and Culture*; see also 'Sir Thomas White of London', above, pp. 100–120.

31. Johnson, *Nine Worthies of London*.

32. Manship, *History*, p. 118.

33. Ibid., p. 53.

34. Ibid., p. 53.

35. Ibid., p. 54. It was restored in 1563, with much more secular motif.

36. Ibid., p. 102. Considering the context in which Manship worked and wrote, there can be little doubt that he had in mind here the two Pu-

ritan lecturers who had been employed by the Borough Council of the day to deliver regular sermons on right behaviour. Richard Cust, 'Anti-Puritanism and Urban Politics, Charles I and Great Yarmouth', *Historical Journal* 35 (1992), p. 3.

37. Manship, *History*, p. 191.

38. Ibid.

39. See, for example, Collinson, *The Religion of Protestants*, esp. ch. 4, 'Magistracy and Ministry', and *Birthpangs of Protestant England;* Underdown, *Fire from Heaven.*

40. Manship, *History*, pp. 191–92.

41. For the Puritan oligarchy and opposition to it in the years immediately following the completion of Manship's work, see Cust, 'Anti-Puritanism and Urban Politics', pp. 1–26.

42. Manship, *History*, pp. 192–93.

43. Norfolk County Record Office MS. C28/1, fol. 265; Henry Swindon, *The History and Antiquities of Great Yarmouth* (1772), p. 413.

44. Summarized in Tittler, 'The English Fishing Industry in the Sixteenth Century: The Case of Great Yarmouth', *Albion* 9, no. 1 (spring 1977), pp. 40–60.

45. Cust, 'Anti-Puritanism and Urban Politics', passim.

46. Manship, *History*, pp. 96–97.

47. Palmer's introduction to Manship, *History*, p. iv.

48. Ibid.

49. Principally in Swindon, *History and Antiquities;* Francis Blomefield, ed., *Essay Towards a Topographical History of the County of Norfolk* (11 vols., 1805–6); Charles John Palmer, *The History of Great Yarmouth: A Continuation of Manship's History of that Town* (1856), and *The Perlustration of Yarmouth* (3 vols., Great Yarmouth, 1872–73).

Chapter 6: Henry Hardware

1. Lawrence M. Clopper, ed., *R.E.E.D., Chester* (Toronto and Buffalo, 1979). See also Collinson, *Birthpangs of Protestant England*, pp. 54–55, in which Hardware exemplifies the Puritan reform of manners in English provincial towns.

2. British Library, Harleian MS. 2125, fol. 45v, as published in Clopper, *R.E.E.D., Chester* p. 198. [Hereafter B.L. Harl.]. All these objects were obviously ceremonial play-figures long employed in Chester's Midsummer festivities. Giants figured prominently in the foundation mythologies of numerous towns, and were frequently represented in local processions. One such figure may still be seen in the City Museum of Winchester. The other figures named here were of more local provenance.

3. E.g. Clopper, *R.E.E.D., Chester*, pp. liv, 526.

4. As Clopper relates, Chester has been unusually blessed with the work of local antiquarians, including Robert and his son David Rogers, Mayor William Aldersey, George Bellin, and especially the four Randle Holmeses, all related. In addition to several important breviaries, Clopper identifies no fewer than twenty-seven surviving and annotated mayors' lists, distributed today mostly in the Chester City Archives, Chester County Record Office, and the British Library.

5. Clopper, *R.E.E.D., Chester*, 526 (but on p. lx he places these events in 1600); Collinson, *Birthpangs of Protestant England*, p. 101.

6. Chester Record Office MS. DLT/B/37, Liber N, fol. 67, published in Clopper, *R.E.E.D., Chester*, 199.

7. Chester Assembly Minutes, Chester City Archives MS. AB/1, fols. 256 and 265.

8. Chester Record Office Ms. DLT/B/37, Liber N, 'The Antiquity of Chester', fol. 67r.

9. P.R.O., PROB 11/121–22 (1613); and Sir George Armytage and J. Paul Rylands, eds., *Pedigrees Made at the Visitation of Chester, 1613* (Harleian Society, vol. 59, 1909), pp. 48, 62, 91, 118–19.

10. Armitage and Rylands, *Visitation of Chester*, pp. 118–19; and B.L. Additional MS. 39,925, fol. 164r.

11. A. R. Myers, 'Tudor Chester', *Journal of the Chester Archaeological Society* 63 (1980), p. 48.

12. P.R.O., PROB 11/121/34.

13. George Ormerod, *The History of the County Palatine and City of Chester* (3 vols., London, 1882), vol. 2, pt. 1, p. 333.

14. B.L. Additional MS. 11,335, fol. 21v.

15. J. Paul Rylands, ed., *The Visitation of Chester, 1580* (Harleian Society Visitations, vol. 18, 1882), p. 11.

16. Ormerod, *History of Chester*, vol. 2, pt. 1, p. 333. This first Henry Hardware was made a Freeman of Chester in December 1546, as a draper; J. H. E. Bennett, ed., *The Rolls of the Freemen of the City of Chester, 1392–1805*, The Record Society of Lancashire and Cheshire, vols. 51 (1906) and 55 (1908), vol. 1, p. 25. He was probably born in the early 1520s, and therefore would have died in his early sixties.

17. Cheshire County Record Office MS. WS 1607, 'Hardware, Henry'.

18. Ormerod confirms this, too, adding that this Henry Hardware, whom we have designated Henry Hardware II, was the first of his line to reside at Peele Hall. Ormerod, *History of Cheshire*, vol. 2, pt. 1, p. 333.

19. Bennett, *Chester Freemens' Rolls*, vol. 1, p. 57.

20. Chester City Assembly Minutes, Chester Archives MS. AB/1, fol. 233r.

21. Chester Assembly Minutes, Chester Archives MS. AB/1, 234v, and 235v; Chester Assembly Files, Chester Archives MS. AF/4/26.

Twenty-one members voted in favour of the £20 fine, only six for the lesser fine of £10.

22. Chester Assembly Minutes, fol. 236v.

23. Chester Assembly Minutes, fol. 245r., 6 May, 38 Elizabeth.

24. Cheshire Record Office, will WS 1607, 'Henry Hardware'.

25. Ormerod, *History of Cheshire*, vol. 2, pt. 1, p. 332.

26. B.L. Harl. MS. 2125, fol. 45v, as printed in Clopper, *R.E.E.D., Chester* p. 198.

27. 'Report of Egerton, Nottingham and Fortescue, 1599' [obviously a report to the Queen, but dated only with the year, 1599], Historical Manuscripts Commission, *Report on the Manuscripts of the Marquess of Salisbury* [hereafter HMC, *Salisbury Papers*], pt. ix (1902), pp. 424–25.

28. Cheshire Record Office, MS. DLT/B 37, Liber N, fol. 65v.

29. HMC, *Salisbury Papers*, pt. ix (1902), pp. 106–7, 113.

30. B.L., Add. MS. 29,780, fols. 136–42.

31. A. R. Myers, 'Tudor Chester', *Journal of the Chester Archaeological Society* 63 (1980), p. 48.

32. HMC, *Salisbury Papers*, pt. ix, pp. 96–97.

33. Cheshire Record Office, MS. DLT/B 37, Liber N, fol. 64v.

34. Andrew B. Appleby, *Famine in Tudor and Stuart England* (Stanford, 1978), pp. 114, 133–44.

35. Cheshire Record Office MS. DLT/B 37, Liber N. fols. 63–66. Appleby, *Famine*, Figure 16, p. 136; Thirsk, *The Agrarian History of England and Wales*, esp. Table 1, p. 820; and W. G. Hoskins, 'Harvest Fluctuations in English Economic History, 1480–1619', *Agricultural History Review* 12 (1964), pp. 28–46.

36. Thus in 1590 freemen were ordered by the mayor of the day to keep a headpiece and halberd at the ready. Cheshire Record Office, MS. DLT/B 37 Liber N, fol. 63. Similar requirements were adopted by the burgesses of Abingdon, Hartlepool, Salisbury, Wells, and no doubt elsewhere as well. Abingdon Corporation Minute Book, Berkshire County Record Office, MS. D/EP7/84, p. 163; Cuthbert Sharp, *A History of Hartlepool* (Hartlepool, 1816), p. 65; Salisbury City Ledger Book, Wiltshire County Record Office, MS. G23/1/2, fol. 258v; 'Manuscript Notes and Extracts of the Borough of Wells', Somerset County Record Office, MS. DD/SAS/SE29 (unpaginated) reference for 23 May, 21 Elizabeth.

37. Cheshire Record Office MS. DLT/B 37, Liber N, fol. 64r.

38. Ibid., fol. 65v.

39. Chester Archives, Assembly Book 1, MS. AB/1, fols. 207 *et seq*.

40. B.L. Harl. MS. 2125, fol. 45r.

41. Ibid.

42. Chester Assembly Minutes, Chester Archives MS. AB/1, fol. 256r and v.

43. Ibid., fols. 256v–257r.

44. Ibid., fol. 258r.

45. By the old style of dating which applied in England at that time, the New Year began on March 25. Our 'new style' or modern system of dating has been employed here, with 1600 beginning on January 1 instead.

46. Harl. MS. 2057, fol. 31v.

47. B.L., Harl. MS. 2125, fol. 45v.

48. Underdown, *Fire from Heaven.*

49. B.L., Harl. MS. 2057, fol. 31v.

50. Cheshire Record Office MS. DLT/B 37, Liber N, fol. 66r-v.

51. B.L., Add. MS. 29,779, fol. 31r.

52. B.L., Harl. MS. 2125, 45r.

53. HMC., *Salisbury Papers,* pt. x (1904), pp. 12, 136, 137, 186, 189, 233, 268, 323, 337, 339, 349.

54. Chester Mayor's Books, Chester Archives MS. MB/28, fols. 65v, 66r-v, 77v–79v. As a county in and of itself, Chester had Quarter Sessions, with the mayor and aldermen sitting as JPs. Beer differed from ale in those bygone days because it had the addition of hops as a preservative.

55. B.L. Harl. MS. fol. 45v. A similar phrasing is employed in other of the mayors' lists which distinguish Chester's recorded past, including B.L. Harl., 1944, fol. 90 r-v.

56. E.g., B.L. Harl. MS. 1944, fol. 90 r-v; Harl. 2125, fol. 45v.

57. B.L., Harl. MS. 2125, fol. 45v.

58. For a sampling of works on Puritanism as a culture, and eminently adaptable to political requirements, see Christopher Hill, *Puritanism and Revolution* (1958), and *Society and Puritanism in Pre-Revolutionary England* (1964); Collinson, *The Religion of Protestants* (1982), esp. ch. 4, *Birthpangs of Protestant England,* and 'Elizabethan and Jacobean Puritanism as Forms of Popular Religious Culture', in C. Durston and J. Eales, eds., *The Culture of English Puritanism, 1560–1700* (1996), pp. 32–57; Keith Wrightson and David Levine, *Poverty and Piety in an English Village, Terling, 1525–1700* (2d ed., 1995); and Underdown, *Fire from Heaven.*

59. B.L., Harl. MS. 2125, fol. 45v., as printed in Clopper, *R.E.E.D., Chester,* p. 198.

60. For the harmony-inducing role of traditional festivities in general, see C. Phythian-Adams, 'Ceremony and the Citizen'; M. James, 'Ritual, Drama, and Social Body'; Susan Brigden, 'Religion and Social Obligation in Early Sixteenth Century London', *P. and P.* 103 (May 1984), pp. 67–112; E. Duffy, *The Stripping of the Altars,* pt. 1; Hutton, *The Rise and Fall of Merry England,* chs. 1–3; and R. Hutton, *The Stations of the Sun.*

61. For London's similar reaction, see Michael Berlin, 'Civic Ceremony in Early Modern London', *Urban History Yearbook* (1986), esp. pp. 18–20.

Chapter 7: Swaddon the Swindler and Pulman the 'Thief-Taker'

I am greatly indebted to two co-workers and one patient reader in the preparation of this essay. Alexandra F. Johnston first brought Handes's account, and thus the tale of his pursuit of Swaddon, to my attention, and afforded me access both to her photocopy of the original and her transcription of this revealing document. Tim Wales did some of the archival legwork and has made useful suggestions along the way. Finally, John Beattie has saved me from a number of gaffes regarding the intricacies of court procedure.

1. From Ralph Handes's expense account, submitted to Temple on 12 May, 1606, Huntington Library MS. STTF, Box 6, no item no. Hereafter referred to as 'Handes's Account'.

2. Considerable attention has been paid to crime in London at a later period, but the substantial treatment of English crime in this period (save for literary-based sources) has often neglected the London scene. Exceptions include J. McMullan, *The Canting Crew: London's Criminal Underworld, 1550–1700* (1984); Archer, *The Pursuit of Stability*, ch. 6; Ward, *Metropolitan Communities*, ch. 3.

3. His eldest brother was fifty-four years of age when he made his will in 1620, meaning that he was born in 1566. Robert, who was not the youngest child, was thus probably born within a decade of that year. The fact that he was entrusted with valuable transactions by his master Richard Sheppard by 1593 probably places his birth as not long after 1566: perhaps around 1568–72. Family Record Centre, London, PROB 11/142, fols., 345–46.

4. The will of William Swaddon the Elder, dated 1602 and proven in 1607, is in the Family Record Centre, PROB 11/109/32.

5. A. W. Mabbs, ed., *Guild Steward's Book of the Borough of Calne, 1561–1688*, Wiltshire Archaeological and Natural History Society Records no. 7 (Devizes, 1953), pp. 1, 12, 19, 36, passim.

6. G. D. Ramsay, ed., *Two Sixteenth Century Taxation Lists, 1545 and 1576*, Wiltshire Record Society (vol. 10, 1954), p. 45.

7. Mabbs, *Guild Steward's Book*, pp. 47–48, 52; and Family Records Centre, PROB 11/142, fols. 345r–346r.

8. Mabbs, *Guild Steward's Book*, passim.

9. 'I have bynne by my father disinherited and my younger brethren and sisters have had all his goodes except a small portion wch I had to bring me into Winchester Colledge', PROB 11/142, fol. 345v.

10. PROB 11/142, fol. 345v.

11. Historical Manuscripts Commission, *Calendar of the Manuscripts of Lord Sackville at Knole*, vol. 1, 1551–1612 (London, 1940), pp. 10–12. (Hereafter HMC, *Sackville MSS.*, vol. 1).

12. HMC, *Sackville MSS.*, vol. 1, p. 12.

13. HMC, *Sackville MSS.*, vol. 2, (1966), p. 2.

14. *Acts of the Privy Council*, new series, 1595–95 (1901), p. 357.

15. HMC, *Sackville MSS.*, vol. 1, p. 19.

16. John Sheppard to Lionel Cranfield, 8 April, 1600, HMC, *Sackville MSS.*, vol. 2, p. 16.

17. Mabbs, *Guild Stewards' Book*, passim.

18. Baynton, a prominent Wiltshire figure, had served as MP for Chippenham (1589), Devizes (1593 and 1604), and for the County of Wiltshire (1597), was knighted in 1601, and served the shire as both JP (1594ff.), and sheriff (1601–2). He owned property in Calne, amongst other places, and if Swaddon did not know him personally, which is unclear, he must surely have known a lot about him. P. W. Hasler, ed., *The House of Commons, 1559–1603* (3 vols., 1981), vol. 1, p. 411; PROB 11/128 fols. 399r–400r, 30 July 1616.

19. For the frequency of deceptive practices and deceitful craftsmen in the London of this era, see esp. Ward, *Metropolitan Communities*, pp. 45–57.

20. Related in Pettus's bill and various depositions in P.R.O., STAC 8/228/4 (1604).

21. Ibid.

22. Ibid., STAC 8/5/6, bill of complaint of 21 November, 3 James I, 1605.

23. This much is related in the bill and depositions in P.R.O., STAC 8/5/6, in which the first document, the bill of complaint, is dated 21 November, 3 James I (1605).

24. Ottley to Cranfield, 9 March, 1605, HMC, *Sackville MSS.* II (1966), p. 158.

25. 'Handes's Account', p. 2.

26. The classic statements of this perspective are Valerie Pearl, 'Change and Stability in Seventeenth Century London', *London Journal* 5 (1979), pp. 8–27, and 'Social Policy in Early Modern London', in *History and Imagination, Essays in Honour of H. R. Trevor-Roper* (1981), pp. 115–31; and Rappaport, *Worlds within Worlds*.

27. For example, Beier, *Masterless Men*, esp. pp. 40–47; Jean-Christophe Agnew, *World's Apart: The Market and the Theatre in Anglo-American Thought* (Cambridge, 1986), passim; Manley, *Literature and Culture*, pp. 1–20. My understanding of this issue has been greatly enhanced by conversations with Joseph Ward.

28. Ward, *Metropolitan Communities*, esp. ch. 1; Keith Lindley, 'Riot Prevention and Control in Early Stuart London', *Transactions of the Royal Historical Society*, 5th ser., 33 (1983), pp. 109–26.

29. These are listed variously as follows: Middlesex Sessions, Sessions

Rolls and Gaol Delivery Files, London Metropolitan Archives MSS. MJ/SR 403–514 (1602–12); Anon., ed. (Typescript) 'Calendar of Sessions Rolls, Sessions Registers and Gaol Delivery Registers' (10 vols., n.d.), 1607–12; W. LeHardy, ed., *Calendar to the Sessions Records* 1612–18 (4 vols., 1935–41); and the London Sessions Records in the Corporation of London Record Office.

30. Typescript 'Calendar of Middlesex Sessions Rolls', vol. 1, p. 143 (29 May, 1608).

31. Typescript 'Calendar of Sessions Rolls', vol. 2, p. 46 (29 March, 1609).

32. Greater London Record Office, Middlesex Sessions Rolls, MS. MJ/SR 444/131 (held February 1607); MJ/SR 455/19, 54, 98, 115 (December 1607); and (Typescript) 'Calendar of Middlesex Sessions Rolls', vol. 1, p. 18.

33. Middlesex Sessions Rolls, MS. MJ/SR 455/98 and (Typescript) 'Calendar of Middlesex Sessions Rolls', vol. 1, p. 18.

34. Robert Shoemaker, *Prosecution and Punishment, Petty Crime and the Law in London and Rural Middlesex, c. 1660–1725* (Cambridge, 1991), p. 23.

35. Shoemaker, *Prosecution and Punishment*, pp. 25–27; Cynthia Herrup, *The Common Peace: Participation and the Criminal Law in Seventeenth-Century England* (Cambridge, 1987), pp. 85–91.

36. This had become common by the Restoration period, and it is likely to have happened in Pulman's time as well. Shoemaker, *Prosecution and Punishment*, pp. 122–25.

37. Shoemaker, *Prosecution and Punishment*, pp. 25–26, 118–25. This assumes that these conditions pertained to Swaddon's time as well as to the somewhat later period described by Shoemaker.

38. His burial, on 11 September, 1617, is recorded in R. Hovenden, ed., *A True Register of all the Christenings, Marriages, and Burials in the Parish of St. James, Clerkenwell* (Harleian Society, 1891), vol. 4 (burials, 1551–1665), p. 130.

39. [Typescript] 'Calendar of Middlesex Sessions Rolls', vol. 2, p. 176 (recognizance of 3 February, 1609).

40. Ibid., vol. 3, p. 186 (recognizance taken 6 March, 1610).

41. Ibid., vol. 2, p. 74 (recognizance of 5 December, 1608).

42. LeHardy, *Middlesex Sessions Records*, vol. 1, p. 21 (February 17/18, 1613).

43. Ibid., p. 228 (8 August, 1613).

44. Middlesex Sessions Records, London Metropolitan Archives MS. MJ/SR/429/11 (26 May, 1605): Pulman, Selman, and Richard Ollington, all of the Parish of St. Sepulchre, stood for Jacob Heyes, who was not from the neighbourhood at all, but from Southwark, south of the River Thames.

45. [Typescript] 'Calendar of Sessions Rolls', vol. 1, p. 267 (26 November, 1608); vol. 2, p. 58 (14 October, 1608); vol. 3, p. 64 (25 August, 1609); vol. 8, p. 38 (18 August, 1611); vol. 8, p. 210 (23 April, 1612); LeHardy, *Middlesex Sessions Records*, vol. 1, p. 26 (27 January, 1613), 51 (1 March, 1613); vol. 2, p. 104 (7 September, 1614); City of London Sessions of the Peace, Corporation of London Record Office MS. SF 28 (August 1609).

46. [Typescript] 'Calendar of the Sessions Rolls', vol. 5, p. 73 (6 September, 1610); LeHardy, *Middlesex Sessions Records* vol. 1, p. 165 (July 1613); vol. 2, pp. 27–28 (20 June, 1614); vol. 3, p. 220 (11–12 April, 1616).

47. [Typescript] 'Calendar of the Sessions Rolls', vol. 2, p. 163 (31 May, 1609); vol. 6, p. 126 (February 1611); vol. 8, p. 42 (2 September, 1611).

48. LeHardy, *Middlesex Sessions Records* vol. 1, pp. 415–16 (8 April, 1614), pp. 453–54 (8–9 June, 1614); vol. 2, pp. 247–48 (19 February, 1615), p. 334 (17 June, 1615), and p. 348 (1–2 August, 1615). One presumes that he acted thus in the capacity of a deputy constable, though no such designation appears on the record.

49. [Typescript] 'Calendar of the Sessions Rolls', vol. 3, pp. 190–91 (2 March, 1609–10).

50. Though Archer adopts a positive view of the justice system operating in London at this time, and of the role of constables within that system, he provides a useful and succinct summary of the views on either side of the question. Archer, *Pursuit of Stability*, pp. 220–22.

51. Ibid., p. 220.

52. [Typescript] 'Calendar of Sessions Rolls', vol. 3, p. 64 (25 August, 1609).

53. Ibid., pp. 190–91 (2 March, 1609–10).

54. See John Beattie, *Crime and the Courts in England, 1660–1800* (Princeton, 1986), pp. 55–59.

55. City of London Sessions of the Peace and Gaol Delivery, Corporation of London Record Office MS. SF 27 (Recognizance taken of Pulman and Elder for the appearance of Elizabeth Lauraunce, 19 May, 1609).

56. 'Handes's Account', p. 5.

57. Ibid., p. 6.

58. Selman is also recorded as serving surety on several occasions, though nowhere as often as Pulman.

59. Hovenden, *Registers of St. James, Clerkenwell*, vol. 4, p. 139.

60. This is agreed upon by several parties in the Star Chamber case of William George v. Robert Swaddon, Nathaniel Craddock, Francis Marten, and William Brett (P.R.O., STAC 8/155/1) including George and Swaddon himself.

61. P.R.O., STAC 8/155/1 and also in the closely related case in STAC 8/92/13. George argued in both cases that he accompanied Swaddon to Cambridge merely to be sure that Swaddon paid him the money he owed

for costs of meals and lodging in his inn. For what it may be worth, George's servant, Jane Picroft, affirmed this version in her testimony in STAC 8/92/13, fols., 4 r and v.

62. See Craddock's bill of complaint in P.R.O., STAC 8/92/13 of 1611.

63. In addition to Craddock and Brett, this included Thomas Kilborne of Huntingdon and John Shawberry of Bury St. Edmunds: both of them deposed to that effect in P.R.O., STAC 8/155/1.

64. P.R.O., STAC 8/155/1.

65. E.g., Beier, *Masterless Men,* pp. 7–8, and ch. 8, which is especially useful in pointing out the discrepancies between contemporary literary descriptions of the 'London underworld' on the one hand and the revelations of the archival record on the other.

66. As summarized, for example, in A. V. Judges, *The Elizabethan Underworld* (1930).

67. E.g., Beattie, *Crime and the Courts;* or Gerald Howson, *It Takes a Thief: The Life and Times of Jonathan Wild* (1987).

Chapter 8: Joyce Jefferies

1. N. H. Keeble, ed., *The Cultural Identity of Seventeenth Century Woman: A Reader* (New York and London, 1994), p. 252.

2. Miriam Slater, *Family Life in the Seventeenth Century: The Verneys of Claydon House* (1984), p. 84.

3. Linda Woodbridge, *Women and the English Renaissance: Literature and the Nature of Womankind, 1540–1620* (Brighton, 1984), p. 239. I am grateful to Michael Schoenfeldt for this reference.

4. Frances Dolan, *Dangerous Familiars: Representations of Domestic Crime in England, 1500–1700* (Ithaca, N.Y., 1994), pp. 14–15, and chs. 4–5.

5. Amy Louise Erickson, *Women and Property in Early Modern England* (1993).

6. Amy M. Froide, 'Single Women, Work and Community in Southampton, 1550–1750', Ph.D. diss., Duke University, 1996.

7. British Library, Egerton MS. 3054, the 'Account Book of Joyce Jefferies' [hereafter cited as 'Diary']. Both the content and context of this document make it virtually certain to have been but the last of several such volumes which Jefferies kept over her adult life. It is suggested in a note placed by the British Library that at least one companion volume had been destroyed by fire in the mid-nineteenth century. Jefferies herself refers in the present volume, fol. 64v., to 'a Lytle thicke booke' in which her agricultural accounts have been recorded; it has also failed to survive so far as is known.

8. Though bound together, the two sections were obviously meant to be considered separate books, because the first is entitled 'A New Booke

of Receights of Rents Anneties and Interest Moneys beginning at St. Mary day 1638 Written at Heryford, at John Fletchers howse', while the second has its own title: 'A Booke of Disbursements begining at St. Mary Day 1638, at Hereford written at John Fletchers House where I now dwell'.

9. Erickson identifies only two other spinsters as having left a personal record, Elizabeth Parkin and Sarah Fell, both of whom lived later on. Erickson, *Women and Property*, p. 192.

10. John Webb, 'Some Passages in the Life and Character of a Lady Resident in Herefordshire and Worcestershire during the Civil War', *Archaeologia* 37, pt. 1 (1857), pp. 189–223; F. R. James, 'The Diary of Joyce Jefferies, a Resident in Hereford during the Civil War', *Woolhope Naturalists Field Club, Transactions* (1921–23), pp. xlix–lx; and R. G. Griffiths, 'Joyce Jefferies of Ham Castle', *Transactions of the Worcestershire Archaeological Society* 10 (1933), pp. 1–32, and 11 (1934), pp. 1–13.

11. Beyond my own effort to examine what it reveals about the activity of moneylending, it has been noted more or less in passing by, e.g., Joan Thirsk, David Klausner, Stephen Porter, and, amongst historians of women, Prior and Erickson. Even then it seems clear that Prior has used Griffiths's antiquarian piece rather than the original and that, save for a single note from the manuscript itself, Erickson has done the same. See Tittler, 'Money-Lending in the West-Midlands: The Activities of Joyce Jefferies, 1638–1648', *Historical Research* 67, no. 164 (October 1994), pp. 249–63.

12. Tittler, 'Money-Lending in the West Midlands'.

13. A. T. Butler, ed., *The Visitation of Worcestershire, 1634* (Harleian Society Publications, vol. 90, 1938), p. 54.

14. W. P. W. Phillimore, ed., *The Visitation of Worcestershire, 1569* (Harleian Society Publications, vol. 27, 1878), p. 58.

15. In April 1650, Jefferies added a codicil to her will of June 1648, and her will was proven by her nephew on 9 November, 1650. The Harleian Visitation of Worcestershire of 1634 has her date of death as 6 November, 1650, which is plausible. M. Fitch, ed., *Administrations in the Prerogative Court of Canterbury, 1631–1648* (Index Library, 1986), see Jefferies, Joyce; A. T. Butler, ed., *The Visitation of Worcestershire, 1634* (Harleian Publications, vol. 90, 1938), p. 54.

16. John Webb claims this to have amounted to 200 marks, but offers no source; 'Some Passages', p. 194.

17. Anne, nee Barnaby, was known successively as Anne Coningsby, Anne Jefferies, and, finally, *Lady* Anne Kettleby, wife of Sir Francis Kettleby. Cf. G. Grazebrook and J. P. Rylands, eds., *The Visitation of Shropshire, 1623* (Harleian Society Publications, 2 vols., 1889), p. 30. The Worcester Visitation of 1634 has his name as *Francis* Coningsby, but this seems to confuse Anne's first husband with her third, Francis Kettleby;

238   Notes to Chapter 8

The Visitation of Worcestershire, 1634, p. 54. Johannes's identity is affirmed in the manuscript genealogy of the Coningsby Family listed as B 56/2 in the Hereford Record Office, fols., 17v–18r.

18. Family Record Centre, PROB 11/129/59, written in 1616 and proven in 1617. It is likely that she gained a considerable amount from her marriages but spent most of it, or gave it to her heirs, before her death. Joyce and her half-sister Katherine each received a variety of personal and household effects, some of which are described, but no specific sum of money.

19. In addition to generous bequests to his sister Katherine and, even more generously, to Joyce, he left 500 marks for the tomb; PROB/11/129/62.

20. Thomas Coningsby had been a companion of Sir Philip Sidney, with whom he toured Italy as a young man, and then of the earl of Essex, with whom he took part in the siege of Rouen in 1591. Coningsby held extensive lands in several shires of the West Midlands and Welsh border country and became one of the most powerful figures in the politics of the region. He served three times as knight of the shire and twice as sheriff for Herefordshire, and as a member of the Council for Wales. He founded a hospital for old soldiers in Hereford City, known as Coningsby's Hospital. He died in 1625, outliving all his sons but one. This was Fitzwilliam Coningsby, with whom Joyce Jefferies also had close relations. *D.N.B.*, see Coningsby, Sir Thomas; P. W. Hasler, ed., *The House of Commons, 1558–1603* (3 vols., 1981), vol. 1, pp. 638–39.

21. PROB 11/148/38, proven 1626. Joyce was named executrix of Thomas's first will of 1616, and of the third codicil, written in 1620. But in the final will of 1623 she is replaced by his son, Fitzwilliam, who had evidently come of age in the interim. Nevertheless, Joyce witnessed the will when it was proven in 1626.

22. PROB 11/129/62.

23. Writing in 1857, John Webb tells us that Joyce lived with her mother until 1617, and then with Sir Thomas Coningsby of Hampton Court, Hereford, until his death in 1625; Webb, 'Some Passages', p. 194. Webb gives no source for this view, but he may well have derived it from additional manuscript sources for Jefferies which are said to have been destroyed in a fire in 1886. This is related in a note, placed in with Jefferies's 'Diary' from a Rev. R. G. Griffiths, dated 18 August, 1932.

24. Hereford and Worcestershire Record Office, Hereford Branch, Ms. O/U 136, 'Mayor's Court Book, 1633–34', see entry for 2 June, 1634.

25. 'Diary', fol. 48v.

26. Ibid., fol. 55r.

27. Ibid., fol. 27v., passim.

28. She was exceptionally generous to Rufford, giving him a hundred

pounds to 'make him a stock', i.e., to provide for him, in 1642. He outlived Joyce, engaged in some moneylending himself, and by the mid-1650s was able to call himself a gentleman; Hereford Record Office MS. O/U 136, a suit vs. John Hackluit in a case of debt.

29. 'Diary', fol. 40v.; Widmarsh Street, or Widemarsh Street as it is to-day, was the chief artery into the town from the north, running across the town ditch and wall through Widmarsh Gate, and therefore existing both inside and outside that boundary. One assumes that values were high for such a main street, but less so for the part which extended beyond the gate.

30. Such fears may have been warranted by the prominent role her close relatives played on the Royalist side: both Fitzwilliam Coningsby, then sheriff of Herefordshire, and his son Humphrey were eventually captured when Gen. Waller's parliamentary army took the city in April 1643; John Webb, *Memorials of the Civil War between King Charles I. and the Parliament of England as it affected Herefordshire and the Adjacent Counties* (2 vols., London, 1879), vol. 1, p. 262.

31. Ibid., pp. 155–56, and n. 4.

32. 'Diary', fol. 53v.

33. Webb, *Memorials of the Civil War*, vol. 1, pp. 256–58.

34. 'Diary', fol. 58v

35. Ibid.

36. 'Diary', fol. 59v.

37. Ibid., fol. 17v.

38. She describes this as 'my brazier furnes' and sold it to the Hereford shoemaker Richard Teagge; ibid., fol. 18v. It may well be the same as the kiln which she paid to have repaired in February 1640; ibid., fol. 36v.

39. Ibid., fol. 18r. There is some ambiguity regarding which houses were pulled down and which were sold, or even whether Jefferies may have sold the titles to those which were pulled down to those who hoped to be reimbursed for the destruction. The earlier reference, dated May 1645 (fol. 17v.), refers to Maud's departure followed by destruction ('for she removed and my howses were pulled downe') and the subsequent reference, of June (fol. 18r.), records the 'several names of those men that bought my howses in Hereford with out Widmarsh gate' which Joyce was constrained to sell or have burned. The term 'howses' here refers, as it of-ten did at that time, both to an actual house and to several other residen-tial premises which were not self-contained buildings in and of them-selves.

40. Webb, *Memorials of the Civil War*, vol. 2, p. 216–19.

41. 'Diary', fol. 70v.

42. Ibid., fol. 72r.

43. B. A. Holderness, 'Widows in Pre-Industrial Society: An Essay

upon their Economic Functions', in R. M. Smith, ed., *Land, Kinship and Life-Cycle* (Cambridge, 1984), pp. 441–42.

44. Succinctly summarized in Peter Earle, *The Making of the English Middle Class* (1989), pp. 158–60; and Holderness, 'Widows in Pre-Industrial Society', pp. 435–36. The latter is unequivocal that '[t]he most prominent economic function of the widow in English rural society between 1500 and 1900 was money-lending'.

45. B. A. Holderness, 'Credit in a Rural Community, 1600–1800', *Midland History* 3 (1975–76), pp. 94–116, 'Widows in Pre-Industrial Society', pp. 423–42.

46. Holderness, 'Widows in Pre-Industrial Society', pp. 423–42.

47. *The Visitation of Herefordshire*, ed. F. W. Weaver (Exeter, 1886); *A Survey of Worcester by Thomas Habington*, ed. J. Amphlett (Worcestershire Historical Society, 2 vols., 1895 and 1899); *The Visitation of Worcestershire, 1634*, ed. A. T. Butler (Harleian Society, vol. 90, 1938); *The Visitation of Shropshire taken in the Year 1623* (Harleian Society, vols. 28, 29, 1889). In addition, I have used the following manuscript genealogies and other sources in the Herefordshire and Worcestershire County Record Office, Hereford Branch [hereafter Hereford R.O.]: The 'Great Black Book' of the City of Hereford; The Mayor's Account Rolls, Hereford, Box l; Hereford R.O., MS. AE 3/4 ('Civic Miscellanies'), vol. 4; Hereford R.O., MS. A 79 ('Herefordshire, 1658'); Hereford R.O. MS. B 56/1–4 (Robert Phillips's Genealogies); Hereford R.O., MS. B 56/12 (Thomas Blount's 'Collections').

48. Clark, 'Debt Litigation in the Late Medieval English Vill', p. 265.

49. Jones, *God and the Money-Lenders*, pp. 72–77. I am grateful to Norman Jones for bringing this to my attention.

50. Tittler, 'Money-Lending in the West Midlands', Table 3.

51. Ibid., Table 4.

52. Craig Muldrew, 'Credit, Market Relations and Debt Litigation in Seventeenth Century England, with Special Reference to King's Lynn', Ph.D. diss., Cambridge University, 1991, pp. 73–76. I am grateful to Dr. Muldrew for permission to cite his thesis.

53. In his study of borrowing patterns in seventeenth-century King's Lynn, Craig Muldrew was surprised to find such a high incidence of the traditional attitude toward lending, in which social obligation and friendship still prevailed over mere profit as the prime motivation. Muldrew, 'Credit, Market Relations and Debt Litigation', passim.

54. For loans from London pawnbrokers, for example, Peter Earle has found rates of 30 percent per annum entirely common and 50 percent not unprecedented, while credit extended to merchants and retailers 'was nearly always offered at a cost higher than the maximum legal rate of in-

terest and often at a rate at three or four times the maximum'. Earle, *The Making of the English Middle Class*, pp. 50, 118.

55. See Tittler, 'Money-Lending in the West Midlands', Table 5.

56. See the classic views on this represented in F. J. Fisher, 'London as a Centre of Conspicuous Consumption', reprinted in P. J. Corfield and N. J. Harte, eds., *London and the English Economy, 1500–1700* (1990), p. 110, and 'London as an Engine of Economic Growth', in ibid., pp. 185–98; and E. A. Wrigley, 'A Simple Model of London's Importance in Changing English Society and Economy, 1650–1750', *Past and Present* 37 (July 1967), pp. 44–70.

57. Woodbridge, *Women and the English Renaissance*, p. 239.

58. 'Diary', fol. 28v.

59. Ibid., fols. 28r., 32v., 39v., etc.

60. Tom Aston, in 1638; ibid., fol. 30v.; Thomas Pickering of Clifton in 1646; ibid., fol. 63v.

61. Ibid., fol. 33r.

62. Ibid., fols. 12v–13r, 50v.

63. Paul Seaver, *Wallington's World: A Puritan Artisan in Seventeenth Century London* (Stanford, 1985).

64. By the anonymous 'J. G., Gent.', 1640 and 2d ed., 1642.

65. D. L., *The Scots Scouts Discoveries by their London Intelligencer* (1639, 2d ed., 1642), Wing no. L.10.

66. Written under the pseudonym George Naworth and published in Oxford in 1645, the same year as Jefferies purchased it; Wing no. W.2650.

67. Thomas Gallen, *An Almanak*, several editions, Wing no. A.1786 etc.

68. William Lilly, *Anglicus, or an Ephemeris for 1646*, Wing no. A.1876a.

69. Not further identified.

70. Published in three successive English editions between 1634 and 1636 by the University printer at Cambridge. I am grateful to Dr. Stephen Greenberg of the U.S. National Library of Medicine for helping to identify this work.

71. 'Diary', fols. 26r. and 48r; for pet-keeping, see Keith Thomas, *Man and the Natural World: A History of the Modern Sensibility* (1983), pp. 110–12.

72. 'Diary', fols. 35r, 62r.

73. Ibid., fol. 65r.

Index

In this index an "f" after a number indicates a separate reference on the next page, and an "ff" indicates separate references on the next two pages. A continuous discussion over two or more pages is indicated by a span of page numbers, e.g., "57–59." *Passim* is used for a cluster of references in close but not consecutive sequence.

the younger, *History of Great Yar-mouth*
Little Mouldsworth, Cheshire, 143ff
Llanthony Priory, Gloucester, 87
Llewellyn, Martin, keeper of Wood Street Compter, London, 162
Llewellyn, Thomas, accomplice of Robert Swaddon, 161–62
Lockups, 75–77. *See also* Blind Houses
London, 19, 31–37 *passim*, 42, 66, 100–104, 113, 132, 156–76 *passim*, 192. *See also individual suburbs*; Merchants
Lud, King, 130
Lyme Regis, Dorset, 66

Manorial administration, 20, 22f, 28, 44, 63
Manship, Henry, the elder, 124–25, 226n10
Manship, Henry, the younger, 17, 31, 36, 121–39; *History of Great Yarmouth* 121–22, 127, 129–35, 226n19
Manufacturing, 7, 10, 33, 111–17
Margery, John, alderman of St. Mary's Guild, Boston, 50
Market places, 54, 64–65, 72, 74, 78, 91, 150, 216n39
Market towns, 9–10, 20f, 28, 210n44
Marketing, 9, 20, 43, 63, 76
Marlborough, Wilts., 71
Marriage, 91–92
Marshalsea prison, London, 48, 52, 163, 167
Marsham, John, Norwich mayor, 97
Marten, Francis, London merchant, 172–76 *passim*
Mary Tudor, reign of, 104, 138
Matthews, William (*alias* 'Wright', John Strange' and 'John Jones'), Swaddon's accomplice, 156, 161, 168, 170
Mayor, office of, 25, 90, 98
McIntosh, Professor Marjorie, 10
Melcombe Regis, Dorset, 11, 78. *See also* Weymouth

Memory, collective, 14–16, 90–97 *passim*, 137–38
Mercers, 86
Merchant Adventurers' Company of London, 114
Merchant hero, 36, 102, 110, 117–20, 132
Merchant Taylors' Company of London, 102–8 *passim*, 118, 219n11
Merchant Taylors' School, 106
Merchants, 36, 44, 63, 66f, 79, 100–103, 110–20 *passim*, 132, 146–47, 157–76 *passim*, 221n7. *See also* Urban society
Messenger, Thomas, alderman of Gloucester, 87
Middlesex, County of, 157
Middlesex Sessions, 157, 165–69 *passim*, 174–75
Midsummer Shows, 16, 18, 140–43, 154, 201
Migration, 7, 10, 21, 33, 201–2
Minsterworth, Gloucestershire, 86
Monasteries, dissolution of, 4–11 *passim*
Money lending, 9, 67, 111, 187–88, 197. *See also* Jefferies, Joyce; White, Sir Thomas, charity
Mountjoy, Lord, Charles Blount, eighth baron, lord deputy for Ireland, 151–52
Muldrew, Dr. Craig, 190
Musical instruments, 142

Nashe, Thomas, writer, 125, 127, 131, 226n9
Neville, Alexander, writer, 131
Newbury, Berkshire, 11
Newcastle, Northumberland, 22, 108, 115
Newgate, London 165
Newgate prison, 168
Noble, Mr., merchant of Newark-upon-Trent, 173
Nora, Pierre, historian, 14
Norfolk, County of, 121–22